Members of the Cast

George Beckman

Published by Books from Graestone, 2021.

Table of Contents

For Ruth who has always believed in me

A leaf in the breeze
Floundering, ignored, unseen
Insignificant

Not Chosen

OUTSIDE THE APARTMENT door, Margo's biggest problem was the "F" on her Biology test. Inside, it didn't matter; her parents were leaving.

Margo leaned on the kitchen table, pressing on her books until it creaked. It wasn't like Father was in the army, or they were missionaries. He dug in the ruins of ancient civilizations.

Father fitted a book into his pack, and Mother's mixer sprawled on the counter. The knapsack and mashed potatoes: two sure signs.

"Your father's grant came in a year early." Mother used her, "isn't this the best news" voice.

Margo couldn't muster an answer right away, finally offering a quiet, "Oh."

With an exasperated sigh, her mother wrestled with a mixer beater held in a headlock by the tangled cord.

"When?"

Mother stabbed at the underside of the mixer, the chrome shaft locking into place. "We'll need to leave soon—two weeks?"

"How long?"

"Well—until June." Potatoes plopped into the colander, earthy steam floating to the ceiling. "You know, Aunt Louise is too sick for you to stay with her—this time."

The real problem hovered like the steamy cloud; Margo couldn't disappear with the vapor or be put into storage with the couch.

The old question returned: Why are you choosing to leave me?

"I've talked to Lena Morrison. They've agreed to take you—for the year." Mother hid her words behind the clatter of mixer blades on the bowl.

A familiar heaviness pressed Margo's breathing, forcing it shallow. The blond Morrison cheerleaders, with their athletic glow, would love this idea! The twins tolerated her, at best. Margo returned the favor, but they took no notice of her not noticing them. In their radiance, other kids gathered like moths. No one flocked to Margo.

"I know this isn't what you wanted—right now."

Margo fought tears of frustration. This was never what she wanted, but her feelings were not important at these moments.

"We don't have many choices—this time."

Margo never bargained at these tense times, but the word many tipped the balance between obedience and rebellion. Her mouth opened, and unplanned words spilled out. "I could stay with Father's uncle in California."

Father stopped adjusting a strap on his pack. He didn't turn toward them, but he paused for a moment. Margo knew because she watched.

Spending a year in California with a man she had only met at Grandmother's funeral brought no comfort, and Margo longed for comfort.

Mother's eyes flicked toward Father. "You know good and well, California is—out of the question." Her mouth spoke the last four words more than her voice.

Do I? Would it be out of the question for you to stay with me!

Words tumbled out when she knew she should stop. "He seems nice to me. He sends a card and money for Christmas and birthdays." *He paid attention to me at the funeral while you paid attention to Father.* They had even let him pay the mortuary.

Mother pushed the cupboard door closed, and it sprang ajar. She rinsed her hands and leaned on the counter, her shoulders hunched. She switched to her, "don't upset your father" voice. "Margo, why would you even think such a thing?" She shook water and the conversation from her fingertips. Mother didn't have a "don't upset Margo" voice.

"You said no dig my junior year! If you get to decide to go on a dig a year early, I should get to decide where I am going to stay!" These words hit, marked by complete silence, and Margo was pleased. Such logic often eluded her when she needed it most.

Father let a book drop, and it slapped the floor. "Margo, that is enough."

Mother, lips tight, pushed both palms toward Margo.

This wasn't an argument that she could win. The outcome had been decided without her input, and the particulars were only minor details in the face of this latest opportunity. She wanted to scream at her father, "Do you ever worry about upsetting me?"

Margo took her books to her room and threw the biology test in the trash. It was supposed to be signed and returned, but she would sidestep Mr. Philips, and he would soon forget.

For supper, Mother served mashed potatoes, pork chops, and false cheerfulness. While Margo did the dishes, Father repacked his books, lost in his world of archeology. Mother made lists.

Back in her room, Margo went to her dresser, tugging left and right until the bottom drawer squeaked open. She took her fourth-grade genealogy project out, laying it on the bed. "Margo McKinney's Family" was written in flowery cursive on the cover.

Fourth grade had been a good year; her parents were only gone for two months in the fall.

Margo's project had four pictures on her father's side. There wasn't even a picture of Grandfather. Father's family was scarce, and she knew better than to ask.

Margo flipped past pictures of her mother's parents, buried before Margo was born, leaving Mother's older sister. She touched Aunt Louise's graying hair in the photo, whispering, "Sorry I haven't written."

The picture she needed to see was of Father's Aunt and Uncle in front of a Christmas tree in California. It came in her card that year, along with a cream knit sweater with forest green drawstring details at the collar, cuffs, and hem.

Even when the sweater no longer fit, Margo insisted on keeping it in her cardboard suitcase. In a sudden move, she pulled the case from the single shelf in her closet and held the sweater close. It was the prettiest thing she had ever owned.

She ran her finger across the clean flowing letters of the note, "Much love from Virginia and Tom." The sentiment always moved Margo. Love from a woman she had never met was welcome in a home where the word love was not spoken and affection rarely shown. She had labeled the picture, "My Father's Aunt and Uncle."

Margo held the picture to the light. Virginia was tall and captivating, looking at her husband with such love, her poise evident even in a photo.

Margo laid the project on the bed. "C-," in red pencil, covered part of the word "Family." Virginia wouldn't be in California. She had died before Grandmother, but the cards kept coming.

In the other room, the TV clicked off, the screen crackling. "John, if she went to California, we wouldn't have the expense of room and board—at the Morrisons'."

Expense! Margo waited. Typical of Father, he said nothing.

They were going to Peru. Storing their belongings. Selling the crummy car. And she was an expense!

Mother tried again. "California might be good for her—a change."

"We'll see."

It wasn't much but pretty big for Father. At least he acknowledged that he had heard.

Margo crawled into bed and pulled her knees to her chest. Father taught a lab until six on Wednesday. When they were alone, she would ask Mother what they had decided.

Wednesday came and went, but words hung in the back of Margo's throat. She dreaded the answer, any answer. She was certain of one thing; Mother would not choose to stay with her.

In history class, an early reddish leaf among green boughs fluttered outside the window. It was Margo's case exactly, an outsider dangling in the winds of her parent's whim. Hurt boiled to anger, but anger didn't change the facts.

Each afternoon she helped Mother pack, thinking, "Today she will tell me if I am staying with the Morrisons or going to California." Margo watched the twins, looking for a sign. They didn't ignore her with any more enthusiasm than usual. She couldn't decide which would be worse, a stranger in California she hardly knew or the Morrison home, full of strangers she did know.

Hopelessness paralyzed her. She turned in no assignments, did no homework. She did what she did best, hid. If she didn't think about it, didn't talk about it, maybe it would all go away. Then a letter from T. Charles Blackwater lay on the table with a plane ticket. There was no hiding from that.

Virginia

THE PLANE STOPPED. The propellers stopped. Margo's breathing stopped.

The layer of smog over Los Angeles hadn't been comforting.

She joined the line moving toward the front of the plane, clumping down the stairs, filing across the tarmac like kindergarteners going to lunch.

"Maggie! Maggie McKinney."

She had forgotten he called her Maggie. T. Charles wasn't as tall as she remembered. At least he still had a mustache.

"Hello, Uncle." Her voice sounded small.

"Maggie, I am so glad you are here. Let me look at you. Ahh—welcome to California."

Margo fiddled with her purse, watching T. Charles. He was handsome in his three-piece suit. The word dapper flickered. He found a porter, and she followed them out to the parking lot.

"How was the flight?" T. Charles asked.

She had been in suspension for five hours. Not in Wisconsin. Not in California. Not anywhere. "Fine."

Wisconsin. The Morrison twins actually talked to her at school. Well, they paused to give their opinion.

Gloria, who seemed to be the spokesperson, said, "So, we hear you are going to California."

Margo nodded.

"Cool." She flipped her hair. "Sis and I won't have to share a room. It didn't seem fair that *you* would have *my* room all to yourself while *I* had to move in with *her*!" She gave her sister a shoulder bounce.

At least coming to California had saved Gloria from any inconvenience.

Wisconsin faded. A pale California sun struggled through gray-brown haze. Not hot. Not cold. Like her, just there.

They stopped at a shiny car that looked like something a Chicago gangster would drive. It had running boards and a rack on the back for her trunk. After the porter loaded her luggage, T. Charles slipped a folded bill into the man's hand and opened her door. She couldn't remember anyone opening a door for her.

Margo looked at the polished dash, wishing she were like Katharine Hepburn in one of the old movies on television, chattering and gesturing. She watched freeway signs go by and said nothing.

T. Charles turned off the freeway and began climbing gentle hills. The houses were further from the street and larger. The car slowed at a house surrounded by green trees taller than its two stories. Double cement ribbons, with grass between, led to the house. Margo arrived, the intruder.

They stopped under a portico that stretched over the driveway. A vine with purple flowers crawled up white pillars. T. Charles came around and opened her door. "Welcome to my home. I hope it soon feels like your home."

Home. In Wisconsin, they said, "the apartment," a temporary place to live until the next dig. How long did you have to live somewhere for it to be home? White siding stretched up from pink flowers in planters. Not long enough.

Margo followed T. Charles through French doors, past polished banisters to a perfect bedroom at the top of the stairs.

"Do you like it, Maggie? There are other rooms."

A window looked into branches, giving it a treehouse effect. The four-poster bed and matching dresser reflected the beauty of the rooms in one of Aunt Louise's magazines. "It's lovely."

Lovely? Even her words sounded foreign. Margo stood in the gorgeous room, overwhelmed by the longing for—for what? Aunt Louise's jack-knife couch? Another apartment?

Left to unpack, she placed her things in drawers that pulled smoothly.

T. Charles made fried chicken with mashed potatoes, the perfect host. He invited her to have a cup of tea in a room that held a player piano. "The Study," as he called it, was peaceful and safe with a fire crackling in a fireplace.

Margo leaned close to a black and white picture of a young Virginia and T. Charles. Virginia wore a stylish hat tilted over short hair, a light-colored curl peeking out in front of her left ear. The camera caught a slight smile, her eyes on T. Charles.

Margo slid her finger across the keys of the piano, all the while practicing the subtle turn of Virginia's lips. Aunt Louise had arranged for piano lessons, practiced on a warbling spinet in her tiny house.

Margo's reverie was interrupted when T. Charles carried in a tray. "I love this picture," she said.

"We were in Santa Monica with friends. It was spring—that was a wonderful day."

She touched the filigree frame. "Tell me about her, please?"

"Virginia." T. Charles poured the tea. "The love of my life."

"What was she like?"

"Original. She wasn't afraid to be different. Rather than following the latest fashions, she had her own style. I could see it. Her friends copied her sense of fashion. It wasn't what was in the magazines—it was just Virginia."

T. Charles gestured toward the photograph. "Pictures never did her justice. You had to see her in real life. Animated, moving—beautiful. No, that's not the right word." He took a sip of his tea. "Fascinating." He smiled. "She was different. Enchanting, at least to me."

Margo bent close to the picture.

T. Charles held out his hands as if to frame the photo. "When she walked into a room, it was as if she knew things the rest of us didn't know. It was natural, not something she made up. She appeared to," he paused, "belong—to be comfortable in all situations."

Margo picked up the picture, trying to imagine Virginia's thoughts.

"I can tell you this, Maggie, you're going to look like her. When I saw you at the airport, I thought you could be our daughter."

Margo's cheeks flushed crimson. Virginia was captivating. Margo wasn't at ease in most situations. The airport, waiting for her luggage, had been awful. Would she ever be captivating?

"She was such fun. Charming."

Margo longed to be fun and charming. "Do you have kids?"

"We were never blessed with children." He gave her a sad smile. "But it was a wonderful life."

Was a wonderful life.

They sat in silence, the tea warming the cheerless musings of each. T. Charles picked up the tray and started for the kitchen. He paused at the doorway. "Cancer is an ugly disease, Maggie. Awful."

Her heart ached for this man she hardly knew.

She went up early to finish unpacking. Instead, she lay in the dark, staring at the ceiling. Another new school.

The Most Beautiful Boy

VEILED CLOUDS HUNG beyond the tree, shrouded in mist. So much for sunny California. Margo pushed the plunger on the alarm before it disturbed the silence.

She leaned close to the mirror, crinkling her lips. Mr. Sandman hadn't sprinkled gorgeous dust on her. She wouldn't have minded going to a new school with more of a figure.

Choosing an outfit for the first day was always tricky. If she wore the dress that looked best, then the rest of the days were downhill after that.

She chose her plaid skirt and white blouse with a Peter Pan collar. The navy jumper and long-sleeved blouse would have to wait for a day she really wanted to make an impression. Long sleeves concealed skinny arms, and the jumper top hinted at a chest.

For once, her hair behaved, but a final inspection showed she fell short of the "dazzling new girl" category.

Margo slid a hand along the polished wooden banister. The house was really something, that was for sure; no jack-knife couches here. Pausing at the bottom, she took a breath.

"I'm in the kitchen, Maggie."

Black and white floor tiles shown like a checkerboard, white cupboards rising to spotless counters.

"Good morning. I thought we'd have hotcakes and bacon. A person needs to start the day off right." T. Charles wore a chef's apron over a dark blue vest.

There were place settings at a red table with chrome legs. Margo perched on the edge of a matching chair.

"There's a pot of tea if you would care for some."

"Thank you." The cup and saucer had tiny blue flowers and gold rims.

"I brought the car around. The school is close enough for you to walk most days, but I'll take you today and help you get registered. School has been in session four weeks."

A month behind on her first day. T. Charles flipped a pancake, her stomach mimicking the feeling. Warm tea soothed the sensation, but not the unease.

After breakfast, Margo brushed her teeth, checking her hair in the mirror one last time. Piano music floated up the stairs. She followed the notes to the living room where T. Charles sat at the long black piano. Subtle chords embellished a haunting melody.

She imagined taking a long nap on one of the couches, not going to school—hiding.

"Uncle?"

"Yes?" T. Charles continued playing.

"Do I look all right?"

He cocked his head. "You'll knock 'em dead. Let me get my coat."

Pretty sure she wasn't going to "knock 'em dead," a mirror in the hall reflected her "pleasant face." Her grandmother's words, not exactly a strong endorsement.

"Will I need a sweater?" The sun had yet to break through the gloom.

"This will burn off. According to the radio, it will be seventy-three today."

Margo ran upstairs and slipped on her white sweater, buttoning the top button.

Outside the French doors, the car gleamed under the balcony. "Uncle, why do you drive such a funny old car?"

He chuckled. "That's not a car. That's an automobile. That's a Packard."

The Packard navigated the warp and weft of streets leading to the school. Leaving the car's warmth, Margo felt a chill that was not from the morning air. Kids milled in small groups, laughing and talking. She didn't feel like laughing.

In the office, there were papers to be signed and questions. Records from two high schools named Jefferson took some explaining. The second Jefferson spelled her last name MacKinney.

"My aunt is sick. So, this time, I'm here—with my great uncle."

T. Charles patted her hand.

When the last of the papers were complete, the secretary tapped them on the counter, straightening the edges. She slipped them into a manila envelope, smoothing it on the counter. "We will call for someone to help you become acquainted with our campus."

Acquainted? Margo nodded. T. Charles said, "Thank you."

"The school day ends at three thirty-five. Will Margo need a bus pass?"

"I'll pick Maggie up this afternoon. In good weather, Maggie will walk."

The secretary wrote Margo McKinney at the top of the envelope.

A large photo of the school, taken from an airplane, hung on the wall, revealing sprawling single-story buildings nestled in green grass. She was definitely not in Wisconsin anymore.

When T. Charles walked to the double glass doors, he paused to put on his hat, and Margo wanted to stop him, ask a question, anything to keep him from leaving.

He looked directly at her for several seconds. "I'll be waiting in front after school."

Margo sat straight-backed as typewriters clacked, the office smelling of ditto fluid mixed with the cedar of sharpened pencils.

The most beautiful boy Margo had ever seen pulled open both doors and placed his hands on the office counter, drumming a rhythm. "Somebody going to Room 12?" He drummed another cadence.

She stood. Tiny freckles peppered the bridge of his nose. Her arms didn't seem to know what they were supposed to do, so she adjusted her purse on her left arm and clutched the binder and admittance packet to her chest.

"You Margo?"

Margo nodded, scrambling to remember what the secretary had said moments before. *Chris? Yes. Chris Ferguson.*

"I'm from the Welcome and Hospitality Club. It is my pleasure to show you around our campus." He held the door for her. "So, I guess you just moved here."

Apparently, he'd run out of "Hospitality Club" talk.

"Yes." This wasn't great conversation either, but an improvement on her standard nod.

Chris moved quickly, and Margo hurried to catch him.

"The paper stapled to your admittance packet will be your locker combination." He looked at a slip of paper the secretary had given him. "Yours is two-forty. Top row, facing the quad. That's good—you won't get books dropped on your head."

Lockers lining classroom walls in outside corridors! She worked the combination and lifted the lever.

"Hey, you got it the first time. I helped a freshman last week. She tried three times and then cried." Chris snatched a sheet of paper out of the locker, wadded it into a ball, and made a perfect jump shot into a trash can. "There's a map in the back of the handbook in your packet."

He had gray eyes. Margo opened the handbook to the last page.

"OK, we're here." He leaned toward her, pointing. "You know, like those maps at a zoo or something; You are here?" He gave her a sideways grin. He had long fingers, and his nails were spotless.

Margo tried for a bit of a smile. He stood inches taller than her but not as slender.

Slender. The kind word for skinny.

Chris took the handbook. "This is the quad."

There were flecks of green in the gray. She forced her eyes away from his.

Would he think her eyes were green? A girl at the second Jefferson had said, "You have green eyes," as if she was surprised.

Margo followed Chris out through a corner of the quad.

"That tall building is the gym. Over there is the girl's locker room. Over on this side is the boy's..." He stopped and shook his head. "I guess you won't need to know where the boy's locker room is."

He gestured with the handbook. "Those are the shop classes. Home Ec. is the wing down there."

A girl with straight black hair came around the corner. "Hi, Chris. I missed Trig Friday—orthodontist. Did he assign the reciprocal functions on page eighty?"

"Just the even numbers. He collected the work from Thursday."

"I did them all. Oh well, they were easy. Thanks. See ya."

Margo forced her face to remain neutral. Functions in Trigonometry? Easy? She had barely managed to pass Geometry last year. What if kids were smarter in California?

"That's the cafeteria." His arm came so close she could feel the warmth.

It wasn't that she couldn't get good grades; it was that she didn't get good grades.

"Over there is the library."

Bells rang, and kids flooded out of the rooms.

"That's the end of first period. There'll be a three-minute bell that lets you know you better get moving if you aren't near your next class." He grinned.

Margo gave him what she hoped was a knowing smile, and they started back toward the quad.

"Hey, Ferg," seemed to be the standard greeting to Chris. "Hey," was his response.

He returned the handbook. "That's about it. Four classes before lunch and two after."

No big surprises. just a new campus with new kids. Three girls gave her the once-over, more than the usual new-girl examination. One glared at Chris, and his cheeks showed tinges of red. She had curves where Margo didn't have places. Margo pretended to look down the corridor. The girls looked back, giggling.

After two more "Hey Fergs," and one "Hey Ferguson," the traffic thinned, leaving them in front of Room 12.

"Your English class. I'm in here first period. Miss Johnson—she's not bad. She doesn't take any slack." Chris started to turn and paused. "I hope this tour has helped. Welcome to Blackwater High."

As he moved away, reality struck. How many times had she traipsed around a new school with an admit packet? Chris proved to be the best "show the new kid around" person Margo had encountered, but the tour was over. He probably didn't remember her name. She watched him for a moment and then followed a group of students into the room. Miss Johnson spoke to two girls. Chris hadn't mentioned how pretty she was.

When the girls went to their seats, Miss Johnson took Margo's admittance papers and read both pages. She flipped back and forth twice. "Margo McKinney," she said. "I'm Miss Johnson. Welcome to second period English."

Margo almost asked to be called Maggie. Was she a Maggie? Maggie sounded small and cute. Margo felt tall and gawky, uncomfortable in all situations, so very different from Virginia.

Miss Johnson walked to a desk near the far wall. "Margo, you may sit here." She turned to another student. "Susan, please get Margo a textbook and a worksheet."

Miss Johnson's red lipstick matched her dress. "We're learning to post proper footnotes for a term paper. We wouldn't want Mr. Keller in History to think we are not teaching anything in English." Her spectator pumps clicked the tile floor as she stepped quickly to the front of the room.

Grandfather

THE PACKARD SAT AMONG modern cars in front of the school.

"So, Maggie, how was Blackwater High?"

Margo did a mental summary of the day and decided Chris Ferguson was the high point. She had seen him at a distance three times, and the thought made her face warm.

"OK, I guess."

T. Charles pushed a button to start the car, the engine hardly making a sound. Margo didn't remember a car that started with a shiny button.

T. Charles changed gears. "Do you like your teachers?"

"Miss Johnson, my English teacher, is very nice. She's pretty." As she thought of the rest of the day, she decided to skip Typing as an item of interest.

"So, Maggie, have you decided what you will study in college? What are you interested in?"

College? Margo hoped to make it to Friday without making a fool of herself. She became aware of the silence. "I haven't really decided." She had never, once, thought about her future. She tried for safer ground. "Uncle, is the school named after you?"

He chuckled. "No. An older cousin of mine, also Thomas Blackwater, gave the district the land for the school before he passed away. Other than that, I can make no claims."

In the study, T. Charles touched a match to the fire he had laid and settled into his chair with a contented sigh.

Beautiful pink flowers floated in a glass bowl. Margo leaned close but gathered no scent.

"Camellias. Virginia always brought them in."

"Tell me how you and Virginia met?"

"We were introduced at a musical. Your grandfather brought her. I will never forget that night, as she came into the lobby on his arm—her faint smile. She looked as if she belonged in that room."

"Virginia knew my grandfather?"

"She was his sister."

Sister! It had never occurred to her how Virginia fit into the family. The information would have been handy for her genealogy project. Mother could have helped more—or maybe not. Perhaps the pressure to shun everyone on Father's side of the family, except Grandmother, was too great.

"Why did Grandmother—?" Growing up, any mention of Grandfather was met with cold silence. "All I know is Grandfather 'ran off'. Where did he go?"

T. Charles sighed. "I don't know. No one does."

It was an unspoken history everyone knew except Margo. Grandmother had been brief but repetitive on the subject. She seemed to enjoy sitting straight-backed in her chair, staring stolidly ahead, declaring, "He deserted us, you know."

One Sunday, Grandmother bitterly recounted the financial trials of raising a child on her own. The story never varied, and even at a young age, Margo could almost recite the telling with her. Mother, who never challenged Grandmother, quietly suggested, "Virginia sent you money all those years."

Grandmother had given a dismissive flick of her hand and said, "Humph. Guilt offering if you ask me."

Margo drifted into a daydream filled with yearning. Virginia had passed away. It was odd, how much knowledge, memory, and—love could be erased by death. Margo didn't miss Grandmother but ached to have known Virginia. The emotion didn't spring from logic but from nostalgia for events she had never experienced. She stirred in her chair.

T. Charles looked up from the fire. "I was a young man in New York, and I worked for the Harmony Music Company. I played the piano to make the master copy for player piano music rolls."

T. Charles gestured toward a polished wooden cabinet that held dozens of long thin boxes. "Sort of like recording, I suppose. Player pianos were like record players today. You could get the latest songs." T. Charles stared into the fire as if the flickering bits of orange drew pictures of the past.

"I also gave piano lessons. One day a young man answered my advertisement—your grandfather."

"What did he look like? There are no pictures."

"Oh, tall, thin, handsome. He had long slender fingers, piano hands." T. Charles went into another room and returned with a glossy photo of two men at a grand piano with the company name in the background.

There was her grandfather, with T. Charles. She clutched the frame with both hands, not blinking. It had taken seventeen years, and she was seeing her first picture of her grandfather. There was a stiffness to the pose, and yet a kindness reflected into the lens.

"The moment he sat down at the piano I knew he was a musician. He was very good. He recorded a number of the rolls in the cabinet, but I'm getting ahead of myself."

Margo stood in front of the cabinet, overwhelmed. *Grandfather played the piano? Good enough to record piano rolls?* She read the end of one of the boxes, "Rose of the Bowery," played by Daniel McKinney, tracing her finger under his name.

"We became friends. Good friends. I gave him lessons, but I sometimes wondered who was teaching who. I got him the job at Harmony—where the picture was taken. He was grateful for the job. He wanted to marry your grandmother." T. Charles leaned back. "And he did. I was his best man."

Grandfather, the deserter, lived in New York? Grandmother lived in Wisconsin. There was so much she didn't know.

"Your grandfather took jobs, playing nights in clubs to make extra money. Your grandmother wanted him to get an office job." T. Charles put his cup and saucer aside. "She didn't approve of the music business."

T. Charles was Grandfather's best man!

"Daniel loved to hear stories about growing up here, near Pasadena—the orange groves. He and Virginia had been raised in Upstate New York—rurally. I think he dreamed of coming out to California. There were music opportunities here, too, you know." T. Charles pushed a log back with the poker. "It would have been an amazing feat to convince your Grandmother to move to California."

Margo doubted anyone ever talked Grandmother into anything.

She held the picture closer and asked what she could never ask before. "Grandfather disappeared before Father was born. How did it happen?"

"We were to record a four-hand version of a song your grandfather had written, 'Uptown Ivories'. Clever tune. The day we were to record, I went early. We both had a key. We did that sometimes, record before anyone got there." T. Charles leaned toward the fire. "But, Daniel never came."

"That's all? No note, no clues?" Hope flickered toward extinction.

"Not a word. I tried to talk to your grandmother, but she said she never wanted to lay eyes on me again. She said I had led him to the devil, that I had encouraged him—that I was the reason Daniel was out all hours of the night."

"That can't be all..."

"I wondered if he owed money. Those were prohibition years. There was gambling in the speakeasys where music was played. There were men who would loan money. If you didn't pay your debts, rough men could hurt you."

"Was Grandfather a gambler?"

"I don't think so. He was quite a gentleman. No, and Daniel wasn't the type to run away. I know he loved your grandmother very much. And with your father due, I don't believe he would have run away from his responsibilities."

Sometimes Aunt Louise had let Margo watch cartoons. In one, the character was dying of thirst in the desert and saw a mirage of cool water and palm trees. He ran and dove into the water, but it disappeared, leaving the poor guy with a mouthful of sand.

She had almost no family, and this man, in this picture, was Grandfather McKinney. She felt a tremendous closeness, and yet it was only a mirage.

"There must be more," she whispered. "There *has* to be more."

"When your grandmother wouldn't see me, I went to see Virginia." T. Charles chuckled. "Of course, I wanted to see her again. We wrote letters to relatives and friends. I asked around at the clubs. Virginia went to hospitals in New York. We never found your grandfather, but Virginia and I fell in love. We were married later that year."

After supper, T. Charles played Grandfather's song on the big black piano. Margo closed her eyes, trying to imagine it was Grandfather at the keyboard.

Later, in her room, she sat at a desk with a fold-out writing table, staring at a blank page in her diary. It was silly; she had not written more than a few entries since the sixth grade.

She started a list:

1. Why does my family dislike T. Charles?

2. Did I ever meet Virginia, when I was little?

3. If Father is so mad because his father left, why does he always leave me?

She decided number two was no and drew a line through it.

Should number four be, "What do I want to be when I grow up?"

She didn't write number four. She crawled into bed, turned off the lamp, and pulled the sheet over her face.

Her Lab Partner

MARGO PRESSED UNRULY hair against her head. She lifted her hand and then bore down again, grinding bent hair into submission.

Vivien Turner had curly hair. It was jet black and bounced when she turned her head in theater class. She turned her head a lot in Theater. Margo tried a damp washcloth. The curly-hair fairy hadn't visited in the night; no bouncy curls.

She tried to concentrate on the improvisation assignment for Theater. Mrs. Kavanagh hadn't said, "It is your first day, so I will excuse you from the assignment until you settle in." Apparently, she didn't know the "easing new kids into class" rule. Margo's assignment was to pantomime trying to start a car. She'd never driven a car. She had watched T. Charles, but wouldn't be pretending to start a car by pushing a chrome button.

She rubbed a towel on the damp hair. At least she didn't have to act as though she was a tall person in a room with a low ceiling. The girl sitting behind her had drawn that card. On her way back to her seat, she grinned at Margo and rolled her eyes. Sharon Jackson.

Margo opened the medicine cabinet, imagining acting like Vivien Turner, looking like Vivien Turner. With the cabinet closed, the vision was interrupted by a damp hair bulge. She brushed it with a vengeance.

A three-by-five card lay at the table with the streets and the turns to get to school. Margo assured T. Charles she would be fine, walking. She slipped the card in her purse as she arrived, watching kids, friends, swirling in groups like fall clouds.

Chris Ferguson came down the hall toward her. He wore a V-neck sweater that fit him perfectly. Margo took a quick breath and entered into yet another of those dreams in which she liked someone who didn't know she was alive. Chris said something to another boy, and they went into Miss Johnson's room.

Margo turned quickly toward the quad. Chris wasn't in her English class! She had Miss Johnson second period! She had come within seconds of stumbling in and making an absolute fool of herself.

Margo moved away, smiling across the quad as if someone had called to her. She fumbled in her binder for the admission packet. How could she have forgotten Biology? Margo flipped to the last page of the handbook. She should have paid more attention to the map and less to Chris Ferguson's tiny freckles.

Sharon Jackson walked across the quad, and Margo hurried to catch her. "Sharon, hi. Remember me? From Theater yesterday?"

"Margo-McKinney-who-can't-get-her-car-started. Hey."

"I'm supposed to be in Room 20. Biology, with Mr. Yeeger?" Margo pushed her hair behind her ear, testing to make sure it was dry. "I'm all turned around."

"Yeager, with an 'A' like in 'make.' He's actually nice. I thought I'd be bored in General Science my freshman year, but he was pretty interesting." She raised her eyebrows. "I got an A! A pleasant outcome!"

Sharon clamped her books to her binder with her thumbs and half pointed with her elbow. "Go straight across the quad. Biology is on the far side of that building."

"Thanks. I'll see you in Theater."

"OK." Sharon sauntered across the quad.

Biology had been a disaster at both Jeffersons. The schools used different textbooks. Margo started the year with the football coach, who plodded through the skeletal system. Before class, he drew football plays on the chalkboard, tapping the O's and X's with the chalk, drawing arrows. Team members gawked and nodded well after the last bell. He wore his whistle around his neck, to remind the class he was the head football coach. It was unlikely anyone would forget because the boys called him "Coach."

Biology at the second Jefferson was taught by a little man who believed in the "Read the chapter, do the ditto, and take the test on Friday" system.

She hurried into the classroom seconds before the last bell. Mr. Yeager wore a bow tie and a starched white shirt. There was no whistle around his neck, and no football plays on the board. The smell of formaldehyde flooded her nose.

He reached for her admittance packet. "Margo McKinney—from Wisconsin." He tore off the first period admit slip.

Margo felt eyes examining her.

"Margo," he said again. "Well—let's see. You'll need a lab partner. We just started the circulatory system, the body's transportation roadways. This is good stuff. Good stuff!" Mr. Yeager lifted on his toes. "Who can help our new student, Margo, with the motto of Biology with Yeager?"

"Think before you ink," the class mumbled.

"You don't sound convinced!"

"Think before you ink!"

The sing-song words didn't comfort her.

"Who doesn't have a lab partner?" Mr. Yeager scanned the room over his glasses.

"I'm without a partner, Sir." A stocky boy at a lab table in the front of the room turned on his stool. He pulled his books closer.

"You do now. With that settled, let's see who managed to make it on time today. Anderson, Baker." Mr. Yeager perched on a stool behind a long table. "Johnson, Little..."

"He should be announcing the assembly," her lab partner said out of the corner of his mouth. "Driver's safety film. Second period."

Margo put the class schedule in her notebook.

"There's an assembly today," he repeated.

Hope flickered. The entire schedule could be thrown off! Theater shortened or canceled!

"Smith? Smith? Where's Jimmy Smith?"

"I think he's sick or something," a boy said from the back.

"Thank you for that most enlightening answer. Well—I'm glad most of you could be here." Mr. Yeager scribbled on a blue pad. In one fluid motion, he tossed the pen onto a pile of papers, held up a blue slip between two fingers, looked at the clock, and said, "Lab reports in the bin."

The clock read eight-ten. Like the Jeffersons, the clocks at Blackwater High had been purchased from Minutes-Take-Hours, Inc.

A boy near the door took the absence slip outside, and others walked from the back, collecting the reports.

The boy next to Margo didn't hand in homework. *Great. With little chance of passing biology, I got the dumb lab partner.*

Mr. Yeager rifled through the papers, drew out two, wadded them up, and made two perfect baskets in the corner trash can. "High school and they still can't get their name on their papers. Easy graders, kids, easy graders." He picked up his stapler.

What Margo needed was a smart person to write her name on their paper.

"Wait! Mr. Yeager!" A girl ran toward the front of the room.

The stapler slammed down.

The girl stopped a few feet from the table. "I was coming," she wailed.

"And yet, you're late."

"We had to go to my aunt's last night."

"And the other nights? This was assigned after last week's lab."

"I don't know."

"Is the ink dry? Tell you what. It's going to cost you fifteen points anyway, so hand it in tomorrow. And Veronica?"

"Yes."

"Work on it tonight. You can't hope to do a complete lab write-up during roll call." Mr. Yeager tossed the stapled papers in his briefcase. "Now, let's see about a little biology."

A wave of hopelessness washed over Margo.

Her lab partner waved his hand. "Sir, I believe there's a note about the assembly on the morning announcement sheet."

"Hey, now we're talking," someone said.

"Joy of joys. Thank you. I was aware of the announcement, but in the interest of biology, I planned to reveal the information at the end of class. Perhaps some hadn't heard."

"Sorry, sir."

Mr. Yeager picked up a half sheet of paper. "Safety Assembly: All students will report to their second period class and go with that teacher—oh my, I hadn't noticed this—go with that teacher to the assembly in the auditorium." Mr. Yeager took off his glasses and looked at the clock. "I can hardly wait to go to an assembly with second period General Science."

"Sir, I have to leave at a quarter till? AV Club?"

"Yes—Audio Visual." Mr. Yeager studied the class. "All right, if we can contain our excitement over the prospect of getting out of second period, perhaps we could open our textbooks to Chapter Two, page forty-three."

Mr. Yeager seemed to brighten at the prospect and began to draw a diagram of the heart on the board.

When Margo's lab partner got up to leave, she was surprised time had passed so quickly. Mr. Yeager showed the path of the blood passing through the heart and gave the class a handout that made sense.

When the bell rang, Mr. Yeager said, "OK, have a good day, class." The students herded toward the door in a rush, carrying Margo with them.

In Room 12, students were excited, but Miss Johnson closed the door and stood in front of the class. She wore a blue dress with a bow collar. "Thank you. Yes, there is an assembly. We'll be going together. I am sure I will not have to ask anyone to leave the auditorium."

Everyone was quiet.

"Good. Wait outside on the sidewalk."

The classes crowded toward the auditorium, bunched like sheep, and Margo had one hour to figure out how to pantomime starting a car.

Superman

THE AUDITORIUM WAS a grand old room with polished wood around the stage, like a huge fireplace mantle. Chris Ferguson sat three rows down and four persons to the right.

Sharon slid in beside Margo. "Hi."

"Hi. Are you in second period English?"

"No. I just don't want to sit with my second period class. Driver's Ed. Almost all boys. They're of the opinion that men are better drivers than women. All have a lot to learn." She rolled her eyes to the left.

Several boys laughed and joked with each other. One tried to stretch under Vivien Turner's seat to kick her heels.

A tall man moved toward the microphone.

"That's Mr. Tyler, the Vice-Principal. Everyone calls him Superman. He always seems to be watching, like Clark Kent, ready to jump into action. He actually is a good guy."

He did look like Clark Kent.

"May I have your attention?" It didn't seem to be a question. "Mr. Simpson, if you know what is good for you, you will stop that." Mr. Tyler fixed his X-ray eyes on the boy bouncing Vivien Turner's seat with his knees.

"This morning we will have a short auto safety presentation and movie by our school nurse, Miss Odegaard. In light of the rise in accidents in our community and the incident last week in the student parking lot, I'm sure this will be of interest to you all." Mr. Tyler's look seemed to ensure that everyone would be interested.

The boy next to Chris Ferguson said something, and Chris nodded.

"Ted Wilson bumped another kid's car," Sharon whispered. "The Driver's Ed boys had eeeendless discussions about the mistakes Ted made." She grinned.

Miss Odegaard looked very stylish in her navy skirt and white blouse with a red ribbon tie under the sailor collar. She stepped quickly across the stage as she came to the microphone. There was a snicker from the back.

26

"I think I'm feeling sick," a boy said. "I may need to go see the nurse."

Miss Odegaard spoke with a lovely Norwegian accent. She stressed the need for auto safety and first aid at the scene of an accident. She shaded her eyes and said, "OK, I think we're abowt to start the movie now."

Spotlights flashed on and off, and finally, the main lights went out.

"Yep. Definitely feeling like a visit to the nurse!"

The projector flashed numbers, and Miss Odegaard straightened the corner of the screen. She stepped aside to admire her handiwork as the screen rattled up to reveal a cluttered stage. She gave a little squeak and jumped back.

The projector stopped, and after spotlights flickered on and off, the auditorium lights came on again. There were groans and laughter.

Miss Odegaard looked up to where the screen had disappeared, and furtively beckoned to someone in the wings.

Sharon leaned close. "Poor Miss Odegaard. It's her first year."

Margo knew how she felt.

"Get Dr. Fix-It," someone yelled.

"Yeah, we want Fix-It, we want Fix-It."

A glance from Mr. Tyler's Superman eyes and the voices died to a mumble.

"Who's Dr. Fix-It?"

Sharon lifted one finger. "Wait. You'll see."

Mr. Tyler went to the microphone. Miss Odegaard looked down at her folded hands.

Mr. Tyler shaded his eyes, looking up at the projection booth. "Alan? Alan, your young assistant is unable to locate the pole used to pull down the screen. Alan?"

Someone stood up and turned toward the projection booth. "Hey, Fix-It, Tyler wants yah!"

"And that will cost you another week on the Broom Squad, Jason."

Jason sat down, shaking his head.

"Barn's Broomies." Sharon gave Margo a crooked smile. "You'll see them around after school, with Mr. Barns, sweeping sidewalks and gutters. Some people are slow learners." She tilted her head toward Jason.

Mr. Tyler shaded his eyes again. "Alan? Oh, here you are."

Margo's lab partner appeared on stage with a long pole. She almost saw the humor of it. Of course her lab partner would be Dr. Fix-It! He stood under the screen and spoke to someone backstage.

"Yay! Dr. Fix-It. Fix-It will fix it."

A boy, who looked like a freshman, brought a chair. Alan stood on the chair and retrieved the screen.

Chris Ferguson shifted in his seat. He had a lovely head.

"Hurray! Fix-It fixed it!" someone yelled. "Bravo!" came from another part of the room, followed by laughter.

Mr. Tyler quieted the crowd and looked at his watch. "Well now, we should be about ready."

The auditorium darkened, the screen bathed by one blue spotlight. It got brighter and then dimmed. *Maybe there won't be time for Theater.*

The movie played well, except for a fluttering effect that lasted only long enough for someone to yell, "Put another nickel in!" Margo's stomach fluttered with the picture.

At least Chris wouldn't be in her theater class. Maybe she would fumble putting the key in the ignition. She had seen Mother do that.

A Pipe Organ?

ON THE WALK HOME, MARGO paused where the last gentle turn eased the lane toward the house. If it weren't enough to have to retake biology again, her lab partner was the laughing-stock of the school. Maybe she would ask Mr. Yeager for another partner.

Theater class had been awful. Margo sat in a chair and pretended to turn a key. She pumped her foot on the imaginary gas pedal and tried the key again. One of the boys whispered, "Wrong foot, that's the clutch."

Margo had laid both arms on the imaginary steering wheel and leaned her head on them. If it had been a real wheel, she would have pounded her head on it. Mrs. Kavanagh started a weak round of applause.

Vivien Turner, who was to portray someone threading a needle, had Mrs. Kavanagh laughing when she pretended to get tangled in the thread. She tried to unwind herself by turning around and around. She wound the thread back on to an imaginary spool only to drop it and chase it across the room.

Margo began walking toward the house again, marveling at her own lack of imagination under the weight of her peers watching. Why didn't she have an imagination like that? She could have tried to open the hood.

In PE, a girl had said, "You really know how to handle the ball." It had been the bright spot in the day. Margo used her advanced conversational skills and nodded.

At noon, Chris had come into the lunchroom. He hadn't seen her sitting with three girls in a corner. It was just as well because the girls turned out to be freshmen. Margo didn't want him to think she didn't have any friends her age, but then she didn't have any friends. Chris laughed easily with the lunch ladies. Remembering the broadness of his shoulders tapering to his tidy waist, Margo walked quickly.

Where the lane met the driveway, she looked up at the house, remembering to keep her mouth closed; a lesson from Grandmother. "Don't let your mouth hang open when you look up. It makes a person look dull."

When she came through the French doors, a single tone could be heard in the quiet house. She moved through the library, letting the sound lead her down a hallway. The house seemed to go on forever. Margo came to a room that held an organ console with several rows of ivory keys. Pipes gathered in clumps against a wall.

"Maggie! Is it time for school to be over already? It seems I just had lunch." T. Charles balanced between rows of metal tubes, some as tall as he. He fiddled behind a pipe and the tone stopped playing. "Sorry, a note was stuck."

"Are you building an organ in the house?"

"I rescued it from an old church being demolished. It seemed a shame to let it be destroyed." He pointed to wads of wires wrapped in black cloth. "These contain hundreds of wires they cut with an ax. I have to test each wire and hook it back to the correct pipe. An odd hobby, I suppose."

Margo shifted her books.

"How was your school day?"

She didn't want an avalanche of questions. "It was all right, we played Basketball in PE."

"I liked running as a boy." He rubbed a smudge on his cheek.

"Would you like me to make tea?"

"Mmmm?" T. Charles bent over a bundle of wires.

"Would you like me to make a pot of tea?"

"Sounds fine. I'll come into the study in a minute. I want to check these connections I just made."

From the kitchen, she heard a musical scale. She laughed when one note tooted like a small child's whistle among others that rumbled like distant foghorns.

T. Charles had washed his face and hands when Margo carried the tray into the study.

"Here, let me show you where the cookies are." In the kitchen, he took the head off a fat bear and put cookies on dessert plates that matched the cups. He winked. "Two cookies won't spoil our supper."

"When did Virginia pass away?" It wasn't a question for polite conversation, Grandmother would have said, and Margo regretted asking.

"Early January 1953—just before dawn the morning of the fourth." T. Charles was somber. "She was ready—tired of the fight." He took a deep breath. "She had been in the hospital but insisted she die at home. Dr. Caldwell checked in the night before to give her a shot for the pain. He said it wouldn't be long."

It was one of the few times Margo agreed with Grandmother. Sometimes, there were things you'd rather not know.

T. Charles gave a tired laugh under his breath. "She worried about leaving me. Worried that I wouldn't—do well. I suppose she was right. For a while, I laid on the couch with the drapes closed. Oh, I kept playing the organ at the church. I didn't starve. Folks bring lots of food, you know."

Aunt Louise had taken a tuna casserole to Mrs. Pacini next door when her husband died. Mrs. Pacini had brought the dish back in spotless condition along with Margo's first biscotti.

"Then, I decided to rescue the organ. It was just something to do but has turned into quite a project." T. Charles stood. "I suppose I had better start supper. Do you like tacos?"

Margo had never had a taco, but during dinner decided she could eat them every day.

T. Charles went back to the organ, and after Margo played several piano rolls Grandfather had recorded, she read her English assignment.

Later, she sat in the study, listening to occasional bursts of music followed by periods of silence. When T. Charles began to play in earnest, Margo thought of Captain Nemo in the movie *20,000 Leagues Under the Sea*, playing the organ in his submarine. She slipped upstairs.

She put her hand on the doorknob to the room next to hers. The rooms shared a bathroom; T. Charles had called it a Jack and Jill. Margo wanted to peek inside, but the organ had been quiet, and she decided to ask.

T. Charles was halfway up the stairs as Margo started down.

"Uncle, what do you have in the room that shares my bathroom?"

"Goodness, a lot of old clothes—things of Virginia's."

"Can I look?"

"Certainly." T. Charles opened the door, the faint smell of mothballs coaxing memories of Aunt Louise's winter coat. He turned on the light. Large square garment bags hung on racks. Against one wall was a makeup dresser with lights around the mirror. A row of large wardrobes lined another wall, with cabinets under the windows.

Margo sat on the edge of the bench in front of the dresser and turned the switch at the bottom of the mirror.

"That's unplugged." T. Charles found the outlet, the bulbs brightening the room.

Margo pushed her hair behind her ears. "Are the dressers full of clothes, too?" She needed to cut her hair.

"Some. Others are costume jewelry. Open one."

There were gloves, necklaces, earrings, and handbags. "Did Virginia wear all these?"

"Oh, no. No indeed. The clothes in the garment bags are Virginia's and the dressers over there. I moved them in here—for now. The rest of these things were part of Virginia's work. She was a photographer. She did women's magazine ads, and these were part of the wardrobe she used. It was all downstairs once, but when the organ came, I moved them up here."

"Did she take pictures in the house?"

"Yes. In New York, she had a studio. When we moved to California, she couldn't see renting a building when we had a house such as this. She had a dressing room and a darkroom in the basement."

"Did famous movie stars come here?" Margo remembered a movie scene with glamorous women being photographed under gleaming reflectors.

T. Charles gave her a shy grin. "Not really. She worked with a modeling agency. A few of her subjects later worked in films. No one very famous. She used the back garden for some of the work."

Every drawer, every corner of the room was filled with things to try on. "Do you mind if I look around?"

"Not at all. Take extra care with these." T. Charles patted the garment bags. "Take a look, but be sure to zip them back in place because of moths. Many of Virginia's things are silk or wool."

T. Charles went to the door. "Have fun. I'm going to turn in. Good night, Maggie."

Her biology reading nagged, but Margo tried on earrings that dripped with purple stones. She settled a hat on her head with a broad rim and a net that covered her eyes. She tilted her head and said, "Hello dahling." She pulled gloves above her elbows and turned sideways in the mirror.

With the help of a partially dried makeup kit, she had to admit she was pleased with the effect. A red "Sabrina" dress of Virginia's almost fit when she gathered it from behind with one hand.

Her mother's words played in the moment. "Don't worry—you'll fill out. You're just a late bloomer." Alone in the room, Margo felt as awkward as she had when Mother said such things. But, for the first time, maybe, there was a chance.

Grace

THE PILLOWCASE WAS smeared with hues of red and pink. Margo turned it inside out, hoping makeup washed out. In the bathroom mirror, without the dress, earrings, and hat, the effect was gone, leaving plain Margo.

In the kitchen, she watched T. Charles bustling around, chattering about the day. Asking Father for a favor was better done after he had eaten breakfast and was no longer grumpy. Pleasantness seemed to be in T. Charles's nature.

Miss Johnson had referred to a character in a short story as "an affable fellow." Margo decided that description fit T. Charles to a "T." The pun tickled her.

"Uncle, would you mind if I borrowed a red beret from upstairs?"

"Of course not! Are you going to wear it to school?"

"Not today." She probably wouldn't have the nerve to wear the beret out of her bedroom.

At school, Margo suffered from the guilt of not studying. She drifted through the morning, settling into her regular pattern of invisibility. Her teachers added to her guilt. After the first three classes, it was hard to justify not caring. The teachers at Blackwater paid attention to their students. Every morning Miss Johnson looked each of them in the eye. Mrs. Kavnagh said, "Have a good day, Margo," after class.

Basketball Girl waited for Margo near the PE building.

"Hey, Margaret. Remember me from PE?"

"Margo." Was she that unremarkable?

"Huh?"

"My name is Margo."

"Oh—yeah. I'm Grace."

Margo offered a lackluster nod.

Grace rubbed her hands together. "You haven't been here the whole year. Where did you come from?"

"I just moved here—from Wisconsin."

"I'm new too. Iowa, only I started at the beginning of the year." Grace moved with the easy rhythm of an athlete. "In Iowa, I played on the Varsity Girls' six-on-six basketball team."

Margo didn't doubt it.

"You play in Wisconsin?"

"I played a little GAA last year. I move a lot."

"GAA?" Grace stopped. "Girls' Athletic Association is nothing but intramurals! They have GAA in Iowa, too. I played *Girls' Varsity*, against other schools."

Grace put her hands on her hips. She was slightly taller than Margo, a welcome change. "Here, they don't have girls' basketball. Not real teams, like the boys have."

Margo considered this information.

After they changed into their gym suits, Grace pulled her aside. "I started last year, at my old school. I was first string—forward. Varsity! As a sophomore!"

Margo watched a girl braid her hair with quick ease.

"Don't you see? There's nothing for me here. GAA is not real basketball. One of the girls told me the GAA girls are *servers* at the spring sports banquet." Grace swept her hand at imaginary tables. "For the boys!"

"Well, I guess it's different in California."

"My grandmother played center when *she* was in high school! My grandmother is old. It was 1920 something." Grace gathered energy. "Don't you see? What am *I* supposed to do?"

Where's the teacher?

"I talked to Mrs. Peters about it, and she said they've never had girls' basketball here."

Margo stepped back, eyeing the locker room door.

"I even went and talked to the Vice-Principal," Grace smirked. "Did you know they call him Superman? Anyway, he said it's up to the school board, and the school board is not in favor of girls' basketball."

Mrs. Peters came out with a bag of basketballs and took attendance. "Bounce passes." She began to roll out the balls.

After PE, Grace followed Margo out of the locker room. "What's your phone number?"

"I don't know." When she wasn't nodding, she was blushing. "I mean, I haven't used the phone yet." Who was she going to call? "It should be listed under T. Charles Blackwater."

"Blackwater? Like the school? In roll call, you're in the M's. McClaran or something."

"I live with my uncle."

"I'll try to call you tonight." Grace disappeared into a crowd.

T. CHARLES WAS WORKING on the organ and didn't hear Margo come home. She went to the kitchen for milk and cookies. Grandmother's words rang in her mind. "Eat. You need to put some meat on those bones." As if she wanted to be skinny.

In her room, Margo was determined to read the assignment in biology. She plodded through seven of the twelve pages before her mind wandered to thoughts of Chris Ferguson. Three times she was a page or two ahead and had no memory of what she had read. T. Charles rustled around in the kitchen, and Margo went down.

"Hello Maggie. How is my girl?"

"OK."

"What have you been up to? I heard you go upstairs a while ago."

"Studying. Biology."

"I was good at numbers when I was in high school. In fact, the teacher had me help other students." T. Charles took placemats from a drawer.

"I can set the table."

"Thank you. Tonight is choir, so I have to go down to the church. You're welcome to come. It'll be about two hours."

"Maybe next week. I need to write to my parents."

"If you're sure you'll be all right."

After dinner, T. Charles made sure all the doors were secure and left. The Packard purred as it went under the portico.

Margo took her biology book downstairs, to be closer to the phone. Instead of reading, she started a letter to Mother and Father, making sure to sound happy and involved.

She jumped when the phone rang, grabbing it before the second ring disturbed the quiet. "Hello?"

"Hello, Margo? It's Grace."

"Yeah–yes." Grandmother didn't approve of "Yeah."

"What are you doing?"

"Nothing. Writing to my parents."

"OK, so—I have this fantastic idea."

"Mmm?"

"Listen. What happens tomorrow afternoon, seventh-period?"

"Pep rally?" Margo looked forward to missing history.

"Right. And a bunch of girls will be dressed up real cute and cheer the 'He-Men' to victory."

The description sounded familiar.

"There are four more football games, but basketball tryouts are before football ends." There was a pause. "Let's try out."

"I thought you said there's no girls' team."

"No, for *the* team. The Big Team."

"Oh?" *In front of the boys?* She sat up straighter, moving the phone to the other ear.

"Don't you see? You're good. Probably good enough for JV. I've been watching some of the guys play after school. They aren't that good."

"I don't know. Won't we get in trouble?" Grace was a steamroller, not to be stopped. Margo could see herself mashed flat, like in the cartoons.

"Might be worth it. Think it over."

Later in bed, Margo allowed herself to daydream about the boys' basketball team. Exercise would give her a better appetite. She could gain weight.

Someone said Chris Ferguson would be captain. Margo watched the moonlight splashing the leaves of the oak outside, imagining the last moments of a game. "Margo McKinney snaps a quick pass to Ferguson, who is up for two!"

Maybe she would get a letterman sweater.

Margo turned on her side and drew up her knees. Probably not possible, even in daydreams.

The Path of Least Resistance

BOYS, NOT OUT FOR FOOTBALL, organized themselves in preseason basketball practice. Chris Ferguson loafed back, spun, and made a set shot that never touched the rim. Layups started.

"See, they're not so hot," Grace said. "The skinny guy, Jimmy Smith? He's missed every shot today."

Margo nodded.

"Sure, there are a lot of good players, but if Jimmy Smith's going out, I see no reason we shouldn't be."

Jimmy bounced a layup off the bottom of the rim.

"We have to begin to practice," Grace said.

"With them?!" She had no intention of practicing in front of Chris. She longed for a chance to see him, but not in her gym suit.

"No. We don't say a word until the first day of tryouts."

Chris rolled the ball gently off the backboard, and it swirled into the net.

"Where?"

"We can use the courts by the girls' locker room after school. Mrs. Peters gave me permission." Grace pulled Margo's chin, so she was looking at her. "Start Monday?"

"When are the tryouts?"

"Three weeks. Plenty of time!"

Plenty of time to say no.

Margo couldn't be sure if Chris recognized her. He looked up once, and she smiled, her face growing hot. Chris gave a slight jerk of his head, rebounded Jimmy's missed layup, and made an easy jump shot.

Margo searched for a way to bring Chris into the conversation without giving Grace the idea she liked him. Like? This was a mad crush.

After a few minutes, Chris left, and Margo lost all interest in watching practice. She waited a few minutes and suggested they leave.

"I think I'll stay for a while. Jimmy Smith has to make at least one this afternoon." Grace made a face. "Hey, I'll call you this evening."

On the way to her locker, Margo saw Chris striding across campus toward the student parking lot. He carried his binder and books under one arm and held his head very straight.

She hurried across the quad and got to the front sidewalk as Chris drove past. Margo wished she knew more about cars. It was an older model but sounded powerful. She was a goner. Even this guy's car was appealing!

Margo walked back to her locker. She picked up *The Elements of Style*, sighed, and put it back.

Sharon Jackson twiddled a dial, three lockers down. "Hey Margo-Who's-Car-Is-Flooded. What are you doing?"

"I came to get my biology book."

"I've been tutoring Melissa Jenkins in Algebra. How's Mr. Yeager?"

"My lab partner is Alan—the AV guy."

Sharon twisted her mouth into a wry grin. "You got Alan Dumont? That's not all bad. Alan's smart." She lowered her head to work the combination. "He aced General Science when we were freshmen. He took a special chemistry last year, so is doing biology this year. Does he still put his homework in the bin before Mr. Yeager asks for it to be turned in?"

Margo didn't know because she hadn't bothered to notice. "Is that your locker?

"No. Just a mathematical test. Forty to the third power. You know, *The Sixty-four Thousand Dollar Question* sort of thing." Sharon shrugged happily. "Just thought I would try."

Margo picked up *The Elements of Style* only to put it back again. She shut her locker.

"So, are you ready for the next Theater assignment?" Sharon asked.

"I don't know. Vivien Turner is so good. How does she think of all those things for her pantomime?"

"Vivien? Oh, she's quite the thespian. She had the lead in *Our Town* last year. Not bad for a sophomore. And she does have bouncy curls." Sharon gave Margo a one dimple smile.

"I can't think of anything clever. I looked like a dope in that chair."

"Hey, want to hear a joke? OK, a woman's car stalls at a stop sign. So, she's trying to start her car, and the guy behind her keeps honking his horn. Finally, she gets out and goes back and says, 'Hey, Mister, I'll honk the horn for you if you'll go start my car.'"

Margo laughed; Sharon made things better.

They reached the sidewalk and stood under the canopy of a huge oak. Sharon looked up into the branches. "I'll see you Monday, in Theater." She held her binder between her knees, pulled her ponytail tight, and fluttered her fingers as she walked away.

Margo fell asleep that night, stewing over why she hadn't told Grace she wouldn't try out for basketball. The answer was simple. When uncomfortable situations arose, she hid. Perhaps she would call Grace in the morning.

SUN STREAMED THROUGH the leaves outside, making shapes and contours, changing in the light breeze. Margo lay in bed practicing the right words to say: I don't think I want to—I don't think I should—I don't think I will have time—.

The sound of the vacuum downstairs disturbed her thoughts, and she dressed quickly.

"Good morning, Maggie! I left a plate in the oven. Can't work without fuel. I have a woman, Mrs. Brice, come on Saturday mornings to help keep the house tidy."

It was surprising how the morning improved with breakfast. Good food, the sun coming in the window, and T. Charles bustling around with a white dust rag trailing from his back pocket made her smile.

When Mrs. Brice arrived, T. Charles announced the basement needed a "spring cleaning."

Mrs. Brice had bright red fingernails, red lipstick, and gold earrings dangling from pierced ears. After introductions, she said, "Might get it done by spring if we start now, Mr. Blackwater. I've waited six years for a chance to shovel that mess out. A hazard is what that basement is. What a person doesn't trip over could fall on 'em!"

The next hour involved Mrs. Brice asking for boxes to be moved and old chairs to be rearranged while she "got at" the cobwebs with a broom. She occasionally held up objects, insisting that T. Charles throw them away. When he agreed, it was Margo's job to make trips to the trashcans in the alley.

Mrs. Brice called a rest break. "I've got to have my mid-morning coffee. Can't work without my mid-morning coffee."

"Maggie, would you care to see Virginia's darkroom?" T. Charles motioned toward a walled-off corner of the basement. "I never did know too much about photography, but Virginia could work in here by the hour." He opened the door and flipped the light switch. The room glowed red.

In contrast to the cluttered basement, the darkroom was immaculate. Trays and equipment lined the counters. Other than two dead spiders, all was in perfect order.

"Virginia designed this herself. These drawers are light proof—these for storage." T. Charles opened drawers that contained lenses, cameras, and dark bottles of murky fluid. "I suppose all these chemicals have gone bad, but this equipment was of fine quality in its day. She had started working with this movie camera." T. Charles touched a brown case.

When he opened it, a lonely camera lay inside. It was as if the darkroom waited for Virginia. Margo shook off a deep longing for Virginia to be there, healthy, taking pictures. Sitting on the couch in the evening. Having girl talk on Saturday afternoons.

At noon Mrs. Brice prepared to leave. "A couple more Saturdays, and this place will begin to shape up. And now, Maggie, you have to keep him from carrying more junk down here. Most things he wants to hide down here could just a well be stored at the dump."

T. Charles gave Margo a quick wink.

Margo ran the vacuum in the study. She decided not to call Grace; she would tell Grace in PE that she wasn't going to try out for basketball.

Bonnie Douglas

GRACE MADE A LIST OF skills to practice. The hardest part was running. The boys jogged six laps around the track each afternoon before they began practice, and Grace insisted they do the same. Margo's lungs burned, and her legs felt shaky.

Why hadn't she told Grace she wouldn't try out? She remained silent, rehearsed words unspoken, further proof of her lack of courage.

One afternoon they met Chris, coming off the track. He ran with that effortless pace athletes have, as if the ground had springs that added bounce to each stride. He said, "Hey," but Margo was unsure if he was greeting her, or Grace, or both of them. She was grateful they were starting their run, so he didn't see her red-faced, panting like a dog.

While her running improved, her grades did not. Mr. Yeager began the skeletal system, and by the time they got to the feet and hands, metatarsal and metacarpal seemed to jumble together in her brain. There was a quiz coming that woke her early in the mornings.

In lab, the trays with frogs pinned to black tar came back out of the cupboards, formaldehyde filling the air. Alan prodded their frog's front foot with a tiny pick. "If we can peel the skin back, we'll see the metacarpus."

Margo scribbled in her binder and backed up a step.

Alan jerked his head. "Come here and look; it won't bite you. You can see the anatomy is simpler than ours, but it's all there. This is the thumb."

Margo dutifully leaned in and held down the tiny foot with the pick while Alan worked with the knife. Her hands would smell for a week.

Mr. Yeager brought around a frog skeleton and a hand lens for everyone to see. "Good job, kids. Margo, make sure you get your lab report in on time."

Margo glanced at her notebook. "Metakarpus," was all she had written.

When the hour was over, Alan offered her hand lotion from a tiny bottle. "Helps kill the smell."

While she rubbed the smooth cream in, Alan scribbled several lines in her notebook.

"Thanks." *Metacarpus*. Maybe Dr. Fixit would fix her grade.

After school, Grace met Margo at her locker. "We can't practice this afternoon. The Broom Squad has court duty."

Margo hid a surge of joy behind a weak smile.

Grace stood on her toes, reaching high. "I think we should go see how the boys are doing. Besides, we still have a week."

Time was running out, and fear turned Margo cold. Her thoughts screamed, "Get me out of this! I don't want to do this!" Instead, she said, "Remember, we haven't made it yet."

"And we never will, with talk like that. Come on! You're good!"

Margo tried to nod with confidence while inside she pleaded, "Please, let's forget the whole idea." It was the perfect moment to say, "I can't go today." She hurried to catch Grace.

"Besides," Grace chatted happily, "I haven't seen Jimmy Smith miss a layup for a while. In history, he was telling Sharon Jackson he's a sure thing for the team—the little bragger."

Mary Suttle from Typing joined them. "Did you hear Chris Ferguson broke up with Bonnie Douglas?"

Bonnie Douglas? Margo had never seen Chris with a girl.

Grace kicked a pebble off the walk. "So she broke up with him. Who cares?"

"No, Chris broke up with *her* and asked for his letterman sweater back."

"Oh, I suppose *he* was wearing her cheerleading sweater?"

"Grace, you're so ridiculous sometimes," Mary said.

They turned toward the gym.

"I bet he wants to date other girls," Mary breathed.

"So, let him," Grace grumbled.

"If he asked me out, I'd go!" Mary said.

I would too.

Mary turned away. "Gotta go."

Why *had* Chris broken up with Bonnie? Would he see them in the stands? Maybe he would look up and smile. That made Margo smile.

They climbed halfway up the bleachers before they found a spot that suited Grace. "It's all psychology. We want to be high enough that the boys look small."

Chris wasn't on the court.

"Watch the passes. They're really pouring it on. At tryouts, they'll probably really burn it in, hoping we muff it. We'll see about that."

Chris Ferguson was not at practice.

"Oh, great going Jimmy," Grace snarled. "What a butterfingers."

Chris had been there at lunchtime. She had learned to spot him standing against the lockers with the other basketball players. Maybe he was sick.

"Oh, great. Layups." Grace began a matter of fact narrative. "First guy with the ducktail, a miss. Look at that hair. He thinks he's so cool. Next comes a hit. Of course, he TOOK FOUR STEPS! Jimmy Smith comes in with his usual flub. Thomas is a hit, but traveling again!" Grace leaned her elbows on her knees, chin up. "Well, that's a big zero so far."

Margo watched the side doors.

"I tell you, we have this sewed up. Any five of the six from my starting team in Iowa would clobber these guys."

Maybe Chris isn't trying out. Margo's interest in basketball slipped to negative numbers. He had broken up with Bonnie Douglas. Did he want to date other girls? Was there another girl he liked?

Margo doubted it could be her. Their paths never crossed; Chris was always across the quad or walking with his friends. Did he even remember she existed?

She was in misery.

Football?

SHARON WAITED BY MARGO'S locker. "Well, girl-from-out-of-state, it's time you joined in with the traditional high school customs. Friday, we're going to the game and then the dance afterward."

"I'll have to ask my uncle." Margo didn't know if she wanted to go to a football game. "I thought you'd think football is stupid."

"Oh, it is." Sharon rolled her eyes. "And the dance will be pretty bad, too. You're watching American Bandstand, right? Very important."

Sharon did a quick dance step. "Football will be endless cheering about things we don't understand. But that's OK. I don't think anyone actually knows what's happening out there. They run into each other a lot."

Sharon said things out loud that Margo only thought.

"Done?" Sharon slammed the locker door shut and twisted the combination dial. "You have to admit the shape of the football is pretty comical. I mean, isn't the very definition of a ball something round? Who thought up that thing?"

Margo laughed.

"Well—they hardly ever kick it. You would think there would be more foot involved." Sharon began to walk backward. "But look, it's the thing. We go to the game. We go to the dance. Who knows? One of the guys lined up against the wall under the clock might get up the nerve to ask a girl to dance. And it's fun watching all the steadies. Some are actually good!"

Were Chris and Bonnie "steadies" who were good dancers? What would she do if someone asked her to dance? When she watched American Bandstand in the living room, she was self-conscious with only the television. What if she were asked by a boy who was shorter than her? It seemed the girls on American Bandstand were short and cute.

"Last week, we got to see Gina Lioni break up with Cid Palmer. It was quite the to-do. She threw his ring at him but missed, and it took all his friends to help him find it under some chairs in the corner. Apparently, they had a 'misunderstanding' about Sharla Collins. All very dramatic."

"I guess I could ask my uncle."

"Hey, the game is with Pasadena. That ought to be entertaining. Last year Pasadena left in the middle of the fourth quarter, and three plays later, we scored our first touchdown!"

Margo grinned. "Are we that bad, or is Pasadena that good?"

"Blackwater just lost three guys for stealing answers to a Physics test, so it could be pretty bad. Back to the game—it'll be cold, and the seats damp with dew. The band will be there in their ill-fitting hats. We will be wishing we were somewhere else. It'll be great!"

Sharon leaned her books against the base of the oak and tightened her ponytail. "Tell your uncle there's a cheer bus. We watch the game, and the dance is in the cafeteria. It'll smell like sour milk in there." Sharon held up one finger. "It *is* well chaperoned. Mr. Keller will be there, wooing Miss Johnson. Tell your uncle he has to pick you up at eleven. They don't let girls go without a parent or a note giving permission to go with someone."

"Miss Johnson and Mr. Keller?"

"Oh, I think so. Come on. It'll be fun."

Testing, One, Two, Three

ALAN LEANED AGAINST a library bookshelf, reading *Popular Electronics*. He didn't notice Margo, but three other boys looked up.

"Alan?" she tried to whisper, but it came out loud and hoarse.

One of the boys said, "Hey, Dr. Fixit. Some girl wants you."

Alan slipped the magazine into his binder and came over. "Glad you're here. I need your help."

Margo sat down. "You said you'd help me get ready for the test. You promised."

"Mr. Evans tried to use the PA system in the auditorium and—well, it didn't work."

Margo had no interest in PA systems. "Alan, I have to have help with the bones quiz!"

"Listen, Mr. Evans told Mr. Tyler, and Mr. Tyler says if the equipment isn't fixed by morning, he's giving me Broom Squad!" A wry grin appeared. "I was supposed to fix the problem two weeks ago. How about it? A half-hour?"

"What would I have to do?"

"Great." Alan started toward the door.

"Just a moment," the librarian said. "Let me see your notebook."

"I'm clean." Alan put the binder on the desk. "Just school work."

The librarian rifled the papers sticking out of the binder and tugged on the corner of the magazine. "And what is this?"

"Oh, yes. I was going to check that out."

"This copy came in today. You know they are not available for checkout for a month."

"How 'bout I promise to bring it back before the library opens in the morning. I'll drop it in the book slot. I have to be at school early—it will be in the slot by seven-thirty."

"Rules are rules. And while we're on the subject, there are four other copies of Popular Electronics missing. Two are checked out to you and are overdue."

"I can bring the overdue in tomorrow as well. I cannot vouch for the missing magazines." Alan paused for effect. "It saddens me to think that someone would walk out with library property."

The librarian folded her arms.

One of the boys moved behind them with a copy of *Hot Rod Magazine*. "Move along, Fixit. Go show a movie." He raised his eyebrows. Margo gazed at a poster behind the checkout desk.

"I'm on the way to fix the public address system in the auditorium. This magazine may help me diagnose the problem." Alan tipped his head and offered the librarian a contrite smile.

The woman returned an unblinking stare.

"Perhaps I should leave the magazine for now." He placed it carefully on the counter and started for the door.

Margo glanced over her shoulder, whispering, "How can you stand there in front of those guys and argue with the librarian?"

"Listen, she knows I know she knows I have a few copies of the magazine. It's all part of the game. Mrs. Ziller is OK. She had the new copy set aside for me when I came in today."

Alan moved toward the history wing.

"I thought we were going to the auditorium."

"I have to make a quick stop. Mr. Mills will have to open the auditorium."

A man stopped cleaning chalkboards in an empty room. He wiped the eraser with a cloth, glancing at Alan.

"Hi, Mr. Mills."

"Hello, Alan. It is good to see you." He gave Margo a wistful look. "Who is your pretty friend? She's not the nice little girl I met before."

Blood rushed to Margo's face. If she was so pretty, why wasn't Chris Ferguson noticing?

"Mr. Mills, I take great pleasure in introducing you to Margo McKinney."

Mr. Mills looked puzzled. "It's good to see you." He slid the cloth along the chalk rail, catching the dust at the end in a battered Schilling Coffee can.

"Mr. Mills, I need to get into the auditorium. I have a note from Mr. Tyler." Alan fumbled in his binder and finally dug a crumpled piece of paper from his back pocket.

Mr. Mills studied the note. "Alan, this says after school," he said slowly. "It's five minutes until four. School is out at three-thirty-five."

"But, sir, it *is* after school."

"Well. I can trust you, can't I? Because the note says after school."

"Scout's honor."

Mr. Mills locked the door and led them to the auditorium. "Make sure you turn out all the lights and that this door closes behind you. I'll come check after I finish the Science Building. I always finish the Science Building at five-thirty."

Mr. Mills looked at the note again. "I'm going to keep this note. I want to keep this note in case Mr. Tyler asks me why I let you in. It says after school." He looked down the corridor. "I have to hurry. I should be in Room 58 by now."

"It'll be OK, Mr. Mills. Mr. Tyler knows I'm going to work on the PA system."

Once inside, Alan moved quickly. "Come on and stay right behind me. I have eyes like a cat in the dark."

On the stage, Alan turned on a light. He wrung his hands like a mad scientist and hunched one shoulder. "And now, Margo, we must get to work."

He pulled a paper sack from under the counter and emptied odd-looking parts next to several boxes with knobs. He flipped one on its back, revealing a snarl of wires.

"Do you know what you're doing? Should you be messing with all those electric things?" She brushed aside three withered balloons and laid her books on the counter.

Alan turned his head slightly. "I built my first radio when I was nine. I built this preamp and amplifier."

Once Alan started to work, time dragged for Margo. She occasionally held a part with skinny pliers.

"Hold this—right there—hold the end up a little more." A trail of smoke came up from the soldering iron.

Alan flipped the box right side up. "This is the grand moment. Go talk into the microphone." He unplugged the soldering iron and plugged in several cables.

She took a step toward the microphone, looking at her feet. "What should I say?"

"Anything. I just want to test the system."

She backed away. "I feel silly."

"Say, testing, one, two, three."

Margo leaned forward. "Testi-" Her voice boomed through the auditorium, followed by a high-pitched squeal. She covered her ears.

Alan made an adjustment and went to the middle of the auditorium. "Say something else."

She leaned in again. "Margo."

"Mr. Evans can't complain about that. Hey, come here. I want to show you something."

Glad to get away from the microphone, Margo joined Alan.

"Sit here. Tenth row, center. I'll be right back."

Alan ran up the steps and behind a curtain. From the side, he appeared, wearing a cape, mustache, and a top hat.

He crept across the stage, and she had to laugh. He was pretty funny, and Margo hissed the villain.

"What do you think?"

"The costume is great. It makes you look like you're in an old movie."

"Come on, try it."

On the stage, Margo moved between three paint blotches, making a small triangle in the spotlight.

"Do some acting."

"I can't act." She wondered if bouncy curls would give her stage presence.

"Sure you can. You're in theater class, aren't you? Pretend you're a damsel, picking flowers." Alan went into the wings and brought out a basket. "Pick flowers. Put them in your basket. Perfect. Let's do a skit."

"I can't." *Why am I even taking theater?*

"You just did. Look, you pick your flowers, and I'll grab your arm and drag you away. We will do a tug o' war, back and forth."

Margo picked flowers, and Alan twirled his mustache, grabbing her arm.

"Put the back of your hand up to your forehead—there you go. Now I pull you. Pretend to yell, Help! Help!"

She let herself be pulled.

"Now, I drag you downstage and tie you to the train track. Just kneel down." Alan tied an imaginary knot. "No, look toward the audience. Never turn your back on the audience."

She pretended to struggle.

Alan brushed his hands together. "That was great. All we need is a hero to rescue you."

Chris Ferguson could save me, lift me, carry me to safety, the dream shuddering to a stop at, *and kiss me*. Margo blushed. *Seventeen and never been kissed.*

"Too bad we can't make a movie of something like this."

"My uncle has a movie camera."

Alan stopped. "What do you mean, a movie camera?"

"It's in the basement. There's a darkroom and cameras and—it's in a case. It's sort of black and chrome."

"Wait. How big is this camera?"

Margo gestured with her hands. "Like so, I don't know. I only saw it once."

"We have to go look at it. Can we go now?"

Margo looked at the clock above the sound cabinet. "Oh, no! It's five-twenty. I have to go." Panic rose in her chest. She grabbed her books and hurried up the aisle.

"Wait. Let me turn off the lights."

"I'm late! Leave me alone! You said you'd help me study, and now I'm in trouble."

"Margo, wait!"

The Packard pulled into the parking lot as she approached.

Alan hurried to the car, opened the door, and Margo got in.

"I'm sorry," she mumbled. T. Charles had been so kind, and if she kept acting like this, she would end up at the Morrisons.

Alan ducked his head into the car. "I'm sorry Margo is late, sir. She helped me repair an important piece of equipment needed for the debate team tomorrow."

"Thank you for staying with Maggie until I got here."

"As it should be, sir. Have a nice evening, *Maggie*. Thanks for helping."

T. Charles maneuvered the car out to the street, the dials on the dash giving a soft yellowish glow.

"I'm sorry, Uncle."

T. Charles made a turn. "It's all right, but I was worried. If you plan to be late, you need to tell me." He patted her hand on the seat. "I was concerned."

Tears burned her eyes. "I'll be more responsible."

"Who was the young man?"

"Just a boy." How many times had the importance of introductions been drilled into her. "Alan Dumont. He's my lab partner in biology class."

T. Charles wheeled the car into the garage. "I waited supper for you. I can warm it up in no time."

No one had ever waited supper for her, but then she had never come home late before.

"Maggie, is something wrong? I'd be glad to listen. You can talk to me. Are you homesick? Can I help?"

She realized that she missed nothing about Wisconsin.

The Quiz

THE ALARM CLOCK INCHED toward six. Margo had studied the drawings after supper, but the bones of the hand seemed impossible. Why hadn't she left the auditorium when the microphone worked? Why had she gone in the first place?

She turned on her side and curled up. Alan was a real rat. He had his project done. He was in the clear.

The alarm lifted her from a heavy sleep, swirling her up as if from a whirlpool.

Mr. Yeager! If she went early, he would help her.

She dressed and went downstairs. "I have to leave early. I'm going to see my biology teacher before school." It wasn't a lie but was a long stretch from the whole truth.

On the way to school, Margo walked so fast she got a side ache. Mr. Yeager's door was open—good old Mr. Yeager. She took a breath at the door and slipped inside.

The room was empty, so Margo perched on her stool. "Quiz" was written on the chalkboard, making her stomach roll. She arranged her handouts on the table and looked at the drawing of the hand.

Someone came in the door, but she kept her head down. If she looked studious, maybe Mr. Yeager would take pity on her.

When Alan sat down next to her, Margo gave him her best glare.

"Listen, I'm sorry about yesterday."

"So am I. You wasted my time, and now you're doing it again."

"Hey, I came to help. I called your house. Your uncle said you'd come here early."

"Leave me *alone*. How did you even find my uncle's number?"

"Sorry. His name was on the admission papers you were fiddling with your first day."

"I don't want your help. Carpal schmarpal—it's all Greek to me."

"Latin, actually."

She felt like slapping the superior look off his face. "Glad you think you are funny! Notice I'm not laughing."

"Just trying to lighten the mood. If you'll give me a chance, I can help you. With Fixit's magical study techniques, it will be easy."

Margo put on her pretend smile.

"Mr. Yeager will have the picture and the names. All you will have to do is draw lines to match them.

Margo gave Alan Mrs. Ziller's unblinking stare.

"Look. There is a simple saying to keep them straight. 'So Long The Pinky, Here Comes The Thumb.'" He pointed to each bone as he repeated the words. It goes in a circle. Match the first letters of the words to the first letters of the bones. The last two are alphabetical."

Margo recited, adding sing-song sarcasm to her tone.

"Now try it with this list I made. Match each bone name. To check yourself, make sure this big one is at the top. Capi means head—think cap.

Margo made the round, matching first letters.

"Good morning Margo and Alan! Always refreshing to see students up early, studying."

Alan stood. "Good morning Sir."

"Morning," Margo managed.

Mr. Yeager went to a cupboard in the supply closet and rummaged through cardboard boxes.

"Go around one more time," Alan insisted. "Remember my techniques. Follow them well, and your scores will swell," he chanted.

"No, I think I've got it."

"One more time," Alan insisted. "Then take a break. Get a drink in the hall, so you're ready.

She went to get a drink as other students began to filter into the room.

Mr. Yeager passed out the quiz. "You can start your test while I take roll. And, let's do our own work. Fred—I mean you."

Margo recited the phrase and connected the lines to the words. She was answering questions on a biology test!

GRACE WAITED BY THE locker room door. "Hey, I was looking for you yesterday afternoon."

"I had to study. Well, I was supposed to study." It didn't matter because Grace had her mind on basketball.

"You're not going to believe this. I got into a free throw contest with a few of the boys after they practiced."

What happened to keeping a secret? "Who was there?"

"Smith, Ferguson, and the kid with the ducktail—Johnny something, and another guy." Grace grabbed her by the arms. "I wasn't first, but I was second."

"Who won?"

"Ferguson. You should have seen him. Dribbling around, skipping and saying, 'The kid does it again.' I could have punched him."

They played hard in PE, and Mrs. Peters complimented their "hustle." Margo continued her hustle to lunch.

Sharon waited at the cafeteria door. "You want to eat outside? You might get a better view."

"View? Of what?" It was hard to believe eating outside in November was even possible.

Sharon pulled her sweater up on her shoulders. "Don't be so serious. Chris Ferguson."

Margo looked away, wishing she didn't blush so easily.

"Don't worry. Secret's good with me. And, you'll see him at the dance." Sharon led the way to the outdoor tables. "Did you talk to your uncle?"

"No, I didn't get home on time, and he came looking for me. Alan was supposed to help me study, and I ended up helping him fix some sound system thing."

"Listen, Ol' Fixit isn't so bad; he's just fourth tier."

"Fourth tier?"

"Oh, yes. High school students are organized into tiers—like the caste system in India."

Margo resisted the temptation to say, "I'm probably an Untouchable."

"First tier are the kings and queens—football heroes, cheerleaders. The 'special' people." Sharon put her lunch sack on a table. "They get elected to the King and Queen's court of Homecoming and the Prom.

"Then there are second tier—they play the lesser sports, are class officers, and the like. They can be in the king and queen's court—sometimes even crowned at the lesser dances. Third, are regular people. Average, I guess."

"Where are we?" Margo wondered out loud.

"I'm thinking I'm an undiscovered second tier."

"If I keep hanging around with Alan, will I be fourth tier?"

"Not the way it works. You don't rise or fall due *only* to association. There's also the 'just famous' factor."

"What's that?"

"Some people in high school are just famous. You can't put your finger on why." Sharon gestured to herself with a flourish. "*I* was famous once, but nobody noticed."

Margo snickered.

"Alas, some people are *naturally* famous, like your Chris."

Margo looked over her shoulder. "Shhh. Don't say Chris outloud."

"No one is paying any attention. Don't worry. There are probably seven guys named Chris within five hundred feet."

"Do you think my Chris, well not my Chris, but the Chris in question is tier one?"

"He may be. He is cute. But he doesn't play football—he's in the band." Sharon held up one finger. "Band can mean a step down for someone teetering on the edge. Chris has a car, but nothing compared to Dirks Hartmann's, the quarterback. Dirks' daddy is rich."

"Chris is in the band? What does he play?"

"Oh, we have to get you to a football game. He's the drum major! He's the guy with the big pole with a silver knob who leads them around."

The Game

T. CHARLES DROPPED Margo off near the busses. "Are you sure you have enough money?"

"It'll be fine."

"I'll be in front of the school at eleven. You have a good time."

"You have to come to the cafeteria to get me. Just go straight up the sidewalk past the office."

"I'll be there." T. Charles gave her his gentle smile. "You look very nice tonight."

Margo had fumbled in her closet before deciding on a red and black plaid skirt and a black sweater.

"Aren't you going to wear your little hat?"

On impulse, she snatched the red beret from the seat, settling it to one side.

"There's my girl," T. Charles said.

Sharon waited near the bus, wearing a blue sweater under her coat. "Hey, nice hat. Wow. Stylish." She leaned close. "Now smile! After all, this is the 'Cheer Bus.' Remember, we're going to cheer on the *big* team at the *big* game."

She turned quickly, and Margo followed her onto the bus.

"Hey, Sharon," one of the Driver's Ed boys said, "you can sit in front of me."

Sharon playfully batted at his shoulder. "I think we'll sit behind you." She winked at Margo.

"Sit by the window. You'll be able to catch the first glimpses of Pasadena and observe the inner bus culture. It's dramatic. After a big loss, girls who know nothing about football will be reduced to tears because of the tragedy of it all."

The hat reflected in the window, making Margo smile.

The football stadium was larger than she expected, and the center seats were filling.

Sharon tugged at Margo's sweater. "This way. We're the visitors. We sit on the crummy bleachers, up there, by the roped-off area. That's where the band sits. You'll have a perfect view."

Laughing, Margo put her shoulder next to Sharon's and whispered. "Don't tease. It's not funny."

Sharon wrinkled her brow, a dimpled smile showing. "Not funny at all. Just a simple matter of fact." She pulled a rag out of her coat pocket.

She wiped the bench and dangled the rag for Margo to see. "Damp *and* dirty. Don't want that on your skirt, do you?" She bounded down the steps and tossed the rag into a trashcan.

A cheer started, and Margo self-consciously mouthed the words. When the cheerleaders put their megaphones on the ground, it spelled "BEARS."

Sharon came back up the steps. "OK, soon we will be treated to the pre-game show."

"What's that?"

"The band, silly! Our band does the first formations when we travel. You get to see Chris in all his splendor. He has gold braids across his chest. It's quite regal." Sharon leaned closer, "The bands are better than the game if you ask me."

The band lined up behind the goalposts, Chris blew three quick bursts on a whistle, the drums played a snappy beat, and the band began to play, marching onto the field.

Sharon pulled Margo's arm. "Up, up. This is the big entrance." Sharon clapped along with the song leaders' dance as the band formed a B, and the cheerleaders jumped and waved their pompoms.

Margo stood with both hands over her heart. Sharon was right; the gold braids were quite regal.

"I knew you would like the pre-game show."

After the band was in the stands, several girls took off their hats to rearrange their hair. Vivien Turner played the clarinet!

The game began. Chris turned to face the band when they played pep songs, and Margo watched him out of the corner of her eye. He set the tall hat aside and smoothed his hair.

She found herself singing along, "On Blackwater, on Blackwater, fight team, fight team, fight."

Sharon gave a look of approval. "School-Spirit-Girl! Make sure you sing Blackwater and not Backwater." She raised her eyebrows. "Backwater High? It doesn't seem to have the same ring as 'On Wisconsin,' does it?"

A clock on the scoreboard stopped inexplicably between some of the plays.

"Those six minutes are going to take forever," Margo said.

"That's the first quarter. We're here for the long haul."

Should have known.

They got hot chocolate at halftime, and Margo nursed hers until the clock poked around to the fourth quarter. Three cheerleaders cried when Dirks Hartmann was helped from the field. His right shoe was off, and he hopped on one foot.

"Enter Wally Wickersham." Sharon was on her tiptoes, peering at the sidelines. "Wally is second tier, but I believe it's because he won't play the big shot. He's in 4-H, definitely not one of the 'special' people."

"He's the substitute?"

"Second-string quarterback—but Wally can throw." Sharon didn't take her eyes off the sidelines. "Wally can think. This game just got interesting."

In the first play, Wally scanned the field. Two Pasadena players charged him, but he stepped easily aside and threw the ball.

"See," Sharon said. "He may not be 'Mr. Cool'— but he is cool-headed."

Watching Sharon watch Wally, and watching Chris left Margo little time to watch the game. Sharon's play by play analysis made the last minutes pass quickly.

Chris led the band in the Alma Mater. Sharon sang along happily, and Margo made a note to learn the words.

On the bus, Sharon was invigorated. "Hey. Not too bad. Wally threw one touchdown pass, and we got six points. 35-6 is better than 35-0. Told you Wally was improperly classified."

In the cafeteria, the tables and the chairs had been removed. Blue and white crepe paper streamers looped out from the center of the ceiling to the sides. A Song Leader jerked a loose one down and wadded it into a ball. Margo stayed close to Sharon and watched the door for Chris.

"OK. There you go. Chris is here."

"Sharon! Shhhh. Do you always just say what's on your mind?"

"Most of the time," she laughed.

Chris walked with his hands in his pockets to other basketball boys under the clock. Margo moved so she could watch him over Sharon's shoulder.

Her heart fluttered when he glanced in their direction. Margo checked over her shoulder, but only two freshmen boys were poking at each other.

Vivien Turner danced with a redheaded boy. Alan moved onto the floor with a girl Margo had never seen.

Even though he was stocky, it was as if he were floating. His feet moved with absolute ease in rhythm to the music. His partner was wrapped in his arms one moment and at the end of his extended hand the next.

Sharon noticed Margo's stare. "Oh, another lesson. You probably thought Alan couldn't dance. I thought it was the Bop, but Alan says it's the East Coast Swing."

Alan twirled his partner twice, she backed into his arms, and they scooted forward, feet in perfect sync.

"His aunt has a studio. He's been dancing since he was three."

Alan put his hands in his pockets, leaning slightly forward, his feet a blur. His partner held out one hand, circling him.

"Who's he with?"

"That's Tina Corti. Alan and Tina have been sweet on each other since seventh grade. Tina doesn't live in the 'good part of town,' but Alan isn't the type to care."

Jimmy Smith asked Sharon to dance. It was a slow dance, and Sharon held her hand lightly on his shoulder. He laughed at something she said.

Margo felt like a dodo, standing by herself. Chris danced with a cheerleader and then went back to the guys under the clock.

Sharon said, "I know you're dying to know. That was Bonnie Douglas. She asked him. I'd say he didn't take the bait. He's back with his basketball buddies, and Bonnie has charged into the bathroom with a bevy of friends."

Great! Bonnie was a cheerleader. When the girls came out of the bathroom, the "B" on Bonnie's cheerleading sweater was stretched tight. Bonnie, the girl who gave Chris a look the first day of school. She had a figure; Margo had elbows.

Jimmy asked Margo to dance. He was shorter than her and looked more uncomfortable than he had with Sharon. Margo suspected they were attempting the foxtrot at Sharon's suggestion.

"So—I guess you're new here?" Jimmy mumbled.

"Yes, Wisconsin."

"Oh."

Chris may have looked their way, at her, but she couldn't be sure.

"I like your hat."

"Thanks."

When the record ended, Sharon said, "Jimmy's OK. He's hovering at a high tier three. He could possibly qualify for a two, but he needs confidence to believe it."

Where was Margo hovering? She had one dance, arranged by Sharon. If it weren't for Sharon, she would be an Untouchable. Well, an Untouchable with a cute hat.

T. Charles was at the door when they came out of the cafeteria.

"Uncle, this is my friend, Sharon. Sharon, this is my Uncle, Mr. Blackwater."

"I'm glad to meet you." Sharon moved quickly and held out her hand. "Margo said she lived with her uncle." She leaned forward. "Margo is OK in my book."

"Yes. Maggie is a delight. I'm glad she's making friends."

Sharon raised her eyebrows. "School-Spirit-Girl is called Maggie." She smiled. "Maggie it is. Oh, there's my dad. Nice to meet you, Mr. Blackwater. See you Monday, *Maggie*." Her skirt and ponytail flared, and she was gone.

When they were in the Packard, Chris's car came out of the student parking lot. Margo couldn't tell if he was alone. She wished she had seen Bonnie Douglas leaving with someone else.

Tryouts

GRACE FLASHED AN ICY stare. "Trying out for the team. What're you doing here?"

"Whadaya mean, you're trying out?" The boy with the ducktail held a ball on his hip.

"We're trying out. That's pretty clear," Grace said between her teeth.

Slowly all the balls stopped bouncing. One hit a foot and rolled. Grace scooped it up easily, dribbled once, turned, and made a perfect set shot, the ball never touching the rim.

"Coach, there're girls trying out. Can girls try out?"

Coach Wiggins ambled over to the group.

"Coach, girls can't be on the team. Come on, Coach, get 'em off the court."

Coach Wiggins motioned to Margo and Grace. "Girls, come over here. We better talk." Margo's face burned.

On the sidelines, she glanced at the boys staring at them. Chris spun a ball backward with both hands, letting it bounce back to him.

The coach pointed at the boys. "OK, outside for a run. To the far fence and back. Hustle!"

Margo looked up only after the boys trotted out the door.

"What's this about, girls?"

"We're out for basketball." Grace put her hands on her hips.

Margo had put off saying no to Grace, and now there was no escape.

Coach Wiggins looked at the court and then at his clipboard. "Out for basketball?"

"Yes sir."

"Why for the boys' team?"

"I was not aware it was a *boys'* team. The handbook says, 'Varsity and JV basketball teams.'"

Margo folded her arms and stepped back. Chris had been one of the last out the door. Dreading trying out in front of the boys shrank amid their disapproval. *Let's just go*, she thought.

"Girls, I can't let you stay today. I have to—I'll need to talk to..."

Grace picked up a ball, dribbled hard, and made a layup. "Come on coach, I can play as good as lots of your guys."

Coach Wiggins shrugged his shoulders. "Nice layup. GAA would love to have you. Are you a junior or senior?"

"Junior. But GAA is..." Grace's face was red. "GAA is not a real team." She tipped her head toward Margo, eyes wide.

"Girls, I need you to write your names down—here on the bottom of this." He handed the clipboard to Grace. "I'll talk to—I don't know. I'll talk to the office."

The boys began to return, breathing hard. They stood in the middle of the court, in groups, watching. Chris was under the basket, with a ball on his hip. Someone coughed.

Margo shook her hair back and handed the clipboard to Coach Wiggins.

He leaned closer. "I can see you're serious." He looked at the clipboard. "Grace. Margo. I'll look into this, I really will. But I can't let you try out today. I'll call you in tomorrow." He nodded. "I will."

Grace turned a complete circle with clenched fists. "This is so unfair. In Iowa, I was first string. Girls' *Varsity*!"

"OK, I..." Coach Wiggins looked helpless. "I gotta start tryouts."

Grace stormed out of the gym, Margo following, finding relief with each step.

"Not fair. This's *not* fair!" Grace paced back and forth. "This is not fair. I'm better than half those guys!" She stomped her foot. "Not fair." She spun toward Margo. "I have to change. You didn't say a *word* in there! Thanks a *lot*!"

Chris Ferguson probably thought she was a weirdo to come to tryouts, and now, Grace was mad at her.

After changing, Margo walked toward her locker. Should she tell T. Charles about what had happened? She had never been called to the office before.

Sharon joined her. "You OK?"

"Oh, Sharon—I just made the biggest fool of myself in front of Chris."

"It can't be that bad. What happened?"

"Grace and I—Grace Thompson, from PE—we went to basketball tryouts."

"OK." Sharon seemed surprised for the first time since Margo met her. "OK. Hmmm, OK. And now I understand why you've been practicing every afternoon."

"Grace made a deal with me. In Iowa, Grace played on a girls' team with other schools. There's no girls' basketball here, so she said we should try out for boy's."

Margo leaned against the lockers. "The coach wouldn't let us stay. Grace is mad because I didn't speak up. Chris was staring at us. They all stared at us!"

"Hey, not to worry. I think it was pretty brave. Wow! I missed this one."

Margo opened her locker. "The coach said they're going to call us to the office tomorrow. Am I in trouble?"

"For what? Hey, you went into the gym. You told the Coach you were there for tryouts. Was there a sign on the door that said, 'Boys only'? You worry too much."

Sharon led the way to the front parking lot. "Have you told your uncle about your plan?"

"It wasn't really a plan." She had only told T. Charles that she was practicing basketball with a friend. "No. I guess I hoped it wouldn't get this far."

What if the school called? Not talking in Wisconsin had become a habit, but with T. Charles taking her in, being kind and interested, he deserved better.

Margo spent the night turning on her side, scrunching her pillow, only to come awake minutes later to do it all over again.

———⊶⊷———

MR. YEAGER TOSSED THE lab reports in his briefcase and looked at the note handed to him.

"Margo, you are to go to the office."

Several "Ooooos" came from behind her. Someone snickered.

A quick glance from Mr. Yeager and the room went silent. Heart hammering, Margo gathered her things.

She sat in a chair in the hall, the office smells reminiscent of her first day. She hadn't mentioned the incident to T. Charles, and now she dreaded him finding out.

The clock dawdled toward nine when Mr. Tyler called her. Grace passed Margo in the hall, giving her a mysterious look. Coach Wiggins and Mrs. Peters were with Mr. Tyler in his office. Margo had scarcely eaten breakfast, and her stomach tightened in protest.

"Well now, Margo," Mr. Tyler began, "we have several questions—the same questions we asked Grace."

The gold pen set on his desk went in and out of focus.

"First," said Coach Wiggins, "why'd you want to try out?"

Margo shook her head in misery. "I don't know." She took a deep breath. "Grace says I'm pretty good. I'm tall. I can handle the ball." She had resorted to sing-song poetry.

"Do you still want to be on the boys' basketball team?"

Margo whispered, "No. Am I in trouble?"

"We're not here to discipline you," Mr. Tyler said. "But this has turned out to be quite—complicated. We simply want to understand."

We're here to help," Mrs. Peters added.

"Margo," Mr. Tyler said, "I've looked at your records. I see you've been to two other high schools."

"Yes. My dad is an archeologist. They're in Peru." Her voice trailed off. Weak excuses wouldn't help for this.

"I also note that your grades are not good. Did you realize you have a D in Biology and History?"

Tears of frustration built in Margo's eyes. "I guess."

"We cannot let you play sports with your grade average. You're ineligible."

Her throat caught, and she gave a little cough. Ineligible!

"It's OK," Coach Wiggins said. "You're not in trouble. Mrs. Peters says you have talent. In fact, I was pretty impressed you came out. But we need to get your academics up to par."

Mr. Tyler smoothed a piece of paper on his desk. "I've asked Miss Gill, your guidance counselor, to schedule an appointment for you. In the meantime, I'll see about getting you help with Biology and History."

Outside, Margo felt light, and the fall air was cool and fresh. She'd escaped! No more basketball! Even hiding her grades from T. Charles couldn't spoil the moment.

The Fall

BEFORE PE, GRACE WAITED for Margo. "Hey, what happened?"

"You first."

"Mrs. Peters actually stuck up for me—sort of. She said there have been girls' teams for years in other states." Grace shook her head. "I didn't think she had that kind of nerve."

"So, will they have a girls' basketball team?"

"There will be a school board meeting. Superman said it won't happen this year. You know, a budget for a coach, and scheduling games. He was actually pretty nice. He has a niece in South Dakota who plays six-on-six." Grace looked across the yard. "So, that's it for me." She started toward the locker room.

"I'm ineligible."

Grace stopped.

"Biology and History."

Grace's face softened. "Maybe now that we won't be practicing, you can study more."

That was exactly the problem. Margo felt guilty. She wasn't dumb, but she needed to do her homework.

News had gotten around, and there were looks of disapproval. Someone bumped Margo in the hall, and she dropped her book. A group of boys surrounded her locker.

"I need to get to my locker." Her voice sounded small.

"I need to get to my locker," someone mimicked.

"Why don't you push your way in? You like to push your way in where you don't belong."

Margo hugged her books tighter, head down. The boys parted, making a path, and she stepped toward her locker. "Home of Supergirl" in runny black paint tarnished the door. A bike padlock hung from the handle. Tears filled her eyes.

"Come on, Supergirl. Break the lock."

"Yeah, show us your super strength."

The boys packed tightly around her, and she turned back. A letterman's sweater blocked her. "Look, Girlie. Don't come around tryouts."

Fear took over. Margo plunged between the lockers and the boys. Someone grabbed her binder. When she turned to pull it loose, her foot caught. She twisted against the lockers trying to get her feet back under her, and went down. Her forehead hit a combination knob on the bottom row, her teeth clacking together.

Blood splattered as Margo reached for her binder. She put her hand over her eye and tried to get up. Someone grabbed her arm. "Come on, help me. She's really hurt."

The next few minutes were vague confusion. She was hurried down the hall and across the quad to the nurse's office. Miss Odegaard helped Margo in and shooed the boys away. She pressed a piece of gauze to Margo's head and wiped her face with a damp cloth.

Later, she gently took the pad away. "There, the bleeding has nearly stopped. Head wounds always bleed a great deal don't you know." Miss Odegaard inspected the cut. "I'm afraid that will need stitches." She put the back of her hand on Margo's forehead. "You'll need to rinse your dress in cold water, so the blood doesn't stain."

T. CHARLES GLANCED at Margo several times as he drove her to the doctor. "Are you feeling dizzy?"

"No. I'm OK." Which was far from true.

T. Charles let out a long sigh, but he didn't seem angry with her.

The doctor assured them it was a clean tear. Margo was bruised and needed stitches. "It's just above your eyebrow and will heal nicely. You're going to be black and blue and may have a headache."

A Gentleman Caller

MARGO SPENT THE AFTERNOON on a couch in the living room. T. Charles made her a sandwich and turned the television to the movie *Lost Continent*. It was a silly film with dinosaurs, and she dozed.

At three forty-five, the phone rang. Sharon had probably run all the way home to call. T. Charles said Margo could talk for a minute as long as she stayed on the couch.

"Wow!" Sharon stopped to breathe. "Are you all right? You left quite a trail of blood on the sidewalk. What happened? The rumors are really flying. Some say you were pushed down. Some say you were slugged!"

"Nothing so dramatic. I tripped over someone's foot."

"The janitors scrubbed your locker door. It's sort of a black smudge. A hurry-up job, but it's the thought that counts."

Margo couldn't help smiling. "What about Grace? Did they do anything to her?"

"I think they were chicken to take on Grace. She'd probably slug one of *them*." Margo could tell Sharon was smiling. "Besides, after you bled all over the sidewalk, the guys had some office time, and more to come, I imagine. It was just a mob." Sharon huffed into the phone. "My grandfather has a quote from Mark Twain. 'No mob has any sand in the presence of a man known to be splendidly brave.'"

"I sure wasn't brave. I was scared to death when they surrounded me."

"Even so, no one in that mob had any sand. Brave people don't need gangs."

After the call, T. Charles came in with a cup of tea. "Maggie, are you sure you are doing all right? He put three stitches in you."

She nodded, forehead tingling.

"Would you like cookies with your tea?"

"I think I'll take a nap until supper." The first day of school, she'd wanted to hide on this couch. She was safe in this house.

T. Charles tucked the blanket around her feet. "You're a good girl, Maggie. I'm sorry those boys did this to you."

Margo leaned her head back on the pillow. "I have a D in Biology." She searched T. Charles's face. "And History," she added weakly.

He patted her foot. "I know, I know. We will work on that later. I'm not very good at being a parent, I'm afraid. We will do better, Maggie Girl."

What a mess. Called to the office. Half the school mad. T. Charles driving her to the doctor, knowing about her terrible grades. Margo turned to face the back of the couch.

She dreamed it was the last day of school. In Biology, Mr. Yeager had written, "Final Exam" on the board. She had no idea it was time for the final and had not read any of the chapters.

The doorbell rang, and Margo startled awake, surprised she wasn't in her bed. She started to get up when T. Charles said, "Stay where you are, Dear. I'll see who it is." He bustled to the door.

When he returned, he said, "There's a young man here to see you. Do you feel well enough for a visitor? He said it's important."

Out of curiosity, she nodded. It was probably Alan. When they called her out of Biology, he had raised one eyebrow. As Margo sat up, she realized she was in her pajamas. She pulled the blanket up.

Chris Ferguson stood in the archway. Margo instinctively ran a hand over her hair. He shifted his feet. "Hi."

"Hi." *Chris Ferguson's in the living room, and I'm on the couch in flannel pajamas!*

"Uncle, this is Chris Ferguson. Chris, this is my great uncle, Mr. Blackwater."

Chris crossed the room and shook T. Charles's hand.

"I am glad to meet you. You'll have to excuse me, I have pork chops on the stove." T. Charles hurried toward the kitchen.

"Listen, I came—I mean, I wanted to see if you're all right." Chris shook his head. "Well, not all right. OK."

"I'll be fine." *Chris came to check on me!*

"Boy, I was really worried. Someone said you went to the hospital with a concussion."

The corners of her lips gave a tiny tug. *He was worried.*

Chris shifted his weight from one foot to the other and rubbed his palms together. "Listen, I was in the crowd." He put his hands in his jacket pockets and then took them out. "I was there. I didn't try to stop them."

"It's all right."

"Yeah, thanks. I don't do stuff like that. Pick on people. I—my folks aren't happy with me. After tonight, my car's grounded except straight to and from school." He crossed and uncrossed his arms. "It's Broom Squad for us. No practice for the week—just laps after Broom Squad. Coach was pretty disappointed."

Margo wanted him to come closer, put his hand gently on her head, near the bandage, look at her with those eyes.

"I'm not going to go to any more tryouts." Color rose in her face. "I'm ineligible. I have bad grades." She glanced up at Chris. "I'm not dumb. I—I'm new here, and I haven't been studying. Probably because Grace and I've been practicing every afternoon." That wasn't exactly true. She sighed. "Bad idea all around, no matter how you look at it." *I sound like Sharon.*

"Hey, lots of kids have grade troubles. I mean, I got grounded for a bad grade once. Poor study habits." Chris looked from the piano to the entry hall and back to Margo.

Does he want to escape? Desperate for him to stay, she said, "Sit down?"

"Yeah. Sure." He sat on the edge of the chair at the end of the couch, leaning toward her. If she scooted a tiny bit, she could've touched his cheek, rosy from the cool evening. The green flecks in his eyes were nearly hidden in the dim light. There were so many questions.

"How did you know where I lived?" *Does him being here mean anything?*

"I helped you to the office. Mrs. Albertson from Algebra saw it all. She told us to stay in the office. I heard the secretary say you lived with your uncle, T. Charles Blackwater. Like the school. I looked it up in the phonebook."

Chris helped me to the office!

"Did I hear my name?" T. Charles asked.

Margo looked up, feeling guilty. *What's there to feel guilty about?* She glanced at Chris's slim hips as he stood, looking quickly away.

"Maggie, it's time for supper. Young man, you're welcome to join us."

"I..." Chris gave Margo a questioning look.

"I already have a place set if you'd like to stay. If you need to use the telephone, it's on the end table."

"My folks know where I am..." Chris took a step toward the phone. "But, I better call."

"You two go away for a minute. I want to go up and change!" *I'm not going to eat supper with Chris Ferguson in flannel pajamas!*

"Are you dizzy? Do you want me to help you?" T. Charles asked.

"I'm fine. You two give me a minute. Scoot." She made shooing motions with both hands.

Margo wrapped the blanket around her, pinching it at her neck, and tiptoed upstairs.

She inspected the bandage. Her head pounded, her forehead was puffy, a dark hue formed over her eyelid. At least she hadn't drooled in her hair.

Why is he staying for supper? I love it that he's staying, but does it mean anything? A tingle of excitement masked the throb above her eye.

Margo washed her face, dabbing around the bandage. *Is this a courtesy stay?* She slipped a dress over her head, brushed her teeth, and combed her hair. *I loved it when he leaned forward and gazed into my eyes.*

After checking the mirror a last time, Margo walked down the stairs, holding her head very still.

At the table, T. Charles said, "It was certainly nice of you to check on Maggie. Are you friends at school?"

Chris glanced at her and pushed a string bean with his fork.

Kindness

T. CHARLES DROVE MARGO to school. She was to go to the nurse during PE for the rest of the week. T. Charles made her promise she would have Miss Odegaard call if she began to feel bad.

Sharon waited at Margo's locker. Peering at her forehead, she declared, "Not too bad, if I do say so. Your eyelid looks a little puffy."

Margo glanced at her shadowed image in the tinted window above her locker. Maybe she should have listened to T. Charles and stayed home. *Did I come so Chris would feel sorry for me? No, I want to see him again!*

She needed somewhere more private to tell Sharon about Chris coming to the house. Sleep had been long in coming, and she woke early, thinking of the evening. She needed time to try to put her jumbled thoughts into words. Margo glanced toward the English building but didn't see Chris.

Morning red mountains under blue sky pushed musings back as reality dawned. She was still Margo, tall and skinny.

"At least you will know which one is yours." Sharon worked Margo's combination and pulled open the door. She stepped back, smiling.

Surprised, Margo cocked her head.

"Come on, Maggie. It is not that tough. I've watched you open your locker plenty of times." Sharon laughed. "It's not like I want to steal your Biology book." She gave the knob a twirl. "And don't leave it on the last number. Even the Driver's Ed pests might guess two numbers."

Margo raised her eyebrows, and a flash of pain shot across her forehead. She touched her hand to the bandage.

"Kidding! Their lockers are mostly on the Science wing. Half are sophomores, chomping at the bit to get their learner's permit. That'll be a scary day. They talk all day long about mufflers and carburetors and floor shifts." Sharon took a skip. "You know a floor shift is the cool thing." She mimicked working a lever with her right hand. "Lots of power and a floor shift."

"Chris's car sounds powerful."

"A '50 Ford with a 265 Chevy with an Isky cam," Sharon recited. "It was his brother's before he went in the Air Force."

This rush of information overwhelmed Margo. Normally cars held no interest, but one wrapped in the shiny Chris-Ferguson-package made her eager for more. If she knew enough to ask what iskycam meant, Sharon would probably know.

Sharon tightened her ponytail. "Hey, gotta go. I'm pushing the 'almost tardy' thing with Mr. Masters. He seems to think coming in at the last second is a sign of a lack of commitment to Trigonometry. I don't want to get a bad name around here!" She walked away, calling to Lisa Henderson.

A lack of commitment was no stranger. It was one of Grandmother's favorite topics when she took Margo to task. Margo slipped into Biology before the last bell.

Alan had been watching for her. "Hey, you're here." He frowned. "Does it hurt?"

"Not really."

"How many stitches?"

"Three."

"It will heal in no time." He studied her closely. "If your eye were going to close, it would have done it by now. Sorry about what happened. Most of the time, these things are stupid pranks. Sometimes things get out of hand."

She hoped he was right, and everyone would forget the whole thing. She'd spent her life being invisible and now would probably make the front page of the school newspaper. Where was the invisibility fairy when you needed her?

Ron slipped up and leaned on their lab table. "Hey, Fixit. The small intestine is twenty-two feet long, but the large intestine is shorter? I don't get it." He glanced at Margo's eye.

"It's not length, Ron. It's how big around the tube is."

"Oh, big tube, little tube." Ron rapped the countertop. "Hey, thanks, Fixit."

"Glad to be of service, Ol' Chap."

"Don't you mind that they call you that?"

"It started last year and caught on. I've never been too crazy about Alan anyway. Not really important in the big scheme of things. Pick your fights, my mom says." He shrugged his shoulders. "Plus, I know how to fix things."

After Biology, Chris came out of Room 12 as Margo arrived. She couldn't tell if he was looking at her or her forehead. He grimaced and said, "Hi."

Margo's brain wilted. *Should I say something, like, "It isn't as bad as it looks?"* It didn't matter because he was gone. *Did he leave English late so he could see me?*

By Fourth Period, Margo was wilting. In the nurse's office, Miss Odegaard gave her ice cubes wrapped in a cloth. She pulled a blanket up to Margo's chin. "I laundered this last night." She smelled like peppermint. "You lie here until lunch. Then you be sure..."

Miss Odegaard woke Margo gently. "You feel like having a bite to eat, 'cause the lunch period bell just rang, don't you know."

"Yes, thank you." She felt along her side for the ice cubes.

Miss Odegaard smiled. "I put the ice in the sink. I didn't want your dress to get wet. You were kinda hugging 'em."

Margo sat up.

"You'll want to get your brush and tidy up a bit." She handed her a warm washcloth.

In the small bathroom, Margo felt as if Miss Odegaard had touched her with a healing wand while she slept. Outside, she squinted in the mid-day haze as she crossed the quad.

Sharon plopped her lunch bag on the table. "How's the head?"

"Miss Odegaard let me sleep. Sleep is better than tumbling. If I turned a somersault, I would just flop on my back and lay there."

Sharon pulled open Margo's milk carton and stuck in a straw. "I was thinking about Amerigo Vespucci, you know from US history." She laid a homemade peanut butter cookie on Margo's sandwich paper.

A bit teary amid the genuine concern of others, Margo shook the feeling away.

"I don't know about Wisconsin, but in fifth, eighth, and tenth grades, we got US history. Lots of explorers. Well, in eighth, there was the Constitution test." She held the back of her hand to her mouth and whispered an aside. "Aced that one. Anyway, Amerigo Vespucci."

Margo nibbled at the cookie.

Sharon bunched the tips of her fingers with her thumb pressed tight and shook them in front of her face. "Ves-a-pucci, so I'm starting a new fad. I'm going to call our country Vespucciland, instead of America. Or Vespucci-a. That makes us Vespuccians. Or does Ves-a-pucceeze sound better?"

Margo took a breath. "Chris came to the house last night."

Sharon leaned forward, sandwich in mid-air. "Hmmm?"

"He came to—to see if I was OK."

"Well, well." Sharon's eyes went wide. "Look at Maggie, the boy maggie-net."

Margo had to chuckle. "Doubt I am a boy magnet. I think he only came to say he was sorry because he was with the boys who—you know."

"That is actually brave of him, I'll say that. Did he come in the house, or was this a 'through the screen door' sort of thing?"

"No, he came in. He..." Margo turned to look over her shoulder. "He..." She leaned forward. "He stayed for *supper*," she whispered.

Sharon laid her sandwich on her waxed paper and tilted her head, her pursed lips pulled into a smile. "I must say, Maggie McKinney, I'm glad I met you. Life at Blackwater can be quite entertaining, but you make it downright fascinating. Chris • Ferguson • stayed • for • supper."

"Shhhh." Mary Suttle was trolling the tables. "My uncle asked. Chris seemed sorta nervous. I sat there like a dope. I wonder if Novocain can make your brain go dead like it does your nerves?"

"Ha! That's a good one." Sharon picked up her sandwich only to lay it back on the waxed paper. "Chris is actually kind of shy when he's not on his turf. Everyone just thinks he's famous."

"Well, isn't he? He was dating Bonnie Douglas. She's a cheerleader and everything."

"More like Bonnie was dating Chris. He was an innocent bystander. Bonnie decided she was going to date Chris at a youth meeting at his church. The class rings had been delivered. She was fiddling with his ring and put it in her pocket." Sharon opened her sandwich and closed it.

"The next day she came to school wearing the ring. She'd wrapped the loop with pink yarn glued down with fingernail polish, and that was it. It fit, and they were going steady."

This was new information.

Sharon took one bite and wrapped the sandwich. "So, let's hear about the evening with a gentleman caller."

Gentleman caller tickled Margo. "He stayed for a while—after supper."

"It gets better and better." Sharon fluttered her fingers on the table expectantly.

"Uncle has this old piano. It plays rolls. It plays itself. Uncle can play—it's complicated. Anyway, I guess Chris had seen one at a pizza place and thought it was great. Uncle let him play several rolls, and Chris seemed to be having fun."

"Chris can play piano," Sharon said matter-of-factly. "And trombone *and* snare drum."

Margo sighed. Sharon was an encyclopedia. "I took lessons for four years, but only when I lived with my aunt."

Sharon stuffed the sandwich in her paper bag. "So, Player-Piano-Boy stayed for a while?"

"Sharon, you won't tell anyone about this—it may not be a big deal." Margo didn't want to sound as desperate as she really was.

"Not to worry. I'm a gatherer." Sharon stood up. "I gather information but I don't gossip."

"You tell me things."

"Maggie, you're different. I give you information. You're new. You'll be permanently assigned to a tier one of these days" Sharon tossed her bag in the trash.

Before she thought about it, Margo did a little jump shot, her head pounding as she landed. The bag arched into the center of the can.

Sharon glanced back, chin tilted to her shoulder. "Besides, what if you ended up a three and with me moving up to a two—how could we be friends?" She turned and rippled her fingers. "Smile."

Chris plays the piano and is in the band. Margo could almost hear Grandmother's stock comment: "Musicians are a flighty bunch." She would be careful to not mention stitches in her next letter.

Porte Cochère

ALAN AND HIS "ASSISTANT," Mike, waited by Margo's locker after school.

Two days hadn't faded the smear on the locker door; a marker so people could find the girl who tried out for boys' basketball. *They should dedicate a page to me in the yearbook.*

Yearbook. Margo wanted to graduate from Blackwater with Sharon, Chris, even Alan. She had no idea where she would be her senior year. Apprehension rolled inside, making her shiver. She laid her books on top of the lockers and waited.

Alan put his shoulder against the locker next to hers. "Hey, I've been thinking about what you said about your uncle having a movie camera. What kind is it? Can you describe it?"

She only half-listened, her interest level scraping zero. "I don't know—it's about like so." She gestured with her hands. "It's black. Oh, it has tubes on the front."

Alan looked at Mike. "This could be a sixteen millimeter."

Mike grinned.

Alan pursed his lips. "Did you see a name on it?"

Margo opened her locker. "I didn't really look at it. It was in a leather case. We didn't take it out."

"This sounds amazing. We have to see this camera. Can we go look at it? Would your uncle mind?"

Did anyone want to spend time with her when they didn't want something? Grace wanted a basketball partner. Alan wanted help with the sound system. Chris came to the house because she conked her head on the lockers. Now Alan wanted to see the camera.

Mother doesn't choose me. That was the one that hurt. Mothers should choose their daughters. She wished Sharon were there. Sharon liked her for who she was.

Alan gave Margo his "I can talk anyone into anything" face. "You did get an 'A-' on the digestive system test." He cocked his head sideways.

Mike nodded. He was older than she thought, just small.

"We could make a short movie," Alan said. "I imagine you could have a pretty good theater grade if you did a movie for your second-semester project."

How does he know about a theater project when I don't?

"Imagine showing a movie to your class in the auditorium."

A movie! "I guess we could look at it. I don't live far. It takes me about ten minutes."

"24 Meredith Lane," Alan recited. "I saw the address when I called the morning of the bones quiz."

"We need to start walking, and you can't stay long. My uncle helps me study in the afternoons."

"Maggie, we're not walking. Your chariot awaits. You're riding home in style."

Mike said, "Alan has a Jeep, '46 CJ2A. It's cherry."

Margo hesitated. Would T. Charles mind if she came home with two boys in a jeep? His first encounter with Alan had ended badly, a moment she was not eager to repeat.

"Hey, it's safe. I'm a careful driver. My Jeep is my baby."

In the student parking lot, the red Jeep sat away from the other vehicles. Margo avoided staring at Chris's car as they walked past. The Broom Squad swept the back basketball courts. A redheaded girl from history class stood next to an odd car that looked like it had melted in the sun. She gave Margo a half-smile, and Margo returned a Sharon finger ripple.

The jeep was aimed toward the courts, and Chris looked up for a moment. *Will he think Alan is taking me home?* That brought a chuckle. Alan was taking her home, but it would be wonderful to ride home with Chris!

Alan pressed a button, the engine coming to life. "Runs like a top."

As they swung around, a glance out of the corner of her eye told her Chris looked up again. The wind blew in from the back, and Margo snatched her hair into a ponytail. She felt quite adventurous driving off in a jeep with the wind in her hair.

Alan didn't go fast, but there was a lot of roaring and shifting each time he slowed for a corner. The gear shift came out of the floor. A floor shift? Did Chris have a floor shift? Margo looked back and lost her ponytail grip. Mike's hair looked like Aunt Louise's Pekingese. Alan made another shift as they neared the driveway.

"Alan is the master of double-clutching," Mike said.

Sharon might know this one.

The Packard was in the driveway, and Mike was out as soon as they stopped. He slipped a comb out of his pocket and swept his hair back as he walked toward the car.

"Oh wow, Alan—it's the Packard. Look at that paint." Mike turned to Margo. "Is this your uncle's main car?"

Margo nodded. Alan looked in the driver's window.

"Alan, this is one of the finest autos made. Thirty-nine, I believe."

Margo felt a bit of pride. "I think the dashboard is the best part."

T. Charles came out through the French doors. "Hello, Maggie. I see your friends brought you home."

"Yes. You met Alan the night—the night you had to come looking for me. This is his friend Mike Russell. Mike, this is my uncle, Mr. Blackwater."

Mike rushed to shake T. Charles's hand. "Sir, your car is beautiful. I don't suppose we could take a quick peek at the engine?"

T. Charles's eyes twinkled. "I always have time to show the engine." He opened one side of the long hood. Mike and Alan crowded close.

"Oh, man. A V12! Look at that, Alan. Massive. This engine is one of the smoothest running engines ever made."

Margo moved closer and looked over Mike's shoulder. She couldn't remember looking at a car engine. In the window's reflection, her hair needed brushing. She ran her fingers back over her ears.

"V12. Dual side-mount spares. Econo-Drive. Look at that grill." Mike turned to T. Charles, his face glowing. "This is really beautiful. You keep her in fine shape."

Alan gestured above the car. "It looks grand under the porte cochère." He shrugged. "Third-year French."

T. Charles chuckled.

Margo repeated porte cochère three times to herself. Sharon would like this one. While T. Charles showed the boys the car, Margo slipped in and put her books on the kitchen table.

She hurried to the sideboard mirror in the dining room and took a brush to her hair. It needed to be it cut—it was too long—like her. She slipped the brush back in her purse.

Cookies on cooling racks made the kitchen smell heavenly. Margo grabbed one and shoved it in her mouth, still slightly warm. She took a swallow of cool water right from the kitchen faucet and hurried outside. *Porte cochère, porte cochère, porte cochère.*

Alan spoke in earnest to T. Charles. "Sir, we've a favor to ask. Maggie told us about a movie camera you have in your basement. We would really appreciate being able to see it. We're in the AV Club at school and are interested in all aspects of theater production."

Margo ran her tongue over her teeth and wiped her lips. Mike sat in the driver's seat, inspecting the gauges.

"Maggie, why don't you go down and get the camera. Boys, Maggie and I usually have a couple of cookies with tea when she gets home. Perhaps you're hungry as well?" He winked at Margo. "Why don't you boys come inside. I have the tea steeping."

Margo hurried downstairs to the darkroom and turned on the light. Her mind ran to Virginia, developing pictures in the red glow.

Mike had decided to have milk with his cookies and chewed happily. Margo set the case gently on the red table.

"There are lights on big stands in the basement, too," she told them.

Alan touched the case. "Bolex H16." He looked at T. Charles and raised his eyebrows. "May I open it?"

"By all means." T. Charles sat back, smiling.

Alan carefully laid the case on its side and lifted the lid. "What a beautiful camera. Three lenses. Sixteen millimeter. Wow." He turned to T. Charles. "May I?"

T. Charles gestured with an open palm. Alan gently lifted the camera out of the case. "These are beautiful lenses on the turret."

Mike looked at the cookies, and T. Charles laid two more on his plate.

After her third cookie, Margo could see that Alan would rattle on about the camera "till the cows came home," and she wasn't going to let him derail her again. "Uncle, we have to start Chapter Seven in Biology."

Alan looked at his watch. "Right. Biology—Nervous system." He placed the camera in the case. "A deal is a deal; besides I have to be at work at five-thirty." Alan gave a flourish with his hand. "Michael, let us away."

T. Charles's mustache crinkled.

Mike stared longingly at the cookies, and T. Charles dropped another in his hand. "One for the road," he said.

They walked the boys out.

"That's a good looking Jeep," T. Charles said.

Alan started the engine and gave the gas a little tap. Mike waved as they backed down the drive.

"Polite boys. Nice to have kids in the house." T. Charles went into the room with the organ pipes. "All right, let's get to this nervous system."

He had moved a chair into the room for Margo. She opened the book and read, "Chapter Seven, The Nervous System."

"Wait, Maggie. Remember, Mr. Yeager said we should read the questions at the end of the chapter first."

It helped to read to T. Charles. He commented from time to time, occasionally reading from notes Mr. Yeager had given him. Margo looked forward to the cozy smell of dry wood and varnish.

When they had finished, she said, "I got a B- on the History quiz I took yesterday. Well, we got a B-."

"I'm proud of you, Maggie." T. Charles's eyes glowed. "Proud of us."

"I raised my hand in history class." This had been a first. "Mr. Hopper had this huge map of North Africa with only the country outlines. He pointed to Algeria, and I knew the answer!"

It was odd talking about school. Her whole life, she had avoided the subject. Magicians called it misdirection. When Mother was fishing for information, Margo had learned to answer without answering, but the true talent was to slip sideways into another subject without making Mother suspicious enough to ask more questions.

"Mr. Hopper followed up by asking me the capital, and I said Algiers!" Margo laughed. "I almost said, 'old Algiers,' because of the song you sing, 'You Belong to Me.'"

T. Charles gave her the smile she loved, and she wished she did belong to T. Charles and his world.

Broaching the idea of spending her senior year in California would require finesse. Margo hadn't opened the latest letter from Mother. She was building her courage to endure happy tidings about the indigenous peoples of Peru. Misdirection would be tricky in a letter.

Drills

MARGO COULD HEAR THE television in the background when Sharon called.

"So, I went by your locker, but you were already gone. I was late 'cause I went to watch basketball practice."

Margo chewed her lip.

"Jimmy asked me to stop by. He's not great, but he has heart."

"Do you like him?"

"I assume you mean like-like and not like. Half and half, I guess. He's a good guy. In History, he read ren-dez-voze, and I tried not to laugh. It's not Jimmy's fault the French can't spell."

Margo coiled the phone cord. "I know. Depot isn't de-pot? That one got me in fifth."

"I wonder if kids in France have problems with spelling. You sure can't sound it out."

Maggie tried for a new subject. "Chris was with the Broom Squad." *Was he watching me in the jeep? Does he even remember when he came to the house?* She couldn't seem to think of much else.

"Yeah, they were a bit short-handed with eight missing." Sharon paused. "Grace was there."

Margo's throat went dry. She hadn't talked to Grace since they were called to the office. Grace hadn't spoken to her, either, but that didn't make her feel any better. "I haven't been to PE."

"Jimmy said they changed her classes, so PE is her last period. Coach Wiggins has her helping with practice."

"Helping! How?"

"She was on the court, running drills. You know, blowing a whistle so someone would run and pass the ball or something."

Blackwater High was a goofy place: called to the office for trying out for basketball, and now Grace was helping coach the team! "Are the boys—is she?"

"Apparently, the boys have sort of gotten over it. Who would have thought? The coach had her take three guys to work on layups. Jimmy made two in a row after she gave them a few pointers." Sharon chuckled. "You know, some of the guys probably wish the school would let her be on the team. She could help them against Pasadena!"

Margo's stomach rolled at the thought of girls on the team, glad it wouldn't be her.

"Grace is really good. For one of the drills, she blows the whistle, they dribble from the middle, pass it to her, and she fires it back when they're under the basket. She puts pepper on that ball.

"Poor Jimmy. His pass to her was wild, but she ran over, batted it down, spun on one foot, and fired the ball back. Jimmy flubbed the basket, but Grace rebounded, making a perfect shot. A couple of guys clapped." Sharon lowered her voice. "Guy clap. You know—they popped their hands together once. That girl can play."

Grace would be there every day when Chris started practicing with the team again. Meanwhile, Margo only saw him at a distance. They never seemed to be at the same place at the same time. She hoped Chris wasn't too impressed with Grace.

Boy Confusion

SHARON TURNED TOWARD her. "Did I see you taking charge of your theater group?"

"I guess."

Sharon dodged a girl fussing with her purse. "What did you decide to do for the skit?"

"Nothing much. A melodrama. Girl tied on the railroad tracks sort of thing."

"Sounds fun. My group is sooo boring. I tried to pep it up, but it's all about Vivien." Sharon bounced on her tiptoes. "I underestimated her. Not only is she a thespian but apparently a writer-dir-rect-tor."

"I'm no writer. I stole the idea from Alan."

"Give yourself more credit. I steal all my best stuff." Sharon stopped near her history door. "Better hurry if you're going to walk by the band room in time to see a certain fella going in."

"Am I that obvious?"

"Hey, it never hurts to promote yourself. You do have your best outfit on!" Sharon leaned close. "Besides, I want to go in. The Christmas Formal is in three weeks, and I need to help Jimmy make up his mind he wants to take me."

Christmas Formal made Margo's stomach flutter. *What if no one asks me?* She had never cared about such things, and now it was paramount. *What if someone does ask? Is there any chance Chris might ask?* She adjusted her jumper straps and stood tall.

When she got to the corner of the building, Chris looked her way as he went into the band room. *Sharon might classify this as a "possible glance."* The thought made her smile.

At lunch, Sharon formed her finger and thumb in a circle as she walked toward the lunch table. "Jimmy will be joining me, well us, at the football game. If that's OK?"

"Won't three be a crowd?"

"No. In this case, three is perfect. A buffer. Jimmy is not ready to go on an actual date. He wants to, but he's still a little gun shy."

"I'll feel dumb there with you with a boy."

"Nope. It will be three kids enjoying the game. Jimmy needs to spend time with me in a relaxed way. No pressure for him." She leaned forward. "Good practice for you, too. No pressure. Don't worry."

T. Charles had spread the jelly all the way to the edges of the bread.

"Besides, this is a double-edged plan."

Margo raised her eyebrows, and the Band-Aid woke her sleeping stitches.

"We will sit by the band again. At first, Chris will wonder if Jimmy is with you or me. This will build a little fire under him. He can't just look. He needs to act."

"I'm not sure he looks."

"Maggie, Maggie. He looks. When he came out of the cafeteria now, he looked. He knows where to look."

And here I sit, blushing again. If I had any moxie, I would walk up to Chris, say, "Hi," and have a conversation.

It didn't matter. She would never have the nerve to waltz up to a boy and flirt. Margo decided she was Nodding Girl. Every time there was an uncomfortable situation, she nodded like a dull-witted dodo.

"Wear your hat. Even Vivien doesn't have a cute hat."

"I have another one. Blue. What do you think? It matches my blue sweater."

"All the better," Sharon said, glancing up.

Mary Suttle scooted in beside Sharon. "Did you hear? Jack Sanders is not asking Bonnie Douglas to the Christmas Formal." She picked up one of Sharon's Fritos.

Sharon gave Margo a knowing wink and pulled the waxed paper closer.

"He asked Grace Thompson. I hear the basketball team has decided she's not so bad after all." Mary fished another chip. "She has those perfect long legs. At practice, Friday, they had a free throw contest. She won!"

Margo found this news made her feel both good and bad. If Jack Sanders was interested in Grace, then Chris was safe. But if Bonnie Douglas was on the prowl, then Chris might be snatched away. Margo leaned forward to ask what Bonnie thought about all of this, but Sharon held up one hand and gave her head a tiny shake, as if to say, "Just wait."

"Bonnie is furious!" Mary said.

Sharon raised her eyebrows as if to say, "I told you so."

"She's dating a football player from Pasadena. She met him at the roller rink. But!" Mary leaned forward and lowered her voice. "She can't bring someone who doesn't go to Blackwater!" She popped another chip in her mouth as content as if she had discovered the cure for the common cold.

Sharon ironed a wrinkle out of the corner of her sandwich paper with her thumbnail, guarding her Fritos.

"Oh, hey, there's Jo-Ann. I need to talk to her." Mary snatched one last chip. "Jo-Ann!"

"Now there's a gossip." Sharon dropped a corner crust of her sandwich in her lunch bag. "Good thing she doesn't 'light for long, or my Fritos would be gone."

"I wouldn't want her to know what I'm thinking."

"Oh, that won't stop Mary. I'm pretty sure she considers you a supporting character. Bleeding on the sidewalk is the kind of thing that puts a spark in Mary's day. Nothing cheers her up like a little tragedy. She's probably the one who started the 'you were slugged' rumor."

Sharon inspected the other corner of her sandwich. "I don't understand why bread has to have crusts," she said disgustedly.

"A result of being baked?" Margo joked.

"If they can slice bread, they can slice off the crust."

Polly's Final Touch

MARGO HURRIED HOME, anxious to show her latest Biology quiz to T. Charles. Mr. Yeager had circled the "A-" and written 'Good Job!'

"A-!" T. Charles beamed. "Oh, Maggie, I'm so proud of you. You must tell your mother in your next letter. Your parents will be very pleased."

Would they? The last letter included a drawing of a basket Mother had bought, with a detailed explanation of how the reeds were dyed. Margo stopped reading halfway through.

"I think I want to get my hair cut. It's too long." She hesitated. "I wonder if I could take a couple of the pictures of Virginia to a beauty parlor. Her hair was perfect."

"Of course we can get your hair cut. Give me a moment." In the den, T. Charles rummaged in the rolltop desk. He laid a business card on the table: Polly's Final Touch.

"This is the beauty parlor Virginia used. Let me call and see if Polly is still there. Polly always cut Virginia's hair." T. Charles's eyes glowed like a child with a new puppy.

Margo ate another cookie. She could only hear part of what T. Charles was saying, but he was talking to Polly.

He came to the kitchen, eyes glistening. "My—Polly had such wonderful things to say about Virginia." He sighed and placed the card on the table.

"Anyway, yes." He turned the card, this way and that. "Polly would love to work on your hair. She will stay after her last appointment tomorrow afternoon."

"Thank you," came out as a whisper.

T. Charles patted her hand. "You are happy, here, aren't you, Maggie?"

"Yes, I really am." She took her cup to the sink. "My friend Sharon said I looked good in Virginia's red beret. Can I wear the blue one to the game Friday?"

"Virginia would be happy to have you wear her things." T. Charles's eyes were moist. "So happy."

Willowy

POLLY GLANCED UP FROM the rollers she was putting away. "Oh, Tommy, she looks like Virginia!"

Polly was a tiny woman with lots of white teeth. She had long red fingernails and smiled when she talked. Sparkly black chopsticks radiated from the bun on the back of her head like two tiny antennas. She clicked over in the tallest red high heels Margo had ever seen, and yet she only came to Margo's shoulder. She pushed the hair back behind Margo's ear. "Oh, my, oh, my. Look at that. Virginia's jaw, skin..."

Polly turned to T. Charles and hugged him. "Tommy, I know I don't have to tell you, but oh how she loved you." She held T. Charles at arm's length. "Look at you! Still a dapper fellow. Virginia didn't want you to become slovenly, you know. As if that would ever happen." She patted his lapels.

T. Charles blushed and took a deep breath. "Polly, this is my grandniece, Maggie. She has admired Virginia's hairstyle in photographs."

Polly pulled Margo's hair back in a ponytail, turning her head from side to side. "Wavy, like Virginia's." Her fingers touched the side of Margo's head. "Just a bit, here." She pulled her lips to one side. "I have girls, with your bones, who go for the curly look. It's too much." She lifted Margo's hair on the left side. "Oh, Tommy, look. She has a natural, gentle marcel, like Virginia. She's going to be beautiful."

Polly led Margo to a chair. "Tommy, you go get some coffee or go to the hardware." She shooed him with one hand. "This is girl time."

Polly stood behind Margo, smelling of lavender, turning the chair left and right. "It's a shame you never saw Tommy and Virginia together. They were darling." She held up a brush. "Now *that* was love! And style! Virginia had a *look*." The brush punctuated her words. "I don't know how many women would see her walking out of here and want a cut like hers—and in the days when longer hair was the style. I wouldn't be surprised to find that

Audrey Hepburn had seen Virginia sometime and copied her hair. Of course, Virginia didn't really have the pixie cut—well it was simply Virginia." Polly turned the chair again, dropping her voice. "She knew just • what • she • wanted."

Margo felt warm inside.

Polly put her hand near the junior Band-Aid over the cut. "What's this?"

"I fell. The stitches are out, but it's still red and a little puffy."

Polly adjusted Margo's head with both hands. "I think we're going to wash and cut first, dry, and see how much wave we have. You know the longer hair pulls straight." She held the chair-back at arm's length. "Oh, Honey, you're going to be quite special."

Margo fussed about being skinny, but Polly leaned over her shoulder and looked at her in the mirror. "Oh, no, Honey, not skinny. Willowy. Believe you me, there are girls all over that high school who wish they were built like you. Lauren Bacall has made a million bucks being willowy."

<hr />

AT HOME, MARGO PUT both hands on the keys of the player piano. She tried to play "Uptown Ivories," handwritten by her grandfather. He had put each note on the paper, and it made her feel closer to him, and yet a lifetime away.

Before he went to choir practice, T. Charles had taken a piano roll out of a cupboard. "I recorded it for Virginia after your grandfather McKinney disappeared.

"Harmony Music never published the roll. Finances were not going well. This is the arrangement for one person. I suppose this is the only one in existence. I don't know why I don't play it more often. It's high time it was enjoyed—that you hear it.

"Your grandfather had hoped the sheet music would sell enough copies to make real money. Virginia believed in the song. She didn't play as well as Daniel, but she had an ear and eye for things. It did sell, but it didn't gain the popularity we had hoped."

` Margo played the roll several times to get a sense of the timing. She imagined Grandfather's fingers on the keys as he had written the song.

Margo watched her legs as she pumped the pedals. Running had put muscle in them. She stopped and looked at the music again. The left hand was difficult, making it hard to believe that one hand could play so many notes. If Chris ever visited again, she wanted to be able to play something.

When she couldn't concentrate another minute, Margo slid the roll carefully into the box and padded upstairs. She put on a beige wool dress of Virginia's. There was a picture in the living room of Virginia wearing the dress with a beret. She gathered the dress behind, snugging it.

Her hair pleased her for the first time since she had started high school. She should have cut it long ago. The scale in the bathroom said she had gained seven pounds.

Margo pulled the dress tight again and swung from side to side in front of the mirror. Willowy. "Hmmm."

She settled the beret on her head. With the part on the right, her hair on the left had soft waves. Margo had looked up Marcel Wave in the dictionary: "To wave the hair by means of special irons." She tipped the hat to the side. No special irons needed. Polly introduced her to Amami Wave Set and showed her how to style finger wave bangs.

The Packard cruised past the house, and Margo hurried into a skirt and blouse. She opened the back door for T. Charles. "How was choir practice?"

"The Christmas Cantata is coming along. You know, the Good Lord did not put enough tenors in this world." He went into the kitchen. "Or, He didn't make composers and arrangers able to understand how high most men can't sing." He laid his music folder on the table. "I need a cup of tea. Care for one?"

"Yes, please."

"I like the blue beret."

She had forgotten the beret and almost took it off. "I love my haircut. Polly showed me a few tricks to make it behave."

"Virginia always said she was the best. She sent more than one of her models to Polly. Once, on the phone, I heard her say, 'I need you to tame one for me.'" He gave Margo a wry smile. "That woman's hair looked like she had combed it with an eggbeater." He put the cups and saucers on the table. "Polly had her looking like she had been uptown all her life."

Third Wheel

SHARON HELD UP ONE hand when she saw Margo. "Okaay!" She made a full circle.

Margo didn't blush.

"I approve. Uncle T took you to the right place. He knows things."

"He took me to 'Polly's Final Touch', on Second Street. Polly is so nice—she did Virginia's hair. Polly and Uncle say I look like Virginia."

"Then she had style. However, *this* is a curious accessory." Sharon patted a rope in Margo's hand. "Hey, gotta hurry. Jimmy actually called last night. He managed to say he would meet me at my locker. I was pretty proud of him—how do I look?"

"You always look good, Sharon."

"And you are always a good friend."

Margo put the rope in her locker and hurried to class. Autumn skies held a warm wind, so odd for November.

Alan said good morning without looking up from his magazine. When he finally did, he paused for a moment. "Nice hairdo."

"Thanks." Margo wondered if Alan had checked out the copy of *Popular Electronics*.

"Have you thought about making a short movie? Mike and I can be the film crew. Your uncle said there's a splicing machine in the basement. It would be a great project."

"I've been thinking about it. I wrote a story about my grandfather for English. There are tons of clothes and costumes upstairs. But..." Margo glanced behind them and leaned closer. "I want Chris Ferguson to be the leading man."

Alan looked up. "Chris? Sure. I'm pretty sure I can arrange that. He's in my debt for helping him with General Science freshman year. He had been grounded—poor study habits."

"But, wait. Don't ask him right away. I mean don't ask him until I'm ready—*we're* ready." She wished she did not blush so easily. "Check with me before you ask him."

"I'm guessing you're infatuated with Ferguson-The-Younger?"

I'm the most transparent person in this school.

Jimmy Smith slipped into his seat seconds before the last bell. He looked over and smiled.

After Biology, Margo turned a corner and nearly bumped into Chris. He was showing the Handbook map to a boy who looked too young to be in high school.

Chris paused to look at Margo. "Oh." His eyes lingered on her hair. "Hey. Here I am, doing my tour again."

Is Chris Ferguson flustered? Margo looked down at the young boy. "It helped me."

The boy looked from Chris to Margo.

"I was new a few weeks ago. It gets better. This is a good school." She gave him what she hoped was an encouraging smile.

The boy nodded and looked away.

"See, Sam. What did I tell you? You'll make new friends in no time. This is Margo."

You could've said 'my friend' Margo? "Glad to meet you, Sam."

Sam glanced up and said, "OK."

Chris looked at her over Sam's head and said, "You should join the Welcome and Hospitality Club. We welcome new students and help other students."

The three-minute bell rang, but she didn't want to leave. "Stick with Chris, Sam. He will show you everything."

A Song Leader, Sherry, with flawless olive skin and dark eyebrows rushed up to Chris. "We love the Band's new song, 'Boppin' at the Hop.' It's perfect, and we've worked out a new routine for it. I hope the Pep Band plays it at the rally." She flipped her long hair over her shoulder.

"Mr. Castellano has it on the playlist." Chris nodded to Sam and said, "I will be right with you."

Margo turned toward English. She couldn't compete with Song Leaders. She slipped into her seat as the bell rang. Miss Johnson glanced up, brushed the hair above her ear with one red fingernail, and winked.

In Theater, Dean, the Sheriff, held up a sign, "Tilly's Train Troubles."

Margo picked her flowers and was captured. Dean had a sign that said "Bad Boy Boggs" when the villain came on stage. Mrs. Kavanagh led the class in hissing and booing. After being tied with the rope, Margo struggled, pretending the train was bearing down on her. Dean made a train whistle sound. Everyone cheered when Tommy rescued her and dragged Bad Boy Boggs to the sheriff.

Margo had grown to love Mrs. Kavanagh's class. They had not spoken a single line of dialog. They learned stage presence and how to communicate with the audience by action. Dialog was to subtly enhance acting. Margo had laughed when Mrs. Kavanagh imitated an actress on TV who shook both arms up and down when delivering her lines. There would be no hand pumping in Mrs. Kavanagh's class.

"That was great," Sharon said after the bell. "I happened to breeze behind Mrs. Kavanagh. 'You got an A!' But, tonight, I suggest we use standard cheers at the game. No booing and hissing."

Sharon looked at the sky. "By the way, Jimmy got brave—we are going to the formal." She twirled. "Going to be a nice night."

Margo did a quick analysis. *I talked to Chris!* Her spirits fell as quickly as they had risen. *What are the chances of Chris asking me to the formal with bronze-skinned beauties like Sherry charming him with Song Leader chatter? She'll be prancing around in front of him at the pep rally!*

Margo was tired of being on the sidelines. Chris or no Chris, if someone else asked her to the prom, the answer would be yes. *Just don't let him be a foot shorter than me. Please!*

<hr />

JIMMY SMITH WAS QUIET as they entered the stadium. Sharon wiped off the bench and ran down to throw away the rag as the band marched toward their seats.

"That's a good hat," Jimmy managed.

"Thanks." *Poor Jimmy's stuck on the hats.*

Sharon talked to three girls at the bottom of the stairs. Chris glanced up toward Jimmy and Margo. Immediately she began to fret that Chris would think she was on a date with Jimmy.

"Wally is up to bat tonight," Sharon reported. "Dirks saw the doctor this afternoon, and he won't be playing. Not a good way to finish your high school career." She batted Jimmy's shoulder. "I know, 'up to bat' is baseball. This is commentary! I should be up in that booth."

Jimmy grinned.

Sharon stood on her tiptoes for a better view. "If I were in the announcer's box, I would not be saying, 'Wickersham is a fine young ath-uh-lete.' The word is ath-lete!"

Sharon turned to the cheerleaders, lifting their megaphones. "We need to make our voices heard. Last game, time for spirit." She nudged Margo. "Come on, we can cheer the team on to certain—well, to a good game."

Jimmy asked if Sharon wanted popcorn, but she said no. After he left, she said, "Popcorn makes me thirsty, and too much liquid in cold weather—you know—and the girls' bathroom here is the worst on campus. They say the boys' is worse, but I don't see how that is possible."

The Azusa Aztec Marching Band began the pre-game show. Sharon put her shoulder against Margo's. "They won Sweepstakes at the big band review. They're the best."

The band high-stepped onto the field to a slow syncopated cadence, drums rumbling. Chris watched, unmoving.

Jimmy came back with popcorn and cups in a box. He offered a soda to Margo. "Sorry, they're smalls." He sprinkled popcorn in the box and handed it to them.

"Thank you, Jimmy." Margo was glad Jimmy sat on the outside instead of between them.

"Small is perfect." Sharon leaned close. "Go easy."

The score was tied during the whole second half. In the last few minutes, Blackwater began to move the ball down the field. Margo got excited and forgot to look at Chris. She finally understood the first down and willed the ball forward. Wally threw several complete passes, and Margo screamed with the crowd. At the goal line, Blackwater did a trick play and scored. Margo missed the touchdown because she thought Wally had slipped the ball to another player.

"I gotta say, that was quite a nice surprise," Sharon said.

"Wally is better than Dirks if you ask me," Jimmy muttered.

A Date

TOMMY ALLEN ASKED MARGO to dance to "The Stroll," and she moved easily down the line, thankful for Sharon's impromptu lesson under the oak.

After the music stopped, Tommy stayed near. Chris went to get a drink of water.

"Hey," Tommy said, "the skit was great."

Margo nodded, "Uh, yeah." Not great, but a nice addition to the nod—she gave it a score of nod-plus. Chris went back to his basketball buddies.

"The Christmas Formal is in three weeks. Would you like to go?" Tommy glanced at Sharon and Jimmy, talking nearby. "With me?"

She was glad the room was not brightly lit. "Yes?" *How long did I stand here before answering?*

"OK. Good. It's a date. Christmas Formal. Good!" Tommy rubbed his hands together. "All right."

A Driver's Ed boy asked Margo to dance a slow dance. They moved to the floor, and when she looked back, Tommy was gone. Sharon and Jimmy danced nearby. Sharon gave her a silly grin.

After the song, Sharon said, "So what did Tommy have to say that was so serious?"

Jimmy danced with Lisa Henderson. Sharon had probably suggested it.

"He asked me to the Christmas Formal."

Sharon raised her eyebrows. "Aaand?"

"I said yes." Margo glanced at Chris and then found Tommy in the crowd. "I didn't know what to say. I didn't want to hurt his feelings."

"Yes. He must have really worked up his courage. Asking for a date is often a task left to a phone call." Sharon leaned closer. "Do you want to go with Tommy?"

Margo glanced at the guys under the clock. "He's nice in Theater. He's taller than I am."

Sharon gave her a crooked smile. "And on this, you give your opinion. Do you want to go with him?"

"You know I wanted Chris to ask me but..." Margo crossed her arms. "I want to go to the formal. I don't want to be left out. I—I don't know." This was her first date, and she couldn't decide if excitement or nervousness would triumph.

"It'll be fine. You'll have a good time. Tommy is a nice guy. I'm going. You're going. Don't worry so much."

The song was over, and Jimmy started toward them, eyes on Sharon.

She tightened her ponytail. "Don't look now, but here comes another chance to dance."

Alan asked Margo to dance. It was a fast dance, and he took her hands and began to move quickly.

"Alan, I don't know how to do this. I'm not a good dancer."

"No problem. Dr. Fixit can fix it. This's not hard. Watch." He let go of her right hand.

"We'll start with the simple Swing. Step right with a little hop, step left, little hop, now back and rock-step." He led her with his hand. "Right, now left, now rock-step. Put a little bounce into it."

Margo watched Alan's feet, mirroring his movements.

"Little steps. You don't have to move all that much until you feel the balance. Right, left, rock-step. There you are. On your toes a bit more." Alan took her other hand and guided her. "There you go. You're a natural."

Margo began to relax by the time the music faded.

Alan turned toward the table where the records were being played, held up two fingers, and rolled his hand over. "OK, one more time. This is 'Jail House Rock.' Elvis. Now we really dance."

She was dancing the Swing! Alan showed her how to twirl into him, look at him over her shoulder and twirl back. She got all tangled up, but somehow Alan moved to make it work.

Tina watched them, smiling. Alan signaled again, and he and Margo danced to "At the Hop." Tina showed Sharon and Jimmy the steps.

Alan might be "Dr. Fixit," but he was a good guy. Tina's boyfriend was dancing with another girl, and she wasn't pouty. Margo vowed to not be pouty if she ever had a boyfriend.

They announced the last dance. Chris glanced in Margo's direction and pushed off the wall, skirting the dance floor. Bonnie put on her smile and intercepted, but Chris said something and stepped around her. He was coming in Margo's direction, and her arms went stupid. She folded her hands in front of her, feeling as exposed as Miss Odegaard when the screen fluttered up. Tommy was moving in her direction, as well.

Chris gave her a half-smile. "Would you like to dance?"

"Yes."

"Put Your Head on My Shoulder" drifted through the room. Margo wanted to lean close and put her head on his shoulder, to whisper in his ear, "Why didn't you ask me to the formal?" Alan and Tina glided around the outside of the other dancers, Tina laughing.

Chris smelled good and Margo wanted the song to last forever.

The lights came on, breaking the magic, and they walked toward the door. *What's Chris thinking? Is Tommy around? Am I supposed to be talking to another boy? Tommy isn't my boyfriend, so I shouldn't have anything to feel guilty about.* The unspoken rules of high school defied her.

"The Welcome and Hospitality Club is on cleanup tonight."

"My uncle will be waiting." She ached for time to pause, giving her extra moments with Chris.

"Sure. Thanks for the dance."

Sharon and Jimmy waited for Margo by the door. Chris stuffed streamers into a trashcan.

On the way home, Margo said, "A boy asked me to the Christmas Formal."

T. Charles considered the news. "I'm not surprised. You're awfully fetching with your new hairstyle and beret."

"It wasn't Chris—the boy who came when I hurt my head." She looked out the window. "I kinda like Chris. I wish Chris had asked." A hint of a smile appeared under T. Charles's mustache. "But this boy, Tommy Allen, is in Theater. He's nice too."

"Did you say yes to Tommy?"

"Yes."

T. Charles turned into the driveway and parked the car under the porte cochère. "I'll put the car away. Why don't you put the tea kettle on, and you can tell me all about it."

Margo used the good cups and saucers. T. Charles smiled when he saw them.

"So, my Maggie Girl is going to the Christmas Formal in California. We'll have to see about a dress."

"I've been thinking about that. Virginia had such wonderful clothes. They're only a little loose."

"You're welcome to anything up there, but those styles are not the latest fad—and we didn't go to many formals."

Margo touched her cup to her lips. "That's just the thing. I think that's what I want. No one is wearing a beret to football games or dances, but I get compliments. I think I want to be original."

T. Charles sat back with a smile. "We will have to try to locate Virginia's alterations woman. She did all Virginia's sewing. Many of the dresses and outfits upstairs are handmade. Mrs. Kim—I'll look in Virginia's address book." He slowly nodded. "I'm sure we can find her."

Before Margo fell asleep, she replayed the evening. She had been asked to the Christmas Formal. Alan staged a dance lesson. Sharon and Jimmy seemed to have a good time together, and they would be at the formal.

Chris asked me to dance! T. Charles wanted to hear the whole story, listening to every word. Perhaps I am willowy.

Tears

MARGO TURNED OFF THE vacuum when T. Charles came down.

"Oh, Maggie! Thanks for vacuuming. I slept a bit late this morning. I think there was too much 'girl talk' last night." His eyes twinkled. "I'll start breakfast."

Margo finished the den and library and was working in the study when T. Charles called her.

"I made extra breakfast. You'll be hungry from working so hard."

Her stomach agreed.

T. Charles had a rose on the table in a tall fluted crystal vase. He sprinkled pepper on his egg. "I thought, later we could go up and look at dresses for the formal."

"There are so many to choose from."

"We don't have to select only one."

It was easy living with a morning person who placed a white rose on the table. "Cultivo una rosa blanca," words learned in Spanish returned to Margo's mind, José Martí's poem of peace. T. Charles cultivated peace in her life.

When Mrs. Brice rang the bell, T. Charles said, "Nine o'clock. I really did have a late morning!"

Mrs. Brice announced it was time to wash windows and mirrors. Margo did the French doors. Mrs. Brice gave careful instructions, "Wipe sideways on the inside and up and down on the outside. That way you can tell which side the streaks are on."

Sharon called soon after Mrs. Brice left. "Can you talk?" Her voice sounded muffled.

"Sure. Are you OK?"

"We need to meet." Sharon lowered her voice. "I can't talk now."

Margo pressed the receiver tight, straining to hear. "I think I can. I'll ask. Where would we meet?"

"There's a—little café on Third Street. Nadine's." There was a long pause.

"Sharon, you don't sound right."

"I can be there at one o'clock."

"I will too," Margo said, and Sharon was gone. A feeling of foreboding settled on her, dark clouds driven by a chill wind.

"Uncle, can I go out for a couple of hours? Sharon and I are going to meet for a soda at Nadine's, on Third Street?"

"Do you want me to drive you? It's more than a mile downtown."

"Thank you, but I think I'll walk."

———————◦———————

SHARON'S EYES WERE red, her face blotchy. When she saw Margo, she leaned forward, her forehead almost touching the table.

"Oh, Sharon! What's the matter?"

Sharon tried to gulp air. She didn't look up. "Ooh, Maggie!" Her shoulders shook. "It's just so—maddening!"

Margo moved over to Sharon's side of the booth. She surprised herself by pulling gently on Sharon's ponytail the way Aunt Louise had stroked her hair when she wasn't invited to Cindy Jamison's sleepover. Sharon wasn't in the sixth grade, and this was bigger than a sleepover.

After a long time, Sharon said, "My dad didn't come to get me last night." She took a shaky breath.

Margo's heart pounded, but she waited.

"He didn't come. Jimmy went home—thank goodness." Her nose was running.

"Finally, no one was left, but me and the teachers. Miss Johnson took me home." Sharon began to cry in earnest.

Margo rubbed Sharon's back. The waitress came by, but Margo gave her head the tiniest of shakes.

After a long time, Sharon looked at Margo with damp eyes. "My dad was laying—on the lawn." The last words squeaked out, ending in a whisper. Sharon wiped her nose with a napkin. She trembled as she took a deep breath. "He drinks. My dad is an alco-" She had the hiccups.

Sharon shook her head slowly. "He drinks. He—I guess he made it partway to his pickup and passed out. Miss Johnson helped me get him up." She hit the Formica top gently with the heel of her closed fist.

She raised her clenched hand in the air, made a small circle, and brought it slowly to rest on the table. She pushed down until her arm shook. She sobbed and sobbed.

Margo's chest ached. Sharon was interested in her problems, but Margo knew nothing about Sharon's life, because she had never asked.

"You can't—tell anyone any—of this. Please."

"I would never. I'm so sorry."

"No, I mean more than just my dad." Sharon sat up. "Everything has to stay secret."

"I'd never say anything."

"We got my dad headed inside. Miss Johnson told me about meetings for those who are affected by drinking. Those were her words, 'affected by drinking.' Alcoholism." Sharon gave a shaky laugh. "There, I said it. My dad is an alcoholic."

Margo reached for another napkin.

"Miss Johnson goes to meetings because of her mother and brother..." Sharon started to cry again. "She was so nice. Dad stumbled inside. I'm not sure he even—knew she was there." Sharon sat back and looked across the room, brushing an eye.

The waitress came, and Sharon said, "One coffee and one?" She turned to Margo.

"Soda, I guess. Cherry Coke?" Margo had never had one.

"She gave me a little card with the meeting time for Alateen. It's for kids. Like me." Sharon handed Margo a damp white card with neat handwriting.

Margo longed for something wise to say. "Miss Johnson is nice."

"So, I'm going to go. Miss Johnson said she could take me. I'm going to go." Sharon seemed to gain strength. "I'm not pretending anymore." She drew another shaky breath. "Miss Johnson goes to Al-Anon, Maggie. She's so pretty. So organized and poised. And because of her mother and brother." She started to cry again.

"You are pretty and organized and poised, too."

Sharon's red eyes searched Margo's face. "You think so?"

Margo felt moisture in her own eyes. "I know so. Sharon, you've—you have been so good. So funny, lighthearted. You helped me when I was new—you're my best friend. The best friend I've ever had."

The coffee and the soda came. Margo took a sip from the straw, sickly sweet washing over her tongue. She wouldn't be finishing the cola.

Sharon blew on her coffee. "I suppose I learned to drink coffee from my dad. I hope that's all I learn."

Margo took another sip and pushed her Coke away.

Sharon pulled her ponytail tighter and sat up straight. "But, Maggie, my friend, believe it or not, that is not the whole reason I wanted to talk." When she breathed in, her whole body trembled. "Well, yes. Now that I've told you, I'm glad you know about—my situation."

She put both palms on the table. Her hiccups had stopped.

"I want to double date for the formal. I want to stay over at your house." She shook her head miserably. "I don't think I could stand Jimmy seeing something like last night."

"I'd love to. Uncle will think it's fun." Margo squeezed Sharon's arm.

Sharon seemed to revive. "OK. Hmmm, OK." She took a sip of her coffee and grabbed a straw from the glass dispenser. "Let's see what Cherry Cola is like."

Margo slid the glass over, a wet trail closing on itself. Sharon took a long drink.

"Wow." She closed her eyes. "Oh, that went up the back of my nose." Her eyes watered. "I'm going to cry again, but from that stuff. Do you like that?"

"I never had Cherry Cola in my life, until today." Cherry Cola wasn't the only new thing in Margo's life that day. All this time Sharon had been happy even when she was unhappy.

A Better Friend

MARGO WISHED SHE COULD tell T. Charles about Sharon. The walk home seemed twice as long as going to the diner.

Upstairs, she took a burgundy dress out of the garment bag. "Is this the one Mrs. Kim suggested? It's beautiful."

T. Charles fingered the material. "This is the dress. According to Mrs. Kim, Virginia wore timeless, classic styles." He leaned toward Margo. "When I told her the dresses were a bit loose on you, she said that was good. She's spent too many years trying to hide lumpy places for too many of her clients." He chuckled. "She's happy to be taking something in rather than letting it out."

T. Charles held up a mid-waist jacket. "Virginia wore this with the dress. It's not for cold weather. It sort of draped on her, open in the front." He turned the hanger. "I guess it doesn't even have buttons." He shook his head. "More for decoration than warmth, I suppose."

"Give me a minute."

Margo ducked into her room and slipped into the dress. A quick look in the mirror pleased her. It fell straight, slightly loose. When she put out her foot, it hit at her ankle. She hurried back.

"What do you think?"

T. Charles looked up from a drawer of handbags. "Oh, you look just—you look wonderful."

"This one almost fits."

"It was one of the last dresses Virginia wore before things got—bad. She had lost ten pounds but insisted we go to a fundraiser. Mrs. Kim took it in a bit." T. Charles held his lips tight and closed his eyes.

"I didn't mean to upset you." She touched his arm.

"Oh, Maggie..." He looked up quickly. "Don't worry. It's a mixture of pain and extreme joy—like much of life. Seeing this dress makes me miss Virginia so deeply—it comes on me quite suddenly and almost takes my breath away. But don't worry. It also makes me feel as if Virginia is here with us. And Maggie, she would be having the best time."

Margo smiled at the mirror.

"Virginia wanted children. We wanted children. She would have been a wonderful mother, but the cancer—she had an operation quite early that made that impossible." T. Charles stood up a little taller and smiled. "It gave us thirty-one years. Wonderful years."

T. Charles took her hand and patted it. "Having you here would have been her delight." He looked directly into Margo's eyes. "Don't fret when your uncle gets a little teary. Tears of joy, Dear, tears of joy."

T. Charles went back to the handbags. "I can't remember which handbag she carried with the dress. There's a picture of us at the gala. A friend took it and gave us a copy. Sometimes she held those little clutches in the hand she put on my back when we had our picture taken. Give me a moment."

Margo sat in front of the makeup mirror and sighed. Sharon's dad drank so much he passed out, T. Charles lost the love of his life. Virginia lost her life. Her biggest problem was—parents who were gone a lot. Somehow, it didn't compare.

Margo's thoughts turned to Aunt Louise. She would write. It was time to think about someone besides herself.

T. Charles held up a small black suitcase when he returned. "Pictures we were always going to put in an album. And then—I just lost interest."

He opened the suitcase on one of the bureaus. "Ha, ha! Look at this! This is Virginia, posing. She was showing a model how she wanted her to stand, and her assistant clicked the shutter."

Virginia had turned to the side, arms folded, face to the camera. She wore an "I doubt it," expression.

"Wow." Margo sorted pictures, putting photos of Virginia in the lid of the suitcase. In picture after picture, Virginia was captivating, whether standing by a Christmas tree or with a group of people.

T. Charles handed Margo a color photo of Virginia and him in front of a large fireplace. Virginia was thin, and her face drawn, her eyes on T. Charles. A small handbag was in her left hand.

He came close. "I'm afraid she didn't feel well. We left after this was taken." He touched her face on the photo. "She looks tired; I shouldn't have let her go." He gave Margo a half-smile. "But when Virginia made up her mind, I could never say no."

Margo pointed. "There's the purse."

"Yes, and I had it here with some others." He handed her a small black beaded bag with a silver clasp.

She opened it and found a tiny handkerchief inside and a lipstick. When she pulled the cap, the lipstick was a perfect match for the dress, waiting for this moment. Virginia had been taken early, robbed of the delight. Tears pressed the corners of Margo's eyes.

T. Charles opened a cabinet at the far side of the room. "These are the shoes. Try them."

Margo had a Cinderella moment when the shoe slipped on her foot. They had a low heel, and she felt like Miss Johnson, in her spectator pumps.

With the coat, she stood in front of the mirror, turning from side to side. She studied the picture and then her reflection. Margo lowered her chin.

They chose several outfits to take to Mrs. Kim. T. Charles said Christmas was coming and to take seasonal things as well.

After they carried the clothes downstairs, Margo went back. Sweaters zipped into clear bags had caught her eye. The third bag held the partner to her fourth grade Christmas sweater. Her eyes burned. It would have been such fun to come to California and go shopping or drink tea in matching sweaters. Margo felt robbed.

Later, she threw the Band-Aid in the trash. It was time to worry about bigger things. She sat at the writing desk, taking time to watch a blue jay fussing with a twig in the tree. She wrote to Aunt Louise, telling her about her bedroom and school. Margo closed with, "I Love You" and slipped the letter in a beautiful card from Virginia's collection.

Margo opened her diary but didn't write. She made a promise to pay attention to the people around her. She would ask Sharon how she was and what she was thinking. Margo breathed a chuckle. Sharon didn't need prompting to find out what she was thinking most of the time. But she would be a better friend.

She wrote, "It is not all about me," and underlined the words. The jay was back, its simple gaze giving Margo hope.

In her notebook, she penned the finish to a poem for English.

Uncle and I restless, stir,
Burgundy dress, he in black,
Our movement and gesture tell.

Virginia, would, so like her
Be watching through the lens-back
Knowing to mark mem'ries well.

The dark jay, messaging, taps
Black beak and eyes against blue,
Holding me with her fixed stare.

Above Virginia perhaps
Is granted this present view
If heaven allows such fare.

Stretching time and memory long,
Keeping generation's song.

Two Beaus

MARGO WALKED TO SCHOOL a few minutes early. She had surprised herself by praying for Sharon at church. It wasn't much of a prayer, but she couldn't remember ever praying for anyone but herself.

Sharon wore her poodle skirt and a starched blouse. Her hair was loose around her shoulders, the sides pulled back with silver clips.

"I like your hair," Margo said.

"You're not the only one who can get a new hairstyle. I cut some bangs. Are they straight?"

Margo studied Sharon's eyes. She didn't look like she had been crying. "Bangs are cute."

Sharon looked toward the mountains and took a breath. "I've been thinking I'm going to miss football. I know I make fun of it, and the ball is a silly shape—but the last two games have been quite successful. Wally made eleven completed passes. That tricky play for the winning touchdown was quite exhilarating."

"I'm wondering if you have a bit of a crush on Wally?" She nudged Sharon.

"Wally? Of course not." Sharon turned to walk backward, white teeth catching the light. "Well, maybe a little. We have known each other since kindergarten. But Wally didn't ask me to the dance. I doubt Wally asked anyone to the dance. Hey, gotta go. See you in Theater."

In Biology, Alan smoothed a sheet of paper on the lab table. It was folded into six squares, like cartoon panels.

"This is the movie idea from your English paper about your grandfather's disappearance." Alan looked up. "Good paper, by the way."

Miss Johnson had written, "Excellent composition, Margo. Keep up the good work."

Alan slid his books to the side. "Each square is one movie scene. The words are what we would put on a card before the scene."

Sunday Comics-like characters made her smile. "Alan can draw!"

"Mike is the artist." Alan shrugged. "I laid it out in scenes."

The story of Grandfather's kidnapping and Grandmother rescuing him from his captors was all there, the way the story should have happened.

Inside, Margo smiled. His disappearance had brought Virginia and T. Charles together.

"This can work, Maggie. The problem is the film—it's not cheap. If we shoot a hundred-foot reel, it will only be four minutes."

"A hundred feet? Is that all we can have?"

"The camera holds a hundred feet. It'll splice into a longer movie, but I've checked prices—this could get expensive." Alan was quiet for a minute. "We probably can't do more than two reels."

Margo pulled the paper closer. A movie! Could Alan get Chris to be the lead in the film? *Will Chris think the story is dumb—think I am dumb?*

Alan liked the plot, but Alan wasn't one of the cool people. *I'm not either.* That was the whole trouble with being invisible. There was no feedback because no one bothered to notice.

Jimmy Smith slipped in the door as Mr. Yeager called his name. "Jim, I think we are dangerously close to getting a tardy. What do you think?"

"It won't happen again, Sir."

Mr. Yeager peered over his glasses at Jimmy for a full ten seconds. "No, I think not."

Margo's eyes were drawn to the sketches, but she folded them in the back of her binder. She mouthed thank you to Alan and turned toward Mr. Yeager, forcing herself to listen to the lab instructions.

In English class, Margo watched Miss Johnson carefully. She seemed as poised as ever. Her patent leather heels clicked as she read the final scene from "The Taming of the Shrew." Margo loved that "Clever Kate" was not tamed, but that the two were playing the others in a game they win. The bell jarred the moment, and Margo sighed.

Chris moved next to her in the hall. *Is he walking beside me, or is the hallway just crowded?* She stole a glance out of the corner of her eye. Chris watched with those gray eyes. A tingle of surprise washed over her.

"Glad to see you don't need the Band-Aid anymore. Does it still hurt?"

"No. The stitches itched, but once they were out, it was fine." *Itched? I have waited for days for a chance to talk to Chris, and the first thing out of my mouth is that my stitches itched!*

"That's good. I'm glad." Chris hesitated. "Well—I have to go the other way."

Chris was only gone a moment when Sharon appeared. "My, my. Look who was walking with Maggie."

"I'm so bad at this." Margo glanced back to make sure Chris wasn't near. "I told him my stitches itched! He walks with me, and I can't think of one thing to say."

"And Chris? I suppose he began a discussion of the Magna Carta and its influence on the Bill of Rights?"

Margo laughed. "He asked how my eye was."

"So, he couldn't think of anything to say, either."

Until then, she hadn't thought about Chris's side of their talk. It hadn't been a sparkling conversation on either side.

"I tell you, the boy is smitten. Chris can be very outgoing and sure of himself. Funny. Around you, he's tongue-tied."

Margo thought of Chris drumming on the office counter and talking so easily her first day. "Maybe he feels bad about me getting hurt and..."

Sharon closed one eye halfway. "And maybe he's smitten."

———————◉———————

AFTER SCHOOL, MARGO intended to entertain Sharon with Mrs. Kim's comment about hiding lumpy parts. Chris stood near her locker.

"Hi, Margo. Can I talk to you a minute? I have to hurry. Practice is starting."

She smiled and waited.

"Yeah, well. I was wondering if you'd like to go to the Christmas Formal with me. As my date."

Margo focused on his light freckles as she struggled with possible answers. "I can't. Tommy Allen already asked me." It was not exactly the clever answer she had hoped for.

Chris blushed. "Tommy. Yeah. Tommy Allen. I saw you talking at the dance."

"Yes." Margo longed for words to let Chris know she wanted to go with him. "Yes, he asked at the dance." *I'm doomed to half-witted remarks.*

Chris seemed undecided. He started to turn, paused, and then took a step sideways. "Well—I gotta go. Coach doesn't like us to be late."

Margo watched his slim hips as he moved away. "Chris?"

He turned. "Yeah?"

"Thank you for asking me."

"Sure." He raised his shoulders and let them fall. "Sure."

What a mess!

Sharon waited by the oak. She came close and whispered, "Well, well. I'll have to get in line to be able to talk to my friend." She looked over Margo's shoulder. "Mary has her radar out—OK, she's spied bigger fish. All clear."

Mary hurried to catch two girls on the sidewalk.

"So, I saw you talking to Chris, and I took the long way around. I'm guessing he wasn't waiting by your locker to find out more about itching stitches."

"He asked me to the formal."

"And there you are! Not one, but two beaus. This is impressive."

"Sharon, you can be proud of me. At first, I couldn't think of a single sensible thing to say, but then I tried your technique. I told him what I was thinking." She couldn't stop grinning. "Well, not *exactly* what I was thinking—but after he started to walk away, I said, 'Thank you for asking me.' See, I learn things from you."

Sharon tilted her head sideways. "It's a good thing that you didn't say what I would have been thinking, which would be, 'Why didn't you ask me last week, you big lug?'"

"Yeah, I suppose that crossed my mind. Probably best I didn't say that."

"All is not lost. Friday night is the first basketball game. Basketball games can be a step up from football. Oh, sure, the gym stinks, and what with the buzzers and the whistles, you could go deaf."

The description brought to mind the crowded old wooden gym at the second Jefferson. "I guess basketball here is the same as in Wisconsin."

"But in Wisconsin, Chris Ferguson wasn't the captain." Sharon gave a mischievous laugh. "Perhaps Tommy will be there and sit by you and make Chris *mad* with jealousy."

"Sure, and Chris'll ask Bonnie Douglas to the Christmas Formal."

"But he will be thinking of you."

Inside, Margo smiled. "Hey, Sharon. Good luck tonight. I hope it's—good." It wasn't all she wanted to say, but it was a start.

Sharon hugged her binder. "Thanks, Maggie."

Eighty, One-Hundred

MARGO FOUND A PIECE Virginia wrote about hats for a magazine. The article said a cloche was perfect for bobbed hair. She chose a white hat with a band that brought out the green in her eyes.

In the mirror, she removed a pin curl clip and pulled the curve forward. She took a deep breath, sitting straight.

Sharon only said the Alateen meeting was OK. Miss Johnson had been kind and not asked any questions. Margo was dying to know but didn't ask questions either.

MARGO SAT BY SHARON in the gym, the buzzer ringing in her ears. Three Driver's Ed boys sat in front of them. Billy Peters kept leaning back against Sharon's knees until she finally rapped his head with her knuckles.

"I have to tell you, Maggie, the one downside to basketball is the uniform. I'm not a big fan of the underarm, so ten guys in their underwear holding their arms up is enough to put me off my feed."

Chris was under the basket, rebounding and firing the ball back out. *He looks good to me!*

Grace sat at the scoring table, controlling the clock. She spoke animatedly to the assistant coach.

The game started, and Margo watched every move Chris made. He often brought the ball down court, and she was impressed with how well he could read the defense.

In the second quarter, Blackwater had the lead, and the coach took Chris and two others out. Four minutes remained in the half.

Sharon nudged Margo's shoulder and gestured with her head. Vivien Turner stood on the other side of the Pep Band, wearing a blue beret.

Sharon rolled her eyes. "Poor Vivien. Where is she going to find a cute hat like the one you have on tonight?"

Margo wished the coach would put Chris back in, but said, "Maybe the coach will put Jimmy in."

"Let's be realistic. We have to be winning by more than ten points for Jimmy to get to play." Sharon sighed. "It's OK. Jimmy doesn't seem to mind. He's just glad he made the team and gets to practice."

The Pep Band began to play, and Sharon patted her hands together, singing along.

"You should take Choir. You have a nice voice."

"You think? I don't know. My brother always thumps on the wall if I sing in my room. Of course, he thumps on my wall if I don't turn off my alarm in the first one second."

Blackwater won by twenty-five points, and Jimmy played the last two minutes. He only got the ball once but managed to pass it to Jack Sanders who laid it up neatly.

"Oooh. I am pretty sure that was an assist," Sharon said. "Yea Jimmy!"

During the Alma Mater, Margo sang, "Hail, Blackwater, Hail, Hail, Hail." She felt a rush of school pride.

At the dance the team was late. Tommy asked Margo to dance, and she showed him the steps to the swing.

One of the Driver's Ed boys asked her to dance. When the record ended, she went back to Sharon. "Who is the boy I just danced with?"

"Frankie Sanchez. He plays saxophone in the band. His brother has a rock and roll group. They played for a dance last year. Frankie isn't car crazy—he's on the baseball team."

The basketball players started to arrive. Bonnie Douglas, still in her cheerleading outfit, rushed over to Chris, talons glistening.

Chris danced with Bonnie, and Margo wished Tommy would

ask her to dance. It was not her best moment, but she didn't want Chris to see her standing like a dope. Frankie came and stood near. He seemed undecided, and Margo said, "Let's dance."

Why would I ever ask a boy I hardly know to dance! At least it isn't a slow dance.

When the record finished, she moved to the side, giving Sharon a "come here" head shake.

"Every time I open my mouth, I seem to say something I regret. I promise myself I won't get into situations I don't want to be in and then..."

Sharon squinted into Margo's eyes. "Join the club—the high school club. Everyone is discombobulated. Isn't that a great word? That is my new word—discombobulated."

"Frankie came over and was sort of standing by me. I got nervous he was going to ask me to the formal, so I opened my big mouth and asked *him* to dance." Margo groaned. "Why would I ever think he was going to ask me to the formal? He probably thought I was fishing for a date to the prom!"

Sharon moved close and held up one finger. "And now the trick is to act like you only asked him to dance. Nothing more. Simply pretend you only asked him to dance."

Chris danced with Bonnie again. Margo didn't see who asked who. When she looked in his direction, he always was looking somewhere else. *Discombobulated is the perfect description of my life. I exist in the dreamland between what I want and what I have, and that isn't a good recipe for happiness.*

"Do you think Chris has given up on liking me? He doesn't ever look at me or seem to know I'm here."

"Oh, he knows you're here. He watches when you're busy with someone else."

"But I'm afraid he'll ask Bonnie to the formal. He keeps dancing with her." Margo was miserable.

"Eighty, One-Hundred." Sharon put on her all-knowing smile.

"Eighty-one-hundred?"

"Eighty percent chance of asking. One hundred percent chance of Bonnie saying yes. You think you're confused. Think about Chris. Bonnie has her claws in him, he likes you, you're going to the formal with Tommy, and Bonnie doesn't really want Chris as a boyfriend because, thanks to Mary's news, she's dating a guy from Pasadena!" Sharon laughed over her shoulder. "Pretty amusing if you think about it." She grabbed Jimmy's hand and led him out to the floor.

They were cute together.

Frankie moved back to Margo's side. "Can I ask you something?'

She put a pleasant look on her face.

Frankie brushed his chin. "Do you think Sharon has been asked to the Christmas Formal? I mean—is she going with Jimmy?"

It was pretty comical, and Margo worked hard to not laugh at herself. *Sharon has two beaus!* "They *are* going to the formal together.

"I'm going to ask her anyway. I want her to know I wanted to go with her. Now that I know the answer, it makes it easier." He twisted his lips. "I guess."

Sharon was right. It was a mixed-up life at Blackwater High.

Tommy asked Margo to dance again, and she enjoyed spending time with him. She wasn't sure she would ever like Tommy as a boyfriend, but he was OK to be with. *Is there such a thing as an in-between-boy, if Sharon is right about Chris still being interested?* Bonnie had her hand on Chris's arm.

The last dance was announced. Margo moved to where Sharon and Jimmy were talking, near the drinking fountain. When Chris tapped her on the shoulder and asked her to dance, she hadn't seen him coming.

"Only You" drifted across the room. Chris's touch sent electrifying waves all the way to her heart.

"I like your hat," Chris said. "I like all your hats."

"They belonged to my great aunt. She had lots of clothes—for her business."

"Sure."

When the song ended, the lights switched on, dissolving the magic in white glare. "Thank you for the dance. I need to talk to Sharon before she leaves."

Chris nodded.

"Jimmy, give me a second to talk to Sharon before I go."

Sharon let her fingers dangle in Jimmy's as he moved away.

"I've been thinking," Margo lowered her voice, "I could have my uncle wait a bit, you know, in case." Chris went out the door. *Why didn't I ask him to wait?*

"I think Dad is OK. He's on the wagon. But thanks." She patted Margo's arm. "Hey, Frankie asked me to the Christmas Formal!"

"Ah, Sharon Jackson, the girl with two beaus!"

Sharon smiled. "Thanks, Maggie. Thank you."

Outside, Sharon's dad walked toward the cafeteria. Sharon wiggled her fingers toward T. Charles.

In the car, Margo asked, "Uncle, what does it mean if someone is on the wagon?" Chris's car pulled out of the student parking. He was alone.

"It's when a drinker has stopped drinking. Unfortunately, sometimes a drinker can fall off the wagon."

Even in the warm car, a shiver went down her spine.

Sleepover

SHARON STRETCHED OUT on Margo's bed. "I declare the Formal a success. Jimmy and I had a good time. You and Tommy had a good time. Jack Sanders and Grace Thompson looked like they were having fun. Alan and Tina were cutting a rug. The decorations almost made me forget we were in the cafeteria." She smiled.

"You know we can't use the gym because of the precious floor." Sharon lowered her voice to sound like Coach Wiggins. "No dress shoes allowed on the basketball court. The floor has just been refinished."

Tommy drove the four of them in his mother's station wagon with a rattly rear window. It was not as elegant as being driven by a chauffeur in the Packard, but it got them there. The boys took them to dinner.

"Sharon, you help me get ready for my major life events. You helped Tommy get a corsage that matched my dress—but you never told me not to order spaghetti on a date."

Sharon sat up. "Yeah, that was an oversight on my part. But, they chose Guido's. At an Italian restaurant, you have to expect spaghetti. Spaghetti is chancy even at a family meal with a fussy grandma or aunt."

Margo knew all about a fussy Grandmother.

Sharon leaned forward. "On a date, it can cause extra difficulty." She pretended to lift a noodle from her chin to her mouth with her finger. "I'll give you this, you didn't suck up a string like *Lady and the Tramp*." Sharon made a slurpy noise followed by a kiss sound.

Margo laughed and turned in the mirror one last time. She hated to take off the dress. Mrs. Kim had done a perfect job. "It fits like a glove," T. Charles had said.

Before Margo got ready for bed, she hung her corsage upside down because Sharon said it would keep better.

"Well, we might as well talk about Chris and Bonnie." Sharon nudged Margo with her elbow.

Margo sighed. "I should hang a sign around my neck."

Sharon laughed. "You're letting your sense of humor out." She leaned on one elbow, propping her head. "All right, here is my analysis. And this study has not been tainted by Mary Suttle gossip."

"What did Mary say?" *This can't be good.*

"Oh, my, what didn't Mary say. Poor Eddie Alvarez. He got her a nice flower, took her to dinner, and the formal—and she spent half the evening gallivanting all over the place. She caught me in the bathroom."

"Did she say something about Chris—or me?" Margo wished Mary's meddling could be about Chris and her.

"Just flitting Bonnie asides. She was in high gear. I think she could tell I was anxious to get out of there, so she had to give the abbreviated version. Forget Mary." Sharon pulled her pillow under her side. "My analysis is that Bonnie and Chris only came together because they both wanted to go to the formal. Bonnie pouted her way through the evening. I don't think that girl knows how to smile—unless she's trying out for cheerleading."

Neither Chris nor Bonnie had seemed to enjoy the dance, and that was sad. If Sharon had taught Margo anything, she taught her to enjoy the moment. Even if you didn't care about football, you could go to the game and have fun.

Margo had danced once with Jimmy while Sharon danced with Tommy. "I sort of wondered if Chris would ask me to dance. He danced twice with other girls."

"Not possible. Bonnie may not want Chris, but Bonnie knows Chris has a crush on you. That fact alone means she would let him dance with any girl in the world—except you."

A crush! The thought made Margo's breath quicken, and she hugged her pillow.

"Bonnie probably engineered every dance. Poor Chris doesn't stand a chance with Bonnie. She likes to get her way and knows how to do it."

Margo weighed Sharon's words and decided if she ever got a chance with Chris, she wouldn't always have to have her own way.

Margo was pretty sure she and Tommy had been on a date of convenience. They had fun dancing, but he hadn't seemed particularly enthralled with her and hadn't kissed her goodnight. She didn't know if she wanted him to kiss her. She had never been kissed by a boy and wanted to be able to say she had. It was stupid, but being a Junior and "never been kissed" was embarrassing.

"I don't think Chris was dazzled by Bonnie's flouncy dress." Sharon shook her head in wonder. "How many petticoats were under that thing? He probably had to put her in the back seat! I mean, everyone had full skirts but not like Bonnie's."

"Batting them down would be a full-time job if she wanted to see the back of his head."

Sharon was not distracted. "Everyone but you, Maggie." She was quiet for a moment. "You weren't afraid to wear Virginia's dress, and it was class all the way. If you'd been at Blackwater High longer, we wouldn't have all been wearing a knee-length white dress with flouncy petticoats."

"Tina had on a dark green dress. I thought she looked cute."

"She made it in Home Ec. They both were cute. Alan looked pretty sharp in his tux. I know he's a stocky guy, but he was like a senator or something—pretty official."

"Tina's nice. She and Alan talked to me a bit while Tommy was getting punch. She's sweet."

Sharon squirmed sideways. "OK. I need to tell you about my meetings."

Margo waited, watching Sharon's pursed lips.

"We have only been to two, but..." Sharon seemed undecided. "This all has to go in the 'don't tell closet' with—the rest of it."

"I haven't even told Uncle."

"Oh, you can tell Uncle T, at least about me. Well, about my dad. Uncle T is great. He was so nice to wait up but not ask a million questions. Uncle T is a gentleman."

It was the perfect description of T. Charles. When they brought Tommy's boutonniere home, T. Charles poked a hole in it with a needle. He insisted she practice pinning it on him twice until she was comfortable doing it. "Keep the pin level, and hit the same hole in the base of the carnation each time," he had said. "The green tape is tough and hard to get a pin through."

Sharon rolled onto her stomach, wadding the pillow beneath her chin. "Miss Johnson picked me up. I couldn't believe my mom actually helped me with this. She talked to my dad. She has a hard time standing up to him. My Aunt Arlene says my mom is a doormat—lets everyone walk all over her."

Doormat. The perfect description of Mother.

"When Miss Johnson came to get me, Tina and her sister, Laura, were with her."

Margo wasn't surprised, and yet she didn't know why. Perhaps Tina didn't cover deep heartache as well as Sharon.

"So, the meetings aren't crowded. But it was sort of nice to have someone I know there. Tina and I are not close friends, but—you know—moral support."

Sharon flopped onto her back and fluffed the pillow under her head. "I don't know what to say about the meetings. It's different, and I'm not sure I can explain. I guess it's good to be with kids who are—like me."

It took three tries before Margo managed, "Sharon, no one is like you. I mean, I know you have your troubles—but no one I know is like you. You're like sunshine around the school. No wonder Jimmy likes you. You make him laugh—you make me laugh. When you and Tommy were dancing, he was smiling." She paused for a moment. "And you care about the kids. And you *don't* gossip. And—you're *not* like the other kids."

A tear rolled down Sharon's cheek. "Thanks, Maggie. I think I'm getting sleepy."

Margo reached over and turned off the lamp but wouldn't be sleeping anytime soon.

Uncle

"UNCLE T, YOU'RE QUITE the chef there, flipping pancakes like a master," Sharon said. "This is nice."

Fresh orange juice was on the table.

"Sharon, Maggie says you are a coffee drinker. I can make a pot."

"Maybe I will try the tea I hear so much about."

"Excellent. Maggie, would you please pour?"

Margo used the cups with blue flowers. "Sorry we just came down. We'll be late for church."

T. Charles turned. "I'm having Lois Sanders play for the choir this week. We don't have to be at church until ten-thirty."

Sharon mouthed, "He's so good to you."

"So, I can tell you girls had a good time. I could hear you laughing last night."

"We didn't mean to bother you."

"Girls, you are no bother. This old house has been quiet too long—the sound of laughter is the best music."

They drove Sharon home before church. When they dropped her off, she said, "I had the best time!"

After church, T. Charles said, "I've been thinking. Your grades are much better. You've attended your first formal dance and had a successful pajama party. I believe we owe ourselves a movie."

"Really?"

"I read in the paper that *Operation Petticoat* is showing. It has Cary Grant and Tony Curtis. Virginia thought Cary Grant was very handsome. From what I read, it's silly—just for fun."

"I'd love to!"

"All right. But first, we should stop for a bite to eat. There's an In-N-Out hamburger stand not far from here."

"I've heard kids talk about it. Wow! Going to In-N-Out!"

———⬥———

FULL OF HAMBURGERS and French fries, they settled in the theater. Uncle bought a buttered popcorn and sodas. They nibbled on popcorn and laughed at the movie.

When they came out, the bright afternoon surprised Margo. She took Uncle's arm.

"Tell me more about the Christmas Formal."

"A girl—Bonnie Douglas was crowned Snow Queen." Sharon had noted that she remembered snow only once. "Chris Ferguson was the Snow King. You remember Chris..."

"Yes, I remember."

"They went together. I don't think they had a very good time. Chris didn't seem to like wearing a crown and having to dance in front of everyone."

"You said you hoped Chris would ask you."

"He did. It was just too late." She leaned against his shoulder and told him the whole story. "Sharon says Chris likes me."

"I'm not surprised. The way you looked last night, I'll bet many of the boys noticed. You need to believe in yourself."

"I'm trying. Sharon is a big help. She's the best friend I've ever had. I..."

Uncle asks more questions about my life than Mother ever did. "In the other two high schools, at the apartment and at Aunt Louise's, I never seemed to feel right. Last year I was back and forth twice. It was—just hard." The other schools faded into the distance.

But, this isn't permanent. Next year could mean—she didn't want to think where she would be next year.

Uncle unlocked Margo's side of the car.

"But here, with you and the school, I feel noticed."

Uncle was quiet on the way home. The Packard purred, and Margo turned on the radio. The station played a Frankie Avalon song, "Venus." She was surprised the radio was not tuned to his usual station, KNX.

When the car stopped at the house, Uncle put his hand on the door handle and paused. "You are noticed, Maggie. You are noticed."

They spent the evening in the study. Margo sat at the piano and tried to work on Grandfather's song. It was difficult, but she had improved. Uncle showed her a couple of fingering tricks.

"Play it for me?"

When Uncle played, it seemed so easy. Even when his fingers were a blur, he was completely relaxed.

"Here, you play the left, and I'll do the right. We'll go slowly."

She surprised herself by getting half of the first page right. "I'll keep trying. I want to use this music for the movie. Alan says the camera doesn't record sound. I want to play the song along with it, like the silent movies."

Uncle moved to his chair and wiggled his feet on the footstool.

"I want Grandfather's music for my movie about him. In the movie, we rescue him, and his music will be part of finding him."

"He would like that, I'm sure."

"But I don't think I'll ever get the song right. Alan says he'll show the movie to my teacher in the auditorium, but the piano is horrible." She took a breath. "If we could get the movie filmed, would you come to school and play for the class, even if the piano is out of tune?"

"We can do one better. Come in the living room."

Uncle padded through the archway and opened the top of a cabinet sitting against the wall.

The nameplate said Packard Bell PhonOcord. "Is it the same company that made the car?"

He chuckled. "No, but you'd think I only bought Packard products." He took a record out of a plain paper jacket. "This machine makes phonograph records."

"It makes records?"

"Virginia and I used to have parties here. Several of our friends played the piano. Some were interested in theater. We made up skits—radio plays." He pulled out another record. "September first, 1949. Ah, our anniversary. Oh, this was fun! We did a short play we'd found. We called it 'Little Nell.' It's very corny."

"Can we play it?"

"Yes. Let's try it on the hi-fi."

The needle scratched and found its place. A tinny voice began, "Twas a dark and stormy night when my Nelly went away." The phonograph arm rocked a gentle rhythm on the record.

When a woman recited, "It's your own Little Nell. Don't you know me anymore?" Uncle pointed to the record and mouthed,

"Virginia." Margo smiled. *Virginia's voice.*

She played all the records. There were silly limericks and two more attempts doing the Little Nell skit.

There were recordings of the piano, and Uncle nodded. He was playing.

Virginia and Uncle played Chopsticks, and the arrangement kept changing styles. When it became syncopated, Virginia giggled, saying, "I can't—I can't do it, Tommy!"

Uncle's eyes were bright.

Margo put all the records back in their slipcovers. "So, we could make a record of Grandfather's song? Will it play on a record player at school?"

"I think your AV friends will be able to figure it out."

"Can we record now?"

"Goodness, let me practice a couple of days—I'm rusty. We may want to wait until you have an idea of how long this movie will be."

"Alan's worried about that. He says every hundred-foot roll is only four minutes. The film is pretty expensive."

Uncle sat down at the big piano, playing chords, lost in thought. He began Grandfather's song, hands moving quickly. After a few seconds, he stopped. "Maggie, would you please get me the music from the other piano?"

Uncle played Grandfather's song three times. Twice he stopped and repeated a section. "I usually fake my way through this part. I suppose I should get it right for the recording."

Later, Uncle went to work in the organ room. Margo took out a record of Virginia reciting, "Hope is the Thing with Feathers," By Emily Dickinson. She wanted to listen again, to have time for the words to become a part of her.

Uncle said Virginia knew many poems by heart, and Margo sat with a picture of Virginia, listening to her voice. The recording was scratchy, but she felt Virginia was talking to her.

I don't want to leave this house, to move, to return to another apartment, another dig next year. Even if next year's dig allowed her to return to California, she felt no longing to spend even one moment in Wisconsin.

Miss Gill

ALAN TRACED ELECTRONIC drawings full of lines and symbols.

"When I came down to breakfast this morning, there were two one-hundred-foot containers of movie film by my place at the table! Uncle got them for us."

Alan stopped his study and looked up. "Two reels? Hey, that's great! That's super. I was going to dig into my savings, but the Jeep needed a new universal joint. That cost me a few dollars."

"Alan, can you do something for me?" She pushed a ten-dollar bill into his hand. "My mother sent me some money. I want to get this sweater vest for Uncle. I clipped this ad from the newspaper. Is it OK, you think? I snooped in his closet, and his suits are size 42. I circled red."

Alan stuffed the money and ad in his pocket. "Consider it done. Tina, Mike, and I were going to the Emporium anyway. We'll bring it Monday when we start practicing the scenes for the movie."

After class, Margo walked easily along the quad. The sky was particularly blue, she had her English paper ready, and was prepared for her history quiz. The calm contrast to her former school struggles was not lost on her.

Chris stood by the door when she got to Room 12. "I wanted to wish you a Merry Christmas."

Her heart quickened. "Thank you. I hope you have a Merry Christmas too."

"Hey, last day before vacation." Chris studied the sidewalk. "Do you think I could come by sometime?" He looked up. "You know, over the holidays? Maybe we could go for a drive or something?"

She didn't blush, but the thought made the tops of her ears feel hot. "Yes. I have a school project I'm working on, but it sounds like fun."

"So, it's OK? I didn't know if you were going steady with Tommy. I don't see you with him much, but Tommy is a good guy. I don't want to..."

"Tommy is fine. We're friends. I think he wanted to ask Dolores Gonzales, but she was already going with Dean Palmer." Margo surprised herself by seeing the humor of it all. "I guess Christmas Formals are just a big mess."

Chris seemed unsure of what should happen next. "I thought you looked pretty in the red dress. It was—my mom said you have class."

Red dress?

Chris put his hands in his jacket pockets. "Mom was one of the parent chaperones at the formal. She asked who you were." He shrugged. "My mom is pretty big in the Parent Advisory Committee."

While Miss Johnson collected the assignments, Margo tried to think which of the parents might have been Mrs. Ferguson. Had Mrs. Ferguson been at other dances? Miss Johnson and Mr. Keller spent quite a bit of time by the punch bowl. They had been laughing. Miss Johnson wore a royal blue wool knit dress, with a wide grosgrain waistband and a bow in the back. Margo hoped they were in love.

Miss Gill called Margo to her office before Theater. Jenny, from History, came out of the office, wiping her eyes.

Two red bells were pinned to Miss Gill's white sweater. "Margo, I wanted to tell you I am very pleased with your progress. I can see you are making an effort in all your classes. Your teachers report that you are showing much more initiative."

"Thank you. My uncle has been helping me with my study skills. Miss Johnson said my writing has improved. I got an 'A-' on my last paper."

"Have you thought about what you are going to do after high school?"

Margo hesitated, feeling unprepared.

"With your improved grades, you might think about Junior College. Are you interested in nursing or teaching?" Miss Gill smiled. "Looking at your typing grade, I'm not sure clerical work is in your future."

Typing was her worst grade, and Margo put her head down.

"Margo? You know I am teasing, right? I only meant that your teacher said you don't seem to be a natural at typing. That's not bad—I have never typed well. I always seem to get the keys tangled if I try to go too fast. I spend more time pulling them apart than I do typing."

Margo laughed. She hated getting ink on her fingers, reaching to pull the "G" and "O" down each time she typed her name.

"I want to get to know you better so we can begin to plan for your future. Which of your classes are you enjoying the most?"

"At first, I was scared in Theater, but Mrs. Kavanagh has shown us so much. We started with pantomimes. Mrs. Kavanagh said she wanted us to learn about stage presence before we started dialog. We've learned about stage and story. She inspires us—me." She considered her subjects carefully. "But, I think I like English best. Miss Johnson makes it all so real."

Miss Gill made some notes on a paper. "This is good. And your Theater and English grades show that you enjoy your work there." Miss Gill tapped her pencil on the paper. "We need to make up the credits you are missing, so you can graduate next year with your class."

Fear crept close. Margo shifted uneasily in her chair, avoiding thoughts of not being at Blackwater High.

"If you take the proper classes in Summer School, you can graduate on time."

The fear descended, crushing her, and she batted back tears. "I don't know where I will be next summer. I—I am here for the school year. Until June."

Miss Gill pushed a box of tissues across the desk, and Margo dabbed at her eyes.

"I am sorry this is so upsetting. But even if you are in Wisconsin, I can put a note in your records. I would be glad to write ahead—perhaps get you registered for summer school."

Wisconsin! The word made her stomach roll. How could it be that she missed it so little. She decided that when you are miserable, and no one pays attention to you, it was easy to forget. Why hadn't the counselors in Wisconsin offered to help when she moved back and forth? She was simply going to school at the first Jefferson on one day and the other Jefferson the next.

Margo wiped her nose, shrugging off the frustration. "Thank you." She met Miss Gill's brown eyes. "Thank you for helping me."

The weight of hopelessness lifted, and outside the sun was shining. Even if Blackwater High was temporary, graduating on time was possible—something she could control in her life.

The Talk

SHARON WATCHED STUDENTS at the outdoor lunch tables. "I love this time of year. All the colors, and it seems like everyone is in a good mood. I know I am."

Margo waited.

"Fifteen days sober," she said.

"Oh, that's good!"

"Yes." Sharon watched three boys playing keep-away with a candy bar.

Margo took a breath. "Chris talked to me. He waited for me by English. He wants to come by over Christmas vacation." She laid her sandwich out. "He thought my formal dress was red. My brain was so clogged with the surprise of him waiting by the room, I couldn't even figure out what he was talking about."

Sharon turned, laughing. "Boys don't know their colors. Burgundy is not in his vocabulary—red is as close as a guy can get. If it isn't one of the eight colors in the first-grade crayon box, they don't know it."

"He kept looking at the ground."

"You could help him a bit," Sharon said. "Listen, guys are nervous when asking a girl for a date—even asking if he can come by. Add to that Chris being a part of you getting stitches, and then him going to the dance with Bonnie—being crowned King with Queen Bonnie. Then you add the whole pressure of, 'What if she says no?' that's in his head."

"How do you know so much?"

Sharon's eyes sparkled in the sun. "Think about when he asks you to dance or wants to say Merry Christmas, and now, that he wants to come visit. He waits until the last second! This is all caused by the 'I like her' condition."

Why didn't I notice? Last dance. Too late for the Formal. Last day before vacation. "Sharon, you're so smart."

"Powers of observation," Sharon said.

"What should I say to him? I also am suffering from 'the condition.' I need some good words."

"Tell him what you really think. Tell him the truth, that you're not upset with him." Sharon tapped her finger on her sandwich paper. "In *Pride and Prejudice*, Mr. Collins says he makes up little compliments ahead of time, but says, 'I always wish to give them as unstudied an air as possible'. He's such a fool!" Sharon wrinkled her nose. "So, don't rehearse too much. Just be natural."

No wonder Sharon knows so much. She reads books that aren't assigned in school. "I never read *Pride and Prejudice*." Margo tried to think of the last time she read a book not assigned in school. It didn't take long, because the answer was never.

"It's high time you did. I'll loan you my copy. If you think the kids at Blackwater are confused and having romance troubles, wait until you read *Pride and Prejudice*. It takes the whole book for Lizzy to admit to herself that she loves Mr. Darcy. That's a real love story."

Sharon put her sandwich paper in her bag. "I might as well tell you, Jimmy and I had a talk before History. This budding romance has about run its course. Jimmy is OK, but his heart is not in it, and mine isn't either."

Surprised, Margo said, "Did you break up?"

"I'm not sure it was that complicated. It's not like we were going steady or anything. Jimmy is one of those guys who takes the road of least resistance. Let's face it—I managed the whole formal date. He's nice, so he went along with it because he wanted to go to the formal." Sharon started for the trash can. "And we had a good time. I think he's afraid he's supposed to ask me to go steady, so he's backing off a bit. This way he can mess around with his buddies over Christmas and not have to worry about girls."

They walked, arm in arm, toward the quad.

"Is this about Frankie asking you to the formal?"

"Oh, Frankie has other stars in his eyes. I saw him holding hands with Sally Kerns after school. I'm thinking they hit it off at the formal." Sharon tugged Margo's arm. "It's OK, honest. I am fine! Oh, almost forgot, don't wait for me after school. We're having a Math Club Tutor's Christmas party." She took a quick skip and hurried toward Chemistry.

Snow capped the San Gabriel mountains. It was a beautiful day, clear and cool. Maybe *Virginia has a copy of Pride and Prejudice at home.* It occurred to Margo that she considered herself home in California.

In History, Mr. Hopper let the class talk after the quiz.

"It will be good to have a little vacation," Jenny said, her cheeks turning pink.

Margo smiled. "Yes. Have a Merry Christmas, Jenny."

"Thanks. You too."

Margo caught Mr. Hopper, staring out the window, and he chuckled. The clock went into super slow gear.

"Class, have a Merry Christmas and a good holiday," he said one minute before the last bell. Other classes already moved past the windows. "Margo, can you come up for a second?"

She approached the desk cautiously.

Mr. Hopper smiled and turned her test toward her, 100% written in red. "Just thought you would like to know." He handed her the paper. "I already entered it in my grade book. Your uncle will be proud of you, as am I. Merry Christmas."

"Thank you. You too, Mr. Hopper."

In the hall, Bonnie, hands on hips, squared off in front of Jenny. "I was just in the office! You ever go crying to Miss Gill again, and you will be walking forever." Bonnie made a shooing motion with both hands. "Go wait by the car. And don't get in! Just wait."

Jenny scurried around the corner. Bonnie turned and hissed, "What are you looking at?" as she passed.

Margo felt suddenly tired. One hundred percent on a test one moment and Bonnie the next. She wanted to go home with no homework for two weeks. To laze on the couch or stand by the fire.

She stopped at her locker. *No! I am not leaving school without talking to Chris. It's time to quit being the girl who takes the path of least resistance. If Sharon can talk to Jimmy, I can talk to Chris.*

With new energy at the thought of seeing Chris again, Margo hurried to a tree near the boys' locker room. Two basketball players said, "Hi," as they went past. Chris was one of the last to arrive.

"Chris?"

"Hey." He slowed.

"I wanted to say something I've been meaning to say..." Ughhh! "I mean, tell you."

Chris looked apprehensive but gave her a crooked smile and came closer.

"Chris, I'm not good at talking to boys. But I want you to know I'm not mad about getting knocked down. I never was mad at you." *Am I making a fool of myself? He might not've even wondered if I was mad.*

Chris brightened. "Hey, thanks. I felt really crummy. I know I learned something that day."

"I wanted you to know. No bad feelings?"

"No bad feelings. Right." He stepped closer. "I'd like to take you out—on a real date, over vacation. I have a big basketball tournament but..."

"Call me or come by. I'd like that." *I sounded natural. Cool?*

Margo hurried home, allowing herself an occasional skip step. *Chris wants to see me over Christmas!*

Margo called Sharon after tea and cookies. "I took your advice. I went and found Chris and told him I wasn't mad. He said he wants to take me on a real date over Christmas."

"Listen to Girl-Who-Has-Starch. Good for both of you! I told you Chris has a crush."

The most wonderful boy likes me! "Well, as long as I'm saying what's on my mind, are you OK? We don't have to talk about meetings or anything—but are you all right?"

"Just telling you about the whole thing sort of got it off my chest. And then the meetings—I've quit pretending alcoholism isn't there, and that is good. I feel like I don't have to hide things, especially from myself."

"I'm glad. You should come over and spend the night again. Uncle can make us popcorn and feed us cookies. Maybe New Year's Eve?"

"Sounds fun. Uncle T will like that. You know he loves to make a fuss."

Bookmarks

UNCLE AND MARGO DECORATED the tree and house. The ornaments showed Virginia's touch, and Margo felt close to Virginia as she placed each of the crèche figurines. She wondered if Uncle had decorated for Christmas since Virginia died. The boxes had looked neglected.

While arranging three angels, she found copies of her history and biology books on a shelf in the library. Bookmarks showed Uncle was reading ahead.

Later Margo sat on a sofa and watched the bubble lights while Uncle played Christmas carols. He played beautifully, and she felt the peace of Christmas. She joined him on the bench, and they sang "Rudolph" and "Frosty the Snowman." *He plays such jazzy chords!* They finished with "Silent Night," the last piano notes ringing long.

Lying in bed, Margo thought about what Sharon had said. It was wonderful to have Uncle make a fuss over her. The thought of leaving Uncle, Sharon, and Chris at the end of the school year chilled her with a deep sadness. How could she go on without these dear people?

Miss Gill was helping her plan her future. Margo had never considered the future, only dreaded the now. *How could I plan when I didn't know for sure where I would be in a few months?*

If I ever have a chance to make plans, they will be California plans.

What if I wrote to Mother and said, "I'm staying in California with T. Charles?" She couldn't imagine writing such a letter.

Sunday, the choir sang the Christmas Cantata. Margo sat, watching Uncle play with skill she knew she would never have. She smiled during the loping rhythm of what Uncle called, "the obligatory camel song." She helped the ladies afterward, pouring coffee and keeping Christmas cookie platters full.

At home, Uncle said, "Cantatas are work. We did a fine job of it, but I need a nap."

Margo found Virginia's copy of *Pride and Prejudice* in the library. A child's marker peeked between the pages. A stick drawing of a girl reading a book looked oddly familiar. Turning it over, "Margo" was scrawled on the back, the "g" standing high on its tail.

Miss Albertson's class. First grade. *Mother must have sent the bookmark to Virginia!* Margo pressed the childish strip against the throb of her heart, knowing it held more than the mark in a book; Mother had been writing to Virginia.

Margo read the top of the page where the marker had been: "An unhappy alternative is before you, Elizabeth. From this day you must be a stranger to one of your parents. Your mother will never see you again if you do not marry Mr. Collins, and I will never see you again if you do."

Margo choked a laugh. Families were complicated. She placed the marker back in the page, settling it deep in the fold, looking forward to when the book would build to that moment.

She was starting chapter three when Chris called, the best call she had ever received. He was coming to dinner, Monday!

Margo, who used to be "Stork." Margo, who boys never gave the time of day. And Chris, the most beautiful boy, wanted to come to dinner.

Even though Margo had promised herself to read four chapters, she sat in complete reverie. *What will I say? How do I act? What should I wear?*

Her date would require lots of advice from Sharon, but Sharon was out of town for the evening.

Uncle helped plan the menu. To celebrate, they baked cookies. The kitchen smelled delicious, and the window over the sink steamed around the edges. Margo felt safer and happier than she could ever remember.

Big News

ALAN GOT OUT OF THE Jeep and whispered, "Mike will put the 'item' out in the tool shed. Your change is in an envelope."

She nudged Alan as they walked. "Thanks. Good work."

Mike came in with a knowing smile, and Margo mouthed a thank you.

Alan was all business and helped stage her part. Mike stood in for the kidnapper.

"Good work, Maggie," Alan said. "Mrs. Kavanagh's methods are perfect for no dialog."

Mike nodded his approval.

Alan became serious after they ran through the scenes twice. "I promised that I'd get Chris Ferguson for the lead man. I don't know if I can come through with that. And then, we need another actor to do the kidnapping."

"Let me work on it."

Alan raised his eyebrows and gave Mike an "I told you so" look.

Uncle fed everyone cookies before the boys left. Margo was slipping the vest for Uncle in her closet when Sharon called.

"Maggie-Maggie! I have big, big news. The biggest of news."

"Let's hear!" Margo held her breath.

"Wally Wickersham called."

"Wally called! Shy Wally?"

"Yep, right before we left for my aunt's." Sharon let the news settle. "You won't believe it. Mary Suttle may have actually helped set the wheels in motion."

"Mary?"

"This gets pretty amazing. Apparently, Mary heard that Jimmy and I had 'the talk.' I think she was digging for the lowdown about whether we were going to elope or rob a bank or something. Anyway, she found out that Jimmy and I've decided to call it quits. Well, not quits—just not make a big deal out of it."

Margo ran the curl in front of her ear between her thumb and fingers. "Mary is a miner of other people's business. She probably interviewed Jimmy and his friends."

"Yes! Can you imagine what a big day it was for Mary?" Sharon was having fun. "Instead of the happy news that we're going steady, she finds that we've decided to *not* date!" Sharon tisk-tisked. "You have to appreciate that Mary must have been elated. A breakup! I'm sure that's how Mary would classify this nugget—and a breakup is way better than a 'going steady' story."

Sharon feigned exaggerated compassion. "Poor Mary. She gets the scoop of the month, and it's the last day of school for two weeks. Oh Mary spends quite a bit of time on the phone, but her specialty is the in-person delivery. Even with the last day hurdle, it has no doubt developed into quite an imaginative tale. When Mary gets a bored look—she elaborates to make it more sensational."

Margo pictured Mary, moving from group to group with this special edition. "Mary's our town crier."

"Ha! Good one." Sharon slurped.

"Are you eating?" Margo needed more than cookies.

"I'm having a cup of tea, and it's too hot. Uncle T is having an effect on me. Besides, coffee gives you bad breath if Mr. Miller's any indication."

Margo weighed this information. "So, tell me about Wally?"

"Yes. So, Mary does everything but hang a light in the church tower. And she happens to blab the whole story to Karen, Wally's sister. Karen tells Wally. Wally stews for two days and calls me on the phone!" Sharon paused with proud finality.

"What did he say? I take it, it was a good call?"

"More than good. I've had a crush on Wally since grammar school. I never thought he would be brave enough to call out of the blue."

"I knew it! You didn't fool me. You said you only had a maybe crush! So, what did he say?"

"We're going to the movies this evening! We're going to see the one Uncle T took you to, *Operation Petticoat*."

"It'll be fun! I'm so glad for you." *Our dates are on the same evening!*

"Poor Wally was already doing the toe in the dirt thing. He said he only has a farm pickup to drive. I told him not to worry."

"Wow. Wally called!" Margo whistled. "You're teetering on tier one! With Dirks graduating, Wally will be quarterback! You've been asked out by an automatic tier one."

"Yes, I have! I need to study tier one wardrobes. But I do not intend to flounce."

"No flouncing. Wally would be like Mr. Bennet protesting against any description of finery. I personally like a good description of finery, but you don't want to tire Wally." Margo continued to tease. "But now you will have to decide if you like the band or football best. If it's band, I'd keep that to myself."

Sharon slurped again. "Ow. There go some tastebuds I won't be using anytime soon. Let me get some water in this." The phone clunked down and rattled to life moments later. "So, any news from Chris?"

"Yes, there is news. It is another big scoop Mary is missing. He's coming for dinner today—at five! I've been dying for you to get back."

"Maggie, you sidestepped the big moment. When? How?"

"Right. Well, he called yesterday evening, and I invited him for supper. I figured we already knew how to eat supper with Uncle, so it is a safe start."

"Safe starts are key. Spaghetti?"

"No, we'll only serve easy-to-eat. No hard to cut meat that could skid off the plate."

"Good plan. Hmm, but think of poor Mary! No way to discover this gold and no school to receive her embellished tale. It's a sad day for her, and she doesn't know what she's missing!" Sharon paused. "Maggie, do you suppose the boys we like have finally noticed what a couple of classy dames we are?"

"It's beyond any of my dreamiest dreams." Maggie surprised herself, sounding like a schoolgirl in love.

"And this is the 'darkest evening of the year,' as Frost has it, even though Mrs. Howard said that's a 'simplistic interpretation.' I should have gotten an A! I choose to think our dates are on the longest winter night, marking sunnier days to come. Nineteen-sixty is going to be quite a year."

The clock chimed two. "Hey, I have to write to my folks and then get gussied up for Chris. I'm trying for a look that will knock him off his feet and yet appear that I didn't really try."

"Oh, this old thing? I just threw it on." Sharon lowered her voice. "I'm wearing my poodle skirt and blue sweater. I have pearls, fake of course. My aunt gave them to me for Christmas last year."

"That'll do the trick. Wally's a goner. He'll never know what hit him."

Margo dashed out a letter to her parents about Miss Gill and how she could make up her credits by attending summer school. She toyed with writing "summer school here" but decided the casual mention was enough.

Mr. Yeager had told the class about putting a frog in water and warming it slowly, and the frog not noticing it was cooking. The summer school nugget was the perfect setup for misdirection, something to draw the eye. She was on solid ground, saying something without actually saying it.

Maggie

MARGO WORE A WHITE sleeveless flapper girl dress. Uncle showed her a loose blue short-sleeved cardigan Virginia had worn with it, and a long rope of pearls!

"Virginia didn't care for sleeveless dresses," he said.

Sharon would've liked Virginia, apparently not a big fan of the underarm. Margo settled a white cloche on her head and looked in the mirror. It was the perfect outfit for her part in the movie.

Her throat went dry when the doorbell rang, and she met Chris at the front door.

He handed her a box of chocolate éclairs. "You wear the coolest clothes. Always something different."

They ate in the dining room using the good china. Chris held Margo's chair. No one but Uncle had ever held a chair for her.

"How long have you lived in this house, Mr. Blackwater?"

"I grew up here. I was in New York City for a number of years. My parents were killed in a car accident, my brother had died in World War One." Uncle laid his knife on his plate. "We came to sell the house, but Virginia fell in love with California."

Margo didn't know about the accident or Uncle's brother. It gave her an uncomfortable feeling that she had not asked Uncle much about his life, something to add to her list.

After dinner, Uncle suggested they move to the living room.

Chris started to pick up his plate, but Uncle said, "Leave everything. You are Maggie's guest."

Chris asked Uncle to play the piano. He played the most haunting and romantic song Margo had ever heard. Chris lounged against a bookcase, and his grey eyes added to the effect.

"That's a beautiful piano, Mr. Blackwater. You play with great expression."

"You sound as though you play."

"Yes. I started when I was eight."

"Would you like to play? This is a Bechstein; it has a lovely touch."

Margo felt uneasy, but Chris traded places with Uncle.

Is Chris comfortable in all situations? If I date him, if he takes me places, will it rub off? Will I be like Virginia, poised, at ease, appear to know things others don't know?

But Uncle never said Virginia *knew* things, only *appeared* to know things. Margo sat on the couch next to the picture of Virginia on the end table. No, Virginia had a great perception of life, music, photography, poetry, and love.

Chris played "Winter Wonderland," and Margo hummed quietly. There was something she missed about Wisconsin—snow. It would have been fun to make a snowman with Chris, and dream by the fire. She pulled herself from her musing when Chris finished. "That was pretty."

Uncle nodded his approval. "You're doing very well, young man."

"This is a beautiful piano." Chris touched a key and smiled at Margo. "Well, happy girl, do you play?"

Margo felt her cheeks straining but couldn't stop smiling. "I only remember one piece, 'Fur Elise.' I'm not sure I can do all of it."

Did I just volunteer to play in front of Chris Ferguson? Yes, and the robot that had taken over her body walked her to the piano. Chris's arm brushed hers as they traded places.

Margo had a false start and then relaxed. She played half of the piece before her fingers got tangled. It sounded choppy and simplistic, but they both complimented her.

Her breathing slowed. *I played the piano in front of Chris, and it was terrible, and he doesn't seem to care!*

Uncle went in to clear the table.

Margo sat on a couch with Chris. "Are you having fun? Is this OK?"

"Everyone seems to call you Maggie. Do you mind if I do?"

"It's fine. I like it better. Grandmother didn't like nicknames, so it has always been Margo—which is silly because even though that is my real name, Margo can be a pet name for Margaret."

Chris smiled. After a moment, he said, "Yes, this is OK. Your uncle is a pretty amazing fellow. And I am having a good time."

He went back and sat at the piano. "It's odd. I've been taking lessons all these years, and I've never played for anyone except at recitals and home. Today I played for you and your uncle." Chris rippled a scale. "Come on, surely you can play Chopsticks!"

Chris is surprised that he played for us—Chris Ferguson, who belongs in the room—at the piano! Do you have to have confidence to act confident? She guessed not.

Margo slipped next to Chris and did the high part. She giggled and thought of Virginia when she fumbled. Chris gave her a nudge with his shoulder.

Uncle came in with a tea-towel on his shoulder. "I'm going to make a pot of tea, but I have soda. Would you kids like a soda?"

Chris said yes, and Margo asked for a small glass.

Chris took a deep breath. "So, Maggie. There's this pizza place my dad took us to. It's over in Hollywood, but not really that far away. It's called M'Goo's. They have a piano up on a platform, and everyone sings old songs. They toss pizza dough in the air. Would you like to go Saturday after Christmas? I won't have practice. I could pick you up at four-thirty, and I'll have you back by nine."

"Sounds like fun. I'll have to ask Uncle, but yes, it sounds wonderful." Maggie tried not sounding gushy, but it was impossible to contain her excitement. *Are we dating? Two dates in the same week sounds like dating.*

When Uncle brought pop with ice cubes, Chris told him about M'Goo's. "I know Hollywood is a few miles, but my car is in good shape. I'm careful, and I will have Maggie home by nine if that's OK with you."

Uncle's eyes checked with Maggie, and he said, "Yes, it sounds like a splendid place to go." He started to go out when Chris asked, "Could you play some ragtime or boogie-woogie?"

Uncle raised his eyebrows but sat down at the piano. His left hand began flying in a quick boogie beat. He looked at them, his eyes twinkling. When he added his right hand, it was fantastic. Chris watched, grinning.

When Uncle finished, Maggie clapped. Chris said, "Wow, you have some chops."

"Listen, you kids don't need me hanging around. If you want to listen to old songs, you can play piano rolls." He started to leave the room.

"Uncle, what is the dance they did when they wore dresses like this?"

"Charleston." Uncle slipped off his loafers and did several quick steps. "Come, try it." The three of them danced in a circle, Uncle counting.

"Oh, my. That's enough for me," Uncle said. He went to the piano. "Here, try it with this." He began to play, and they struggled to keep up with the beat.

Later, Uncle went to the kitchen. Maggie put on a record and showed Chris the swing steps.

"I saw you doing this at the dance. I wish I had been your partner. Alan makes it look easy with his fancy footwork."

Maggie sat down and patted the couch next to her. "I've a favor to ask."

Chris sat down, his knee close to hers. She wanted to reach out and hold his hand.

"I'm making a movie—a project for Theater Class. Uncle has a camera, and we have film." She watched to see how Chris was taking the news. "Alan and Mike Russell are doing the filming, and I need..."

Maggie folded her hands in her lap. "I need actors. I want you to be in the movie. We can't record sound, so you won't have to remember lines."

His eyebrows jumped. "Me? I'm not sure I'm any good at acting."

———⊶◉⊷———

THAT NIGHT, IN FRONT of her diary, Maggie had something to write about. Sharon had a movie date with Wally. Chris had come to dinner. When she explained the plot and told him about Grandfather McKinney, Chris had agreed to be in the movie, and come to practice the next two mornings. They were going to M'Goo's on Saturday!

Maggie closed the journal. Why write about it? She was living it. Miss Johnson encouraged her students to become Renaissance people; to have talent and knowledge in many fields. Miss Johnson was taking a watercolor class.

Virginia had been a Renaissance woman. Maggie opened *Pride and Prejudice*.

My Living Room

MAGGIE RAN TO THE DOOR when Chris rang.

"Hi. Thanks for coming." She was excited but tried to not act like a ninnyhammer.

He shrugged his shoulders. "I told you I may not be any good at this."

She presented a fedora to him as if it were on a platter. He put it on at a jaunty angle. *He's good already!*

When Alan arrived with Tina and Mike, he showed Chris and Maggie where to stand in relation to the camera.

"For the last scene, when you are reunited, you should hug," Alan said.

Chris hesitated. Maggie wanted to put her arms around him so badly but stopped a step away. Mike gave a nervous laugh.

"We can work on that later," Alan said quickly.

Chris winked.

Maggie's breath caught, and her mind went foggy, but she kept her head up and tried for an insightful smile.

The morning went too fast, and Maggie walked Chris to the door. "Did you have fun? Was this OK?" She wanted to say, "Will you be back?"

"Sure. Same time tomorrow?" Chris plopped the fedora on her head. It slid down, and she peeked at him from under the brim. He adjusted it with both hands, tipping it to the right. "Perfect."

She floated back through the living room.

Uncle played piano rolls for Alan and Tina, while Mike sat reading a history of Packard automobiles. Maggie washed the glasses, cups, and bowls. Alan joined her and dried.

"Your uncle is telling Tina about New York before the depression." He threw the towel over his shoulder. "It's good for her—no one talks at her house." He gave a weak laugh. "I've about half raised her, and what do I know?" He leaned against the counter. "I didn't mean—you know what I mean."

Maggie knew about not talking, at least not talking about what anyone was really thinking. "Tina's great, Alan."

━━━●━━━

WEDNESDAY, THE HOUSE filled with kids. Sharon and Wally's movie date had been a success, and Sharon asked Wally to be in the movie. "It's perfect for Wally," she joked, "no talking!" They held hands when they got out of his old pickup.

Maggie met Chris at the top of the drive with the fedora at the same angle he had left it the day before. He lifted it off and put it lightly on his head, pushing it back with one finger. The moment didn't seem to require words, which was good, because Maggie had no voice.

Alan insisted they work each scene again and again. Mike reported how many seconds each scene took and wrote it in Alan's binder.

Sharon suggested the sideways, one arm hug for the last scene, and Maggie slid in like a timid crab. Alan laughed. "Maybe we can have you behind a screen. You know, a silhouette of the hug."

"Or kiss," Tina teased.

Chris and Maggie blushed. She didn't want to have her first kiss to be in front of everyone, but it was all she could do to keep from throwing her arms around him and turning her head to the side, slipping in under the hat, and kissing him. She didn't know for sure how to "plant a kiss" on someone, but movies made it quite romantic.

Later, Sharon and Tina lettered the word cards. Uncle played Grandfather McKinney's song. He and Mike worked it out to be exactly three minutes long so it would fit on a record. Chris watched, fascinated.

The last time through the song, Alan and Tina began to dance. Uncle was tickled. "Let's go into the living room where there's more room, and I can see you without craning my neck."

At the big piano, Uncle played and laughed. He never missed a beat, his eyes darting from person to person. Tina worked with Wally while Sharon danced with Alan.

Uncle said, "You kids might think this is silly for an old man, but..." He began the song "Great Balls of Fire," his fingers dancing on the keys.

Maggie put her back against the archway, taking in the scene. Alan swung Tina between his legs. She squealed, was back on her feet, and they did the coaster step. Wally clumped along, but Sharon helped him.

Sharon rescued me. She walked in the auditorium and sat down beside me, and began chatting. She pulled me into school life and that started everything that led to now. It nagged Maggie that she hadn't rescued Jenny being chewed out by Bonnie in the hall. *I just was glad it was Jenny and not me.*

Chris reached for Maggie's hand, and they joined the dancers.

When the song was over, Sharon said, "Uncle T, you're the coolest uncle. My uncles just sit when they come over." She hugged him around the neck.

Uncle played "Jingle Bell Rock," and Alan and Tina sang along. Sharon danced with Mike, who surprised Maggie by dancing well.

It was like American Bandstand, and it was in her living room. Maggie smiled inside. *My living room.* Four months earlier, California had been the furthest thing from her mind. It was difficult to comprehend that this was a moment on loan. Mr. Yeager said dreams only last a few seconds but seem longer. Were these moments like a dream, fleeting, only to evaporate when her parents returned? Maggie shivered. No, she would always remember the smiles, music, and laughter, even in Wisconsin.

Uncle began the song he had played when Chris and Maggie tried the Charleston, and Alan and Tina knew the dance. Tina did a thing, covering her knees, hands switching. Alan and Tina lined everyone up and showed them the steps.

"Slow down, Uncle T." Sharon fell onto a couch. "Enough dance lessons for me." Her face was red, and she laughed. Wally sat down beside her, and she grabbed his hand.

"It's eleven-thirty," Uncle said. "We have to keep Chris on a schedule. We're having tuna sandwiches—I know tuna is not as good as a hamburger, but it's lighter. Chris has to be at practice in an hour and a half." He and Tina went to make the sandwiches.

Chris and Maggie moved a chair and coffee table back into place, Wally jumping up to help.

Uncle served potato chips and soda. Maggie had never heard him whistle, the melody floating on the air as he moved between the dining room and the kitchen. The boys glugged their pop, and Uncle filled their empty glasses.

Maggie stood on the porch when Chris left and listened to the car start. He ducked forward, grinned, and she waved. In the background, Sharon, Alan, and Uncle were singing "Angels We Have Heard on High." Maggie found Tina in the kitchen and helped finish the dishes.

"Thank you for inviting me," Tina said. "Your uncle has such a nice house. He's good to us."

Maggie slipped the plates into the cupboard. "Coming here is the best thing that has ever happened to me."

Sharon towed Wally into the kitchen. "Thanks for everything. We have to go. Wally has to do some spraying." Sharon's eyes only left Wally long enough to give them a single dimple smile.

Chris Ferguson has been here three days in a row. Who would have thought?

Straighten Up!

ALAN AND MIKE WENT into the kitchen to study the camera instruction book. At the big piano, Uncle and Tina began singing "Silver Bells." Tina had that big Rosemary Clooney sound coming out of a little person. Uncle didn't swoop around as much as Bing Crosby, his voice tender and rich. Maggie cocked the swinging kitchen door back and put the kettle on to boil.

She sat at the table and watched Alan. When the piano was quiet, she started toward the living room. Tina sat beside Uncle on the piano bench, with a box of Kleenex in her lap. Uncle said something quietly, and Tina nodded, blowing her nose.

Maggie slipped back to the kitchen, closing the door, and made the tea, setting out cups. She poured Mike a glass of milk.

Uncle came through and gave Mike two cookies. Tina's eyes were red when she joined them.

She turned to Uncle. "Thank you, Mr. Blackwater, for the food and the music and—everything."

"You're welcome, Dear. You can call me Uncle T. Everyone else does."

After a quiet tea, Maggie and Uncle waved as the jeep rolled down the driveway amid swirling leaves against a blue, blue sky. Santa Ana winds were becoming Maggie's favorite times, making Southern

California's winter like an extended fall, with its rich textures.

"Why was Tina crying?"

"Kids have problems sometimes. Your friend Tina is a vivacious little girl, but she's not immune to problems."

And Uncle always helps make things right.

"Thanks for the snacks and the perfect morning." It seemed it was a day for tears. "I never had friends at the apartments in Wisconsin. Not like this. This is such a happy house."

"It's happy because you're here. We used to have lots of people over, and lately it's fun again." Uncle carried the potato chip bowl into the kitchen. "Was it silly for me to play rock and roll?"

"No, it was great! I hadn't heard you sing like that. You're as good as Jerry Lee Lewis any old day. Your Bing was pretty good too!"

"I don't know about that, but it was fun. Tina and Alan sure can dance. They should enter a contest."

"Alan's aunt has a studio," Maggie said. "I love to watch them. They're so good it looks like it's rehearsed, but it's not. At the school dances, they make it up as they go. I think they're cute together."

"You all were cute. Poor Wally doesn't say two words, but he seemed happy to try to learn the Swing. I think he's crazy about your friend Sharon. When she's telling one of her funny stories, he never takes his eyes off her."

"I think the feeling is mutual."

Maggie started for the stairs. "I love you, Uncle."

"I love you too, Maggie Girl."

That night she sat in front of her diary. Tina had problems. Sharon had problems. Maggie sighed.

When she was eight, she had come home from school, and Mother was edgy. Father had his knapsack on the floor.

Grandmother had come to say goodbye! She should have noticed something was unusual the past few days, but the apartment was always tense when Grandmother visited.

Mother told Maggie about the new opportunity, the new dig, and Maggie threw a fit, crying and screaming. She had been invited to go to a Brownies meeting with a girl in her class at school.

Mother has been quiet while Father fiddled with his books. Maggie lay face down on the couch and sobbed.

Grandmother stood over her. "I think it is time you grew up, young lady!"

Maggie looked to Mother and found no comfort, and the fire of panic enveloped her. Father continued to sort his books on the shelf. When she turned, Grandmother was a wall of stone.

"I mean it! Straighten up! Sit up, this minute. This is a wonderful opportunity for your father to do research for his thesis. You should be proud."

Maggie stared at Grandmother's crossed arms, scarcely able to breathe.

She learned a lesson that day. When Father wanted something, Mother went along. Sharon's words, "road of least resistance," played in Maggie's mind. It was easier for Mother to let her daughter cry than to go against Father—or Grandmother.

Grandmother had been gone five years, but the old rules were still in place.

Maggie closed the diary and crawled into bed. How could she ever tell her parents she wanted to stay in California? Mother wouldn't protect her. Panic came, as it had when Grandmother said, "Straighten up!" Maggie's chest burned.

She took a deep breath, shaking her head slowly. "No," she whispered. This time was different. Uncle, her teachers, Miss Gill, and her friends were all on her side, and in them, she found comfort.

Maggie didn't know if she *straightened up* or not, but she was no longer eight years old, and the panic melted away. She lay back and thought of singing "Silent Night" with Uncle. She fell asleep in heavenly peace.

M'Goo's

SHARON ANSWERED ON the first ring.

"Did you have a nice Christmas?"

"Yes, very." Sharon lowered her voice. "Dad was sober. He really is trying. How about you?"

"It was only Uncle and me, but it was nice. He's like me—not much family. Mother sent him bow ties. She sent me packages too, and I gave Uncle the vest from the Emporium. I helped cook the ham." *And mashed potatoes that were not a peace offering from Mother.*

"Ready for the big date?"

"Ready and nervous." Maggie hugged the red sweater Uncle had given her. "Sharon, how do I know if I should sit by Chris in the car or sit on the passenger side?"

"Easy one. Here's how it works. If he takes you around to the passenger side and opens the door, you sit there. If he takes you to his side, slide in, and sit in the middle next to him.

"One time when Martin Simpson let me in on his side, I kept right on sliding. When I got to the door on the other side, I got a shock." Sharon was playing with the phone cord.

"Dates are easy. The boy has to decide everything. He has to ask. He has to decide where to go. He has to decide which side of the car he wants you on. You just take his cue."

Maggie pondered this bit of advice. Tommy had let her in on the passenger side during the formal. At least she did that right.

"Next, we have the good night kiss problem. This is a tough one. If you don't want to be kissed, have your key out or open the door, say thank you, and go in."

"I've never been kissed."

"My first kiss was in the third grade. We were playing hide-and-seek over at Jeannie Bell's house. Pete Webber and I both dove under a bush and bumped heads. We looked up, saw each other, and kissed. It just seemed like the thing to do."

Sharon made everything seem easy. She made her life seem so carefree.

"Has Wally kissed you?"

"Yes, indeed, he has. First time was in the pickup when he brought me home after the movie. It took a while. I guess he didn't want to have my parents come out if we kissed on the porch. I thought I was going to have to kiss him, but he finally got up the nerve." Sharon paused. "It was nice. What time is Chris coming?"

"Four-thirty. Uncle said he's read good things about M'Goo's. I better get moving."

———◦———

A LETTER FROM MOTHER lay on the dresser, unopened.

Maggie jumped when the doorbell rang. She settled the red beret on her head; the sweater was a perfect match. Uncle answered the door, and Chris stepped into the entry hall. Chris wore slacks and a V-neck sweater with a stripe across the chest.

"You look nice," Chris said.

"Thank you. You do, too."

Uncle kissed Maggie on the forehead and told them to have a good time.

Chris opened the passenger door, and Maggie got in. She couldn't decide if she was disappointed or relieved. She settled on disappointed, but it was nice that Chris was being a gentleman.

He started the car and shifted gears. *He has a floor shift.*

The car was louder than the Packard. It ticked and chugged as if struggling at stop signs. As soon as Chris touched the gas pedal, the engine came to life, and the car moved easily up to speed. He was so cool as he leaned forward to ease the gearshift into another gear.

"You want to listen to the radio?"

Maggie started to nod but said, "Yes."

Chris turned the knob and moved onto the freeway as "Mr. Blue" filled the car.

"I've never been to Hollywood."

"We're not going to the part of town where the movie stars live—but my cousin Ted saw Jimmy Stewart one time."

Maggie tried not to gawk on Hollywood Boulevard. Hicks from the sticks rattled around in her brain. Traffic kept them from going very fast, and she saw the big red M'Goo's sign ahead. Chris turned, and Maggie saw a flash of white in the window of the old building.

They stood outside as a man twirled a huge disk of pizza dough. When he tossed it into the air and caught it on one fist, it seemed to stretch forever, not tearing. M'Goo's was going to be fun.

Inside, the ceiling was high, and there was sawdust on the floor. On a platform in the middle, a fellow wearing a boater and a red garter on his long-sleeved striped shirt hammered the piano. Chris took Maggie's hand and navigated to a table close to the platform.

A waitress handed them a menu and a large folded card: "Sing Along With M'Goo." They sat reading the jokes on the menu. Maggie unfolded her song card to the words of dozens of songs, while Chris ordered pizza and two sodas.

Another tune started, and Chris smiled. "The piano man is really good, like your uncle."

Dough flew behind the counter, the aroma of pizza and singing filling the room.

The piano player called, "Number 55, Five-Foot Two." They found it on the card and sang along. Chris had a strong voice.

Maggie didn't know if it was the atmosphere, but she ate two and a half pieces. Chris ate four. "Isn't this great!" he said.

"The best," she replied. *The best day ever.*

On the way to the car, their fingers slid easily together. He opened the driver's door, and Maggie slid to the middle. He slipped in beside her. "Having a good time?"

"This is really fun. I've never seen a place like M'Goo's. All ages singing and laughing."

Chris looked at a wristwatch hanging from a knob. "Eight-fifteen. We better get moving."

Maggie watched his feet as he worked the pedals and moved her knees to the side so he could shift. He smelled like Aqua Velva and pizza. Maggie slid down, leaned her head back, and smiled.

"You said I should join the Welcome and Hospitality Club. What do you do, besides show new kids around? I don't think I'm ready for campus tours."

"We help kids who have problems. I take a boy, Johnny, to the bus after school. He is in a wheelchair, and I push him down to the loading area every day after school. We get along fine."

Maggie did a quick evaluation: Sharon tutored kids in Math, and Chris helped kids with big problems. What did *she* do but worry about herself?

Chris walked Maggie to the front door, touched her shoulder, and kissed her lightly on the lips.

Maggie's first kiss, and she thought she might float away.

Chris put his hand behind her neck and stroked her cheek with his thumb. "Maggie, this was really fun. I didn't want to be with Bonnie at the Christmas Formal. I'd rather have been with you."

"Bad timing." Her heart quickening, she squeezed his hand. "Good night," she whispered.

In the entry hall, she hung her hat on the hall tree and found Uncle among the organ pipes.

"So, Maggie. I can see you had a good time."

"Yes. It was so much fun."

"I'll make tea, and you can tell me all about it. Or would you like a soda?"

"I'll have tea, please."

Maggie babbled on and on. "Here is the 'Sing Along With M'Goo' song sheet they give out. We sang and sang."

Uncle opened the card. "All the old songs. Some of these were popular when your grandfather and I were young. Virginia would have loved M'Goo's."

"Can you play one?"

"Which one would you like?"

"Number twenty-one, 'Let Me Call You Sweetheart.'" Chris's eyes had caught the light as they sang.

Uncle sat down and played with no music. They both sang, Maggie looking at the card and Uncle with his eyes closed.

That night before bed, Maggie picked up the letter and turned it over in her hand. If it was like the usual letters, she didn't want to read about the rich history of the people living high in the Andes. If it contained plans for her future, she was not sure she could stand to read about that either. *Not tonight.*

Potsherds

AFTER CHURCH, MAGGIE called Sharon.

"So, the date? Success?" Sharon asked.

"Well, not having been on many dates, I'm not sure I can give an accurate analysis."

"OK, let's take the issues you had going into the date. Where did you sit?"

"My side going—his side coming."

"Good date, so far! How about the kiss? I'm guessing you weren't fumbling with your keys?"

"Keys were the last thing on my mind. We kissed on the porch. I'm giving the kiss a hundred percent, not that I have comparison kisses." *One-hundred percent is as good as it can get, but our date was two-hundred percent.*

"Oh, don't worry. The song says, 'A kiss is just a kiss,' but a good kiss does not need comparison. On the other hand, a bad, sloppy kiss is unforgettable. Uck!"

"Ew. This was not a sloppy kiss. It was a tender, sweep-me-off-my-feet kiss."

"So, excellent kisser. Tell me more."

"M'Goo's is fun. The menu is full of funny stories. It says Grauman's Chinese Theater is 999 ½ footprints from M'Goo's."

Sharon laughed. "I like this place already."

"The song sheet says M'Goo made Hollywood famous, and he was glad to do it."

"I think we need to go to M'Goo's some time!" Sharon paused. "So, plans for M'Goo-Guy? More dating on the horizon? The Christmas Basketball Tournament is this week." Sharon began to tease. "The choices are: the not attend, the attend one, or—the attend all."

"Chris said the games start Monday. I guess it's a pretty big deal. Should I go? Should I want to go? Is Chris expecting me to go?"

"These are excellent questions. Do you want to go?"

"I want to see Chris."

"Wally says it's an elimination tournament. That means that if you wait until Wednesday, Blackwater might have lost early and not be playing." Sharon was having fun. "But, if you go Monday, and they're champions, you may be committed, and you will be there all day three days. That would be too many armpits for me."

"Do you think you could stand one game?"

"Sure, I can do one game for my friend. I wouldn't want you to look forlorn up there."

"So, what should I do?"

"I suppose you could fuss about it or—you could ask Chris."

Sharon made things simple.

"I want to invite you and Wally for New Year's Eve. Uncle will make popcorn, and I don't know what. Afterward, you can stay the night."

"Uncle T spoils you. Well, he spoils us. Sounds super." Sharon lowered her voice. "I happen to know a certain fellow is going to call about seven-thirty. I'll ask him."

That evening, while they ate popcorn, Maggie asked Uncle when he got the Packard. He told about Virginia ruining the engine of an overheated LaSalle by putting water in it when it wasn't running.

"She was upset with herself and checked a mechanic's book out of the library, determined to learn more about automobiles." Uncle shook his head in amusement. "She was so serious and asked question after question, many to which I had no answer."

"Uncle, what's a LaSalle?"

He chuckled. "A cheaper version of a Cadillac!"

"She took our mechanic to lunch! He told me later, Virginia had a list of questions and a steno pad to write the answers. From that time on, she marked the calendar with dates for oil changes, learned to check her own tire pressure, and insisted I show her how to change a tire."

Uncle leaned forward to demonstrate. "She couldn't get the lug nuts loose, and so she carried a piece of pipe in the cars to use as leverage—a 'cheater.' She helped a woman change a tire on Colorado Boulevard one day! Came home proudly showing me her 'mechanic hands.'"

This was the final proof that Virginia was a Renaissance woman. Maggie had never met her, and yet her absence in the house was palpable. When she looked, T. Charles had written "oil change" on the calendar.

When Chris called, Maggie said, "I had a wonderful time last night."

"Good. I did too."

When she asked about the tournament, he said, "We're playing our first game at eleven tomorrow. Walk down if you want. Then we will see how it goes—it is a long three days. I have to help because Blackwater is hosting the tournament."

"Sharon and I will come in the morning."

Maggie wandered into the living room and practiced the piano. Uncle had given her a copy of "Fur Elise," and she was determined to memorize it. She tried her grandfather's song but sighed with frustration. It was simply too hard.

Maggie went up to bed early. She picked up Mother's letter several times, only to put it down again. At ten twenty-seven, she opened the letter and sat on the edge of the bed. Her hands shook.

Dear Margo,

Just a short note to wish you a Merry Christmas. Sorry we are not there to spend the holidays with you.

Your father has uncovered some potsherds, unlike any previously found in the region. This is confirming evidence helping to prove your father's theory about striated potsherds—

She skimmed to the bottom of the letter.

Your father says to tell you, Merry Christmas.

Love, Mother.

Maggie let the letter fall to the floor and curled up on her side. It was always about the dig. Mother hadn't responded to any of the things she had written about in her letters: the formal—better grades—Sharon.

Maggie shook her head slowly. She couldn't remember her father ever writing to her. She didn't know what she wanted to be when she grew up—but it was nothing like him.

Could I be a Renaissance woman?

Father certainly wasn't a Renaissance man. Oh, he was a college professor, but if the subject wasn't archeology, he rarely said anything. Mother put gas in the car.

In her diary, Maggie wrote, "When I learn to drive, learn to change a tire."

Movie Music

SHARON AND MAGGIE SLIPPED into the stands. Men walked importantly back and forth, consulting clipboards. Grace ran the clock. The pep band and cheerleaders weren't there, and Maggie found she was disappointed. Most of the spectators were parents or players from other teams.

Alan stretched the microphone cord. Maggie went down and invited him and Tina for New Year's Eve. "I wonder about Mike. I'd like to invite him, but will he feel funny not having a date?"

"Mike has a crush on Tina's sister, Laura," Alan said. "Tina says the feeling is mutual."

"Good! Then invite them too."

The party was more on her mind than the game, but each time Chris scored, Maggie felt a tingle of pride. *That boy out there likes me!*

Blackwater won, and Chris introduced Sharon and Maggie to his parents. Mrs. Ferguson had tiny freckles across her nose, and Mr. Ferguson was an older version of his son. She caught Mrs. Ferguson glancing at the scar line above her eyebrow, perhaps uncomfortable about the "incident."

On the way to the oak tree, Sharon said, "Chris has good parents. Nice of his mom to tell you she wasn't coming to any more games until the championship. She knows this could be a deadly week."

They said goodbye under the tree. Clouds had blown in over the hills with a beginning wind. Maggie wrapped her arms around herself and hurried home.

She curled up by the fire with *Pride and Prejudice*.

In the late afternoon, wearing Virginia's "mechanic's" bib overalls, Maggie helped Uncle finish the final wire connections to the Swell organ. He taught her how to solder wires together, and she completed two octaves while Uncle made supper. He said her hands were steady and quick. After the silver solder snaked around the twisted wires, she wrapped each connection with black tape. Alan would be impressed.

Maggie walked to the game on Wednesday, anxious to tell Alan about learning to solder, but one of the other AV club members was doing sound duty.

At the scoring table, Grace nodded when a man pointed to notes on a clipboard. Maggie was glad Grace had a way to be near the sport she loved.

Bonnie Douglas sat with the girl with the platinum hair. Bonnie looked at Maggie, said something, and the girl laughed.

When Maggie went into the bathroom at halftime, Bonnie leaned close to the mirror. As Maggie moved toward the stalls, Bonnie said, "What are you looking at?"

Electricity went through Maggie. She hadn't looked at Bonnie. "Nothing, sorry." Sorry. *What am I sorry for?* Maggie waited in the stall until she heard the bathroom door swing closed. When she came out, Bonnie wasn't in the gym.

Blackwater didn't win, but Chris came up for a few minutes after the game making it all worthwhile. A daydream carried her home.

There was a letter from Aunt Louise, but it wasn't in her handwriting. Jean Frasier explained Aunt Louise couldn't write—she was failing. Maggie's heart failed a bit with her. Jean wrote that Aunt Louise had shed a tear when she read Maggie's letter to her. Maggie was comforted that Aunt Louise had understood who had written.

Grandfather's song floated through the house, changing into variations of the melody.

"Uncle, what are you playing?"

"I was thinking about your movie. The PhonOcord can't cut a record long enough for the film, so I'm going to borrow a friend's tape recorder. See what you think." Uncle played the end of each movie scene, shifting to new variations.

"You're so good you should have been a professional musician."

"When I was in New York, I made my living from music, but it's a hard life. If you play in the clubs, the hours are terrible. There's always someone who's had too much to drink being obnoxious. Virginia encouraged me to take a degree in Applied Psychology."

"You never told me you went to college. Are you a psychologist?"

Uncle rested his right ankle on his left knee and nodded. His right hand fiddled with notes, his forearm propped on his right knee until another song fell under his fingers. Then he put both feet down and played. Notes lingered in the air.

Until recently, Maggie only thought of Uncle puttering around the house, doing projects. Paying attention to others had its benefits!

"Where did you work?"

"I treated some Hollywood folks, but I worked for the Veterans Administration during the War. Then there was the Korean War." Uncle stared across the room, lost in thought.

"Lots of boys came home, having seen and done things they should never have had to see or do. Some I helped. Others, I couldn't." Uncle sighed. "I retired when Virginia got sick."

"No wonder you're so good with Tina—and with me."

"I didn't do much for Tina. Mainly I listened. That's important. Listening—and hearing. But you—you're my girl."

Uncle played a perfect run on the piano, every note crisp and clear. "So, do you like the movie accompaniment? Once the movie is done, I can make the music fit each scene."

"It's perfect. You think of everything."

Uncle got up. "I think we need to plan the New Year's Eve party. Look at these." Uncle emptied a bag of party favors on the table. There were little pointed hats and noisemakers. He put a blowout horn to his lips and blew the paper toward Maggie's ear. She giggled.

They looked through a box of Virginia's recipes. "I think we can manage these Hamwiches," he said.

In her room, Maggie wrote a long letter to Aunt Louise. She told about the Christmas dance and M'Goo's. She wrote how good Uncle was to her and about the movie.

It seemed inadequate. Aunt Louise couldn't talk since the stroke. Now she couldn't write; the letter was all Maggie had for her.

In her diary, she wrote, "Ask Alan to show me how microphone cables are connected."

New Year's Eve

CHRIS KISSED HER GOODNIGHT on the front porch. "Really a fun party."

When he drove away, vapor trailed lazily from the exhaust pipes, wisping to nothing.

Whoops and shouts were still going on in the distance. Even though it was California weather, Maggie was suddenly cold and went back inside. Sharon had said goodnight to Wally a few minutes before by the French doors, and his old pickup rattled down the driveway.

Tina kissed T. Charles on the cheek, and she and Alan, bundled in big coats, piled into the Jeep with Mike and Laura. T. Charles and Maggie waved good night from the French doors.

Sharon carried bowls into the kitchen. "Great party Uncle T," she called.

"Leave all that until the morning, Sharon. You girls go up to bed."

"No, Uncle T. You go to bed." She hugged him around the neck and kissed his cheek. "You go get your beauty sleep. We are cleaning the kitchen." She patted his vest. "That's an order."

Uncle chuckled and started up the stairs.

"Uncle, I love you. That was the best party I've ever been to!" Maggie supposed it was a silly thing to say because she had never been to a party, but she knew she loved Uncle.

There had been more food than anyone could ever eat. They danced to records and then begged T. Charles to play the piano. Alan and Tina taught everyone new steps for the Swing.

Sharon ran the dishwater. "I thought Tina was going to giggle herself to death in the Ball of Wool game. Where did Uncle T come up with those games?"

T. Charles had given everyone a Clorets mint before the game. "My wife, Virginia, used to say it's more fun to play with a fresh mint smell!"

They knelt on opposite sides of the kitchen table and tried to blow cotton balls off the other team's side. The game did not last long.

Tina hyperventilated and giggled so much they had to help her to her feet.

After the dishes were done and the living room was back in order, the girls went up to bed.

They lay a long time talking about Reverend Crawley's Game and Wink Murder. Reverend Crawley's Game was Maggie's favorite because she and Chris had to try to squeeze together between Sharon and Tina's arms. They all had fallen into a pile and laughed until it hurt.

Sharon had been the best at Wink Murder, so sly that it was hard to catch her "killing" someone with a wink.

Maggie's eyes traced tiny lines on the ceiling, thinking of Chris in his cone hat, happily rubbing her nose with his blowout horn. Uncle turned on the TV at midnight, and they sang Auld Lang Syne with Guy Lombardo's orchestra. Chris kissed her lightly on the lips—the greatest kiss ever. He said, "Happy New Year, Maggie." And it was.

<hr />

MORNING SUN SILHOUETTED Sharon in the bedroom window. She was beautiful.

"Are you OK?"

She turned and smiled a half-smile. "Yes." She sighed. "I wonder how things went last night—you know, with my dad. New Year's is not an easy time."

Maggie twiddled a quilt tie.

"Silly of me. Nothing I can do about it one way or the other." She turned back to the window. "You know, for a long time, I thought it was me. If I could be good enough, he wouldn't drink." She sighed a half-laugh. "Then one time I got straight A's, and he celebrated. If I got a "C," he got mad and drank. If I got "A's" he got happy and drank."

Sharon traced the windowsill. "I need to take care of myself, and I guess I knew that. I can't do anything to stop my dad if he's going to drink. But it has been eight weeks. One more day is possible."

"Right. We just have to hope for the best." Maggie paused. "Uncle said one of Virginia's favorite old hymns was 'How Can I Keep From Singing.' She wanted it sung at her funeral. She was really sick and dying, and she was thinking, 'How Can I Keep From Singing.' I wish I had known her."

Sharon turned. "Look on the bright side, right?" She jumped on the bed. "Let's sneak down and see if we can get breakfast ready before Uncle T gets there."

They did and tapped on Uncle's door with a tray of food. He sat up in bed and declared it was the first time he had breakfast in bed in a long time.

Maggie made two trips, with TV trays and plates. Each time she came back, Uncle was laughing at one of Sharon's commentaries.

"You know your friend thinks all bowlers should get a strike every time," he said.

Sharon brushed her hair back and clipped it with a barrette. "Hey, same ball, same alley—every time! No wind. No sun."

They laughed, and Maggie said, "Yes, Sharon sees things in a funny way. Don't get her started on the shape of a football."

Sharon lifted her nose. "I cannot help it if a football doesn't meet the definition of a ball."

Sharon gave her analysis of the party, and Uncle wiggled his feet under the covers. After a while, he told them to skedaddle. "Let this old man get cleaned up and dressed."

Downstairs Sharon and Maggie had one more game of Ball of Wool, laughing until their sides hurt.

Uncle padded down the stairs. "I guess we slept through the parade. I had planned to wake you girls and turn on the Television."

"Next year, Uncle T, next year."

Maggie's heart caught. There might not be a next year. The thought of not being in this house made her throat close.

Practice

MRS. KAVANAGH MET MAGGIE at the door of her classroom. She thumbed through the folder Maggie handed her after vacation. "This is quite an ambitious plan you put forth for your project. I like what you call picture panels. In film, this is called a storyboard. I see that you have several students already agreeing to be cast and crew. You mention you have access to wardrobe." She paused. "I must say I'm impressed."

"Thank you. We've been working on it over vacation. It is only about eight minutes. There is no sound, so it will be like an early silent movie."

Mrs. Kavanagh pinched her watch at the band hooks. "Class is about to begin. I would like to meet with the students who are going to work on this project. Could we meet here, Thursday after school?"

"I can try. It might be hard for Chris Ferguson—he has basketball practice."

In PE, they were learning to run the 440 relay. Maggie was the third leg, standing in a daydream until Dolores Gonzalez tapped her on the shoulder with the baton. When Maggie looked up in a daze, Dolores gave a snort of disgust and ran on. They got last place, and Maggie got four laps.

Visions of the movie flooded her mind as she hurried to their lunch table at noon. From now on, she would put the film and Chris aside when she went to class.

Sharon inspected the contents of Wally's sandwich. "You see what I mean? That is a sandwich that you can be proud of. That's meatloaf in there. Mine? Peanut butter and jelly."

Wally closed his sandwich and took a big bite. When he held it toward Sharon's mouth, she took a nibble.

Alan and Tina slid into the bench across from Maggie.

"Mrs. Kavanagh talked to me, and she wants to meet the cast and crew after school, Thursday, in the Theater room. Do you think you can come?"

Alan and Tina glanced at each other and nodded. "I can be there for a little bit. I'm pretty sure Mike can too—I usually take him home."

Wally and Sharon nodded.

"I'll talk to Coach Wiggins." Chris winked.

It took a moment for Maggie's brain to restart. "Thanks—thank you." She took out the carrot sticks Uncle had cut for her.

"I should get a cameo," Sharon announced.

"I've been thinking it wouldn't be a bad idea to have some extras for the street scene." Alan gave Tina a tiny nod.

Sharon held her head in an exaggerated pose. "It'll actually help the movie in later years when I'm famous. People will want to see me *before* I was discovered!" Sharon swept her hand toward an imaginary marquee. "With a special cameo appearance by Sharon Jackson."

Wally shook his head. "Maybe you should eat your peanut butter and jelly sandwich before you rush off to Hollywood."

"No one understands the pressures of being a star!"

Jenny lingered near, smiling at Sharon's antics, and Maggie started to invite her to sit with them when Bonnie grabbed Jenny by the arm. "Come on, slowpoke." Bonnie gave Maggie a cold stare.

It took about two weeks to get from Tuesday to Thursday afternoon. Even the after-school clocks became lethargic. Maggie slipped into her seat in Mrs. Kavanagh's classroom.

Mrs. Kavanagh asked everyone to take a seat, turning a student desk toward them. Chris slipped in the door. "Sorry I'm late, and I have to leave in about ten minutes."

"Thank you all for coming. I've read Margo's proposal and looked at the storyboard and the plot summary. Margo, this is quite an undertaking, but I see you have a team."

"Mrs. Kavanagh, I know I gave you the folder, but everyone here has helped. It is a team effort. Alan and Mike did the storyboard, Tina and Sharon made the cards. Everyone is involved."

"Well, it is impressive."

Alan leaned forward. "We're pretty serious, Mrs. Kavanagh. We have worked on this over Christmas, each scene timed to the second. Maggie's uncle is providing music."

"Tuesdays and Fridays are the only days we can all be together after school," Maggie said.

Mrs. Kavanagh wrote a note. "I do have a couple of concerns." She laid down her pencil. "I will not be able to be there every afternoon, but I want you to understand, I'll be dropping in regularly." She paused and looked at each person. "If I ever hear of horseplay or any nonsense, that will be the end of this project."

Heads bobbed.

"I've spoken to Mr. Mills, the afternoon janitor." Alan fixed his blue eyes on Mrs. Kavanagh. "He will let us in and lock up—if we have a note from you. He's pretty particular about needing authorization. I'm aware of the times the auditorium is in use for Debate, and we have six weeks before play practice begins. Perhaps you could sign us up for Tuesdays and Fridays?"

Mrs. Kavanagh covered a smile. "I'll look at the schedule and give Margo the dates you can use the auditorium."

Alan cocked his head. "We'd like to use several of the flats stored above the stage—we'll be very careful."

"I don't mind you using the flats. Perhaps I will teach you how flats are made." She tapped her pencil. "We'll stretch a few—in fair exchange."

"Yes," Alan said.

"Margo, perhaps you and I should meet again, tomorrow afternoon? I have a few suggestions that may help the transitions between scenes."

MRS. KAVANAGH'S INTERPRETATIONS smoothed the scenes, and Mike reported they only added twenty-two seconds. Mr. Mills opened the auditorium twice a week. One Tuesday, he arrived early to lock up and sat in the back row to watch.

They worked on the set when Chris had to be on the game bus. Alan and Mike practiced with the camera, aiming the lights. Sharon painted detailed backgrounds on five flats, Maggie in awe of Sharon's ability to bring life to the scenes.

Maggie settled into a routine she loved: studying with Uncle, games and dances with Chris, double dating with Sharon and Wally.

It rained early on a Friday, and low clouds hung against the mountains after school. The cast and crew sat in a row in the front seats of the auditorium. The mood matched the weather.

Alan broke the silence. "I think we're ready. We have timed these scenes and timed these scenes. Why am I so nervous?"

That made Maggie nervous. She depended on Alan to know what he was doing and that all would go perfectly.

"Because we only have one shot," Mike said. "We have eight minutes of film."

Maggie stood. "Alan and I talked to Mrs. Kavanagh. We have arranged for extra time, Tuesday, for a dress rehearsal. It's a home game, so Chris won't have to leave early for the game bus. Everyone in their places, in costume. We will film on Friday because the team has a bye."

Mr. Mills shuffled down the aisle. "Alan, you know it is almost four-fifteen. At four-fifteen, I have to lock up. So you have to put things away—because I have to lock up at four-fifteen."

Alan assured Mr. Mills they would hurry.

Mr. Mills lingered. "I like your play."

Maggie thanked him, but his mind was on the clock. They put the lights and camera tripod in a closet.

"See, Mr. Mills, four-fifteen on the dot," Alan said.

"That's good, Alan, because I have to lock up by four-fifteen. I have to finish the Science wing by five-ten."

"Thank you Mr. Mills," Alan said. "We'll see you next week, on Tuesday. Remember, we'll need the auditorium until five that day."

"Yes." Mr. Mills pulled a card from his pocket. "I have it written down. Next Tuesday at three-thirty-five, right after school, until five."

Dress rehearsal. *Ready or not, it's coming.*

The Muddy Place

"I HAVE IT ALL WORKED out," Sharon said. "Wally and I'll come and get you Saturday at noon. We go out to the ranch where a dirt road runs on two sides of the big grove."

Maggie hadn't seen Sharon this excited in a while.

"Wally's dad is letting me practice driving a stick shift. He and Wally will be working in another part of the grove, but I can practice for an hour or so. Wally will take us home."

THE GROVE TREES WERE huge, much larger than the orange trees in the backyard. The smell of orange blossoms filled the air as they walked to the pickup.

Wally opened the door for Maggie. "It sticks a little." He smiled and went around to Sharon's side. "You know the route. If you have any trouble, you can walk back to the house and wait for us. Mom and Karen are in town."

Sharon watched Wally jog easily to the tractor, where his dad waited.

"You really like him, don't you?"

"Yes! Wally doesn't have a mean bone in his body. He knows all about Dad and the meetings. Things like that don't bother him."

Sharon gripped the steering wheel. "If the Driver's Ed boys could see me now." She worked the shift lever. The gears ground, and she squirmed in the seat, trying to push the clutch down further.

Maggie rolled down her window.

"I'm sure it would help if Mr. Wickersham had a floor shift. I'm sure a floor shift would be easier." Sharon found a gear, the pickup bucked, and was quiet.

She gave Maggie a look. "Don't laugh. I do that all the time. I've no idea why they can't make clutches that sort of ooze into gear—would that be so hard?"

Sharon turned the key, and the pickup jumped. "I do that all the time, too." She wiggled the shift lever and started the engine.

"Are you sure you can do this?"

Sharon rolled her eyes. "I took my driver's test in my mom's automatic and got a ninety-five percent. I'm a good driver. All cars should be automatics."

Sharon looked over her shoulder, and the pickup moved away from the barn. "I practice looking over my shoulder. Mr. Wilson said I'm very aware of my surroundings when driving." Sharon turned onto the lane beside the trees. "There, see. Once I get moving, the shifting and clutch part get better." The engine revved as she reached to push the shifter into another gear. The speedometer bounced around ten.

"Mr. Wilson also said I'm very good at braking." The pickup began to buck, and Sharon jammed in the clutch. "There, saved it. I hate stopping because you have to do all this complicated stuff at once. But I'm getting it."

"You're certainly not speeding. I haven't seen anything above ten miles an hour."

"Dad said I have to practice on my own before I can drive his pickup. Wally said to pretend these cement standpipes are stop signs." The pickup bucked to another stop.

Maggie covered her mouth and looked out the window.

"I see you laughing. Wait until you try driving the Packard. You'll see this clutch and gas pedal and shifting takes some doing." Sharon wiggled in the seat again and tugged on the gear shift.

"I'd be afraid of denting Uncle's beautiful car. It is so long, I'd never get it parked."

"You just need practice. I drove this lane the other day with Wally. I did pretty well. It was muddy at the turn, and we were slipping around sort of like bumper cars at the fair."

After three trips out and back, Sharon eased into an open area at the far corner the grove. "Look, Wally made me some lines to practice parking. See, he even put a board over there to be the curb."

She carefully pulled into the "parking place." She turned off the ignition and reached for the door handle. The pickup jumped one last time, and Sharon gestured at the dash with both hands. "Apparently, the engine does not get the message that the key is off for a while. You'd think it would know off is off and take immediate action."

"I think you're doing better. The last few stops have been well-executed if I do say so myself." Maggie made two tries to get her door open.

"You have to lean into that thing. Bump it hard with your shoulder. If you don't get a bruise, you probably won't get out." Sharon came around and jerked on the handle as Maggie hit the door with her shoulder. "This door made it easy to decide where I was going to sit on our first date!"

Huge oranges hung from the branches between white blossoms. "Wally said we could pick oranges off the corner tree." She got a knife and blanket out of a box in the back. She picked two oranges, cut off the ends, and etched the peel in quarters.

They sat on the blanket and looked at the shiny leaves. Juice ran down Maggie's fingers.

"Oh, look, I forgot." Sharon ran to the pickup and brought back a rag. "Me, the bench cleaner at the football stadium, and I forget a rag for our hands."

Sharon threw her peelings under the tree. Maggie looked around for a trash can and then, feeling foolish, tossed her peelings away.

Maggie laid back on the blanket and looked at the blue sky. The scent of orange blossoms, the glossy leaves, and the sky made her realize she rarely spent time outside, just looking.

"The football coach talked to Wally. He wanted to make sure he was going to play next year. He wants him to be quarterback." Sharon sighed. "I guess he's going to play. He's so funny about it. Being quarterback is not a big thing to Wally. Dirks made it the deal of the year—well, he and his dad."

When Chris and I played "Around the World," he didn't laugh when I had to shoot granny-style from the top of the key. He was more interested in talking than our game.

Sharon rolled onto her side. "Wally really knows what he wants to do. He's going to go to Cal Poly, up in San Luis Obispo. They have a great Ag program. He'll come back and run the ranch."

"Isn't that a long way from here?"

"Yes, and I don't know how I feel about that. Wally is—oh, you know I've had a crush on Wally since elementary school. I don't know if I'm in love—but I have never wanted to be in a place where Wally wasn't."

I must be in love with everyone here. I don't want to be where Uncle and my friends aren't.

They folded the blanket, and Maggie took a deep breath. This moment, this place was perfect. Wisconsin was much further than San Louis Obispo. *What if I never saw the people of my new life again?* The thought caused an ache deep inside that seemed unbearable.

They got in the truck on the driver's side, and Sharon started the engine. "Boy, this thing turns hard." She struggled with the steering wheel, backing to the right. The truck hit a bump, and Sharon's foot began bouncing on the accelerator. The pickup roared in spasms, and they wheeled around. The truck came to an ungraceful stop off the dirt track.

"Oops. That wasn't good." Sharon laughed and changed gears. The engine roared, but the truck only shuddered. Sharon glanced at Maggie and worked the shifter, but the pickup didn't move.

"Wally told me to not get off the road back here." Sharon pulled her lips sideways. "Might as well see how stuck we are."

She opened the door and stood on the running board. "I found the muddy place!" she said cheerfully.

Maggie slid out on Sharon's side. Sharon jumped to dry dirt. "Only the rear wheels are stuck. It is in a low spot. Maybe if I back up a bit, I can get going."

Maggie jumped off the running board and looked at the muddy tire.

Sharon fought with the gear shift. "Tell me how I'm doing." The pickup whined and moved back a few inches, mud flying off the tires.

Maggie stepped back. "I think forward might be better."

"I'm going to really gun it!" The old muffler howled, and the pickup sank down.

"I don't think that's helping. The tire is digging a hole."

Sharon turned off the engine and looked down from the running board. "Wow—almost touching the ground." She stepped off and surveyed the situation. "That looks pretty stuck. Wally will have a great time with this."

Maggie couldn't help but chuckle.

"I see you. I know this will be very entertaining to everyone." Sharon pretended to pout. "This old truck has hard steering and jumps every time I try to get it to go."

They walked back on the dirt road. As they came near the turn, a large engine chugged closer. Wally came around the corner on a big tractor with fenders that looked like torpedoes.

He stopped near the girls and jumped down. "We had to work on the spray rig and came back. We heard the truck roaring and figured you might be stuck."

Sharon wrinkled her lips and patted his dusty shoulder. "No teasing me about this! I was backing up, and the steering wheel didn't want to go straight without a fight. That pickup is hard! My foot was bouncing around on the foot feed, and the next thing I knew it found a mud hole. That truck was looking for trouble!"

Wally laughed. "Come on, you two, I'll give you a ride."

Exhaust blatted out of a pipe at the side, and Maggie stepped back. "How fast does it go? It looks streamlined for a race."

Wally smiled. "The fenders are so the branches slip past the wheels in the grove. I'll go slow."

"Come on. It'll be fun," Sharon said.

Wally helped Maggie up beside the steering wheel, where she gripped a metal shield. Sharon stood on the hitch with her arms around Wally's waist.

There was a gentle rocking as the big machine lumbered along. Sharon peeked around Wally's shoulder and winked.

At the pickup, Wally smiled. "You did a pretty good job, but at least the front is not in the mud." He lay on his side and hooked a chain under the front of the pickup.

"Sorry you're getting all dirty," Sharon said.

Wally brushed at his jeans. "All in a day's work. Mom does lots of laundry."

Sharon hugged him. He moved his arms helplessly as if to pat her shoulders but didn't touch her blouse. "You're going to get dirty."

"Can't help it. You're so great about this."

Wally reached in the window of the pickup and straightened the front wheels. Sharon pointed, made a muscle with her right arm, and winked at Maggie. Wally took the truck out of gear and opened the door.

"OK, keep it in neutral, and don't start it. The tractor will do the work."

Maggie moved back, expecting a big moment, but with hardly a chug, the tractor had the pickup on dry ground.

Back at the barn, Mr. Wickersham met them.

"I'm sorry I got your truck tires so muddy, Mr. Wickersham."

"Don't worry—that truck was never very clean until you came along. Wally washes it every time he takes you somewhere!"

Childhood Tales

LEAVES SKITTERED ACROSS mid-winter ground, and Maggie pulled her collar up against the wind.

"Where's Chris?" Sharon wondered.

"I don't know. Miss Gill called me in, so I came from the office." Maggie took her sandwich out of her lunch sack. "I do have a bit of fun news. Uncle has a friend who plays the organ at the Moonlight Rollerway, and he needs a substitute for this Saturday. Uncle is going to play, and as part of the deal, he's getting passes for us. You are all invited. We can skate all evening."

"Oh, I like this," Sharon said. "You know I could become a world-famous figure skater with a little more practice."

Wally leaned around to look in her face. "You do know that figure skaters skate on ice?"

Sharon held her head up. "I could follow in Carol Heiss' footsteps to the Olympics. All I need to do is convert from roller to ice."

Wally laughed and stood up. "Sure, and all I have to do is switch from football to baseball, and I'm Don Drysdale." He ruffled Sharon's bangs and tossed his bag in the trash.

Tina wadded her sandwich papers. "Skating sounds perfect, Maggie. I'm cleaning houses, so I can't come until after four." She gave her lunch bag to Alan. "I have to get to Home Ec early to preheat the ovens. Someone can have my dessert."

Tina and Alan had jobs and responsibilities. Maggie wondered if she should have a job? Did soldering wires for the organ count?

A pink Puff-Ball lay in waxed paper. Alan pushed it toward Sharon, who shoved it back.

Sharon pointed to the Puff-Ball. "Now see, I never understood these things as a snack. My brother wolfs them down. I usually eat the outside first. One is pink, one is white, and I can't tell any difference. Then all I have left is the dry chocolate part with white goo in the middle. I couldn't get that down without lots of milk."

Wally gestured for her to continue with raised eyebrows.

"And, yes. Some of you know my feelings about school milk in cartons!" Sharon shook her head at Wally. "I know it amuses you, but yes, it all stems from Kindergarten." Sharon rolled her eyes. "There are lots of things Wally could remember about elementary school, but he likes this story. I got sick one day after they gave us our milk and snack."

Alan pulled one corner of the wrapper, inspecting the Puff-Ball. "Keep going, I want to hear this."

"I'm glad you all find this so entertaining. They brought those little cartons of milk down on a cart, from who knows where. I'm sure they took their sweet time."

"Too warm?" Wally prompted.

"Well, if you insist, yes, it wasn't cold. What with the smell of stale Tempera paint already gagging me, that milk was awful. Mrs. Thompson insisted, 'Drink your milk boys and girls,' and I threw up!"

Alan stuffed everything into Tina's lunch bag and pushed it to the middle of the table. Wally unwrapped the Puff-Ball, took a huge bite, and eyes on Sharon, chewed happily.

She hit him playfully on the arm. "I don't know why you think that story is so funny. I was in misery, and I had to go to the nurse. I didn't like her anyway because the last time she had come to get me, she told my mother I needed a shot."

Maggie gave Sharon a wide-eyed smile. "I'm guessing you're not a big fan of shots."

Chris joined them. "Are we talking about Sharon's dislike of shots?" His eyes met Maggie's. "Cried in second grade even before it was our class's turn."

"Hey, I have tender arms."

There was a chorus of "Awwww."

Sharon feigned hurt feelings. "And maybe we should hear the story of Chris and the hearing test?"

Maggie looked up eagerly. "Yes! Let's hear about Chris and the hearing test."

Chris pretended to pout. "Hey, I was a little kid. I didn't want those things on my ears, and I tried to pull it off. A piece of hair got caught in the little chrome slider. It hurt."

Maggie nudged Chris. "I'm glad you're brave now." She patted his arm.

"Chris, you're leaving out the best part!" Sharon said.

They waited.

Sharon mimicked a little boy voice. "He said, 'Those things are going to make me balded,' as he rubbed his little head."

Chris gave them a superior look. "I was having trouble with the irregular form of some words." He glanced at Maggie. "Hey, if a man can be balding, why can't he be balded, when he's done balding?"

Sharon stood. "That was the first bell, and it's a hike to Chemistry."

Maggie watched the faces at the table. They had these great stories, a history together. She yearned to have been part of those scenes. If life was but a poor player, the thought that her current role might be a cameo in their lives nagged her. *I don't want my lines to be a bit part, played by a character actress who moved back to Wisconsin.* "Remember Maggie, from our junior year?"

Chris walked her to her locker. "Coach wants us to eat at four-thirty, so I'll have to leave the dress rehearsal early. I'm sorry to mess it up. I'll still be able to pick you up in time for the JV game."

"It'll be OK, Chris. You worry too much." *Like I don't.*

A Lack of Commitment

MAGGIE KICKED OFF THE blankets and turned on her side again. The dress rehearsal and filming crowded her thoughts. What if the film came back blank? How could she ask her friends to do it all again? How would they afford more film?

"A lack of commitment" was one of Grandmother's favorite lines. Maggie hated it when she heard her grandmother's voice in her head. "You wanted fancy ice skates, and how long did that last?" Maggie hadn't dared to say winter had passed, and it was early summer.

"You wanted a bicycle, and there it sits by the door, collecting dust." Maggie hadn't reminded Grandmother that she had been with Aunt Louise for six months, and when the bike came out of storage, the rear tire was flat—that the tire was still flat.

Had I just gone along—let Alan's suggestion pull me into this?

Maggie folded her pillow in half. *Did I do this to spend time with Chris? To feel important?* Even with the covers off, she felt hot.

If the film didn't turn out, would Grandmother visit her in her dreams with folded arms? "A lack of commitment is what it is. You wanted to make a movie, and how did that turn out?"

A shiver made her squirm. She was playing Grandmother in the movie, but she didn't feel like Grandmother when she was acting. Maggie sat up in the dark. When she and Chris were practicing, she felt like they were Virginia and Uncle! "Now that was love," Polly had said.

Virginia and Uncle were committed to finding Grandfather. Virginia searched, wrote letters. She and Uncle sent money. She probably wanted to know her brother's child.

Grandmother hadn't shown the will to search for Grandfather.

Maggie huffed a laugh to herself. "It was lack of commitment, Grandmother. That's what it was—a lack of commitment," she whispered. "Oh, we all know you were pregnant with Father. You were left alone when Grandfather ran off. I've heard that old record so often it sounds as scratched as the Little Nell plays."

No, it wouldn't do. Maggie settled back in bed, whispering. "A lack of commitment is what it was Grandmother, plain and simple. Why didn't *you* look for him? You wouldn't even allow Uncle to help! You showed a lack of commitment, plain and simple."

Maggie saw Grandmother differently for the first time. Anger built in her. In the movie, she would play a *committed* Grandmother who would *not* give up. She would search for and *find* Grandfather. "You'll see who is committed, Grandmother. You'll see who is committed!"

Her nails dug her palms from clenching her fists.

Frumpy

ALAN, MIKE, AND MAGGIE met Uncle in the front parking lot. He had the costumes in three suitcases.

"Thanks, Uncle." Maggie kissed him on the cheek. "Come in and watch for a few minutes?"

"I'd like that, but I can only stay for a bit. I'm on my way to get the tape recorder."

Uncle thinks of everything. She couldn't remember Father ever picking her up at school—ever coming to school, for that matter.

In the auditorium, Sharon held her dress against her and twirled. "My moment is here!" After she changed, she came out and twirled again. "My cameo is about to happen. The world will soon discover me!" Embroidered ruffles fluttered.

Wally, with his black cape, hat, and fake mustache, looked evil indeed.

Sharon peeked out from behind a curtain. "Help me, help me."

Mrs. Kavanagh came in with a clipboard.

"Uncle, I want you to meet my Theater teacher, Mrs. Kavanagh. Mrs. Kavanagh, this is my great uncle, Mr. Blackwater."

"I'm very glad to meet you, Mr. Blackwater." Mrs. Kavanagh surveyed the stage and nodded her approval. "Margo has learned a great deal in Theater. This should be exciting."

She went to Sharon. "This dress could fit a little tighter in the waist."

"I'm sorry I didn't get to it," Tina said. "I still had to finish altering my dress."

"Alas, I am not domestically inclined," Sharon quipped. "My mother has forbidden me to touch her sewing machine. I jammed the bobbin so badly my dad had to pry it out with his knife." Sharon shrugged. "Apparently, when you fill a bobbin, you don't wind it by hand." She wrinkled her nose. "I wound it the wrong way."

"Leave the dress on the table after rehearsal, and I will take it in." Mrs. Kavanagh pinched the material on the side. "Not much, about an inch."

They stepped through each scene, Mike calling the seconds.

After the first run-through, Uncle said, "This is starting to come together. Maggie, I'm going to go. I'll try to be home by the time you get there. Is that OK?"

"Yes. I have my key. And thank you again." She kissed his cheek.

Mrs. Kavanagh had them do one more run through. Mike reported that each scene was within five seconds.

Mr. Mills sat in the back row and watched the last scene. He clapped when Chris and Maggie appeared to kiss behind the screen.

Mrs. Kavanagh had said, "No kissing on school grounds." She suggested that Chris take his hat off and hold it between the screen and the backlight, the shadow hiding the "kiss."

Chris took off the overcoat and turned to leave. He winked and placed the hat on Maggie, making her shiver.

Mrs. Kavanagh talked with Maggie while the others changed back into their school clothes.

"This is going very well. I can see Alan and Mike have carefully planned the camera work." She moved left and right, studying the set. "It was good to meet your uncle." She changed the angle of a flat. "I can see he is taking good care of you."

"Yes. I love living with him here in California." She wanted to be able to say, "I am going to stay permanently." *Maybe I will bring it up with Uncle.*

Sharon handed Mrs. Kavanagh her dress and wiggled her fingers to Maggie as she and Wally went up the aisle.

Mrs. Kavanagh made small corrections as to how Maggie should position herself in relation to the camera.

Mr. Mills came to the stage. "I am going to have to lock up."

"Oh, I'm sorry, Mr. Mills. I will close up today."

"I like your dress young lady. It reminds me of the old days." Mr. Mills' eyes seemed to lose focus. "They used to wear dresses like that."

"We all probably need to go," Mrs. Kavanagh said.

The clock read four-fifty. "Yes. Thank you, Mr. Mills. Thank you, Mrs. Kavanagh."

Maggie hurried toward her locker. Bonnie Douglas, Jenny, and the girl with the platinum hair were in the corridor.

"You think you're so special, don't you?" Bonnie's voice oozed sarcasm.

Maggie looked over her shoulder to make sure Bonnie was talking to her. The quad was empty. *There's probably a set of instructions for teachers: "When Margo McKinney goes near her locker, make sure you are nowhere in sight."*

"Oh, I'm talking to you, Margo McKinney. Or maybe I should call you Maggie. Because you think you're so special."

"I..."

"Cat got your tongue? You seem to be able to talk to Chris Ferguson pretty good. You didn't have any trouble asking him to the Sadie Hawkins Dance."

Maggie moved toward the lockers, but Bonnie blocked her way, narrowing her eyes. "I've had just about enough of you. You come here from Wyoming or West Virginia or—wherever with your little hats and odd little outfits. What's *this* you have on today?"

It didn't seem to be a question. Her locker was a magnet for trouble. Would she end up with more stitches? Was the office even open?

"You play all shy and quiet. So superior. You leave the dances in that car. You know what I think? I think you look frumpy in these getups. I can't believe you'd wear something like *this*." Bonnie gestured up and down the flapper girl dress. "I see you're fast friends with Tina *Cor-TEE*. Everyone knows she's from the wrong side of the tracks by just looking at her."

Startled, tears pushed at Maggie's eyes. She stood taller. *Do not let her see me cry. Do not let her see me cry.*

Bonnie bumped Maggie's arm as she passed. "Chris and I are going to the Sadie Hawkins dance this year. He only said yes to you because he feels sorry for you."

Maggie looked to Jenny, but she stepped back, turning as if to leave, not meeting her eye. *I deserve that—I was no help when Bonnie had her cornered.*

Maggie reached for the combination knob but sensed Bonnie was still behind her. She turned, and Bonnie leaned toward her, looking up, hands on her hips.

"You think you can come into this school, hang around with Sharon Jackson, Tina Corti and Dr. Fixit, *and then* ask Chris Ferguson to the dance? You should stick to your own kind."

"They are my friends," Maggie said quietly.

"Yeah, they're real high tone friends. Sharon's dad is a drunk, and Tina's dad skipped town. You choose real good friends." Bonnie spun and walked away, the girls following.

"They are good friends," Maggie whispered. "They're the best friends I have ever had."

Maggie's hands were still shaking when she got home. She went straight for the teakettle.

Uncle followed her, putting cups and saucers on the table. He laid cookies on a dessert plate. "What's wrong, Maggie Girl?"

"After practice, Bonnie came up and said the most horrible things. She said I was frumpy and my friends are—" She hated that she cried so easily. "She said Sharon's dad is a drunk and Tina's dad—" Maggie had the hiccups. "And—and I don't deserve Chris." She slumped at the table.

"Maggie, sometimes people can say mean things. When kids are angry, they can be very cruel."

"She's one of the beautiful girls. Popular. What does she have to be angry about? She's a cheerleader and has big bosoms, and all the boys think she's so perfect." Maggie put her forehead on her arms.

Uncle snorted. "She's probably jealous."

"Of what?" Her voice sounded hollow.

"You."

Maggie raised her head. "She's just mad because I asked Chris to the Sadie Hawkins dance."

"Yes, she's mad. Because?"

"Because Chris is going with me?"

"Yes, Chris likes you." Uncle paused. "And how do you think she knew Chris is going to Sadie Hawkins with you?"

"Probably heard Mary Blabber-Mouth Suttle gossiping about it."

"Do you think Chris has been telling anyone?"

"I doubt it. We thought it would be fun."

Uncle poured the tea. "So, how do you think Bonnie knew?"

Maggie pulled her cup close. After a long time, she quietly said, "Bonnie asked him to go with her."

"Yes, Bonnie asked him."

Maggie nibbled at a cookie.

Uncle turned his cup and saucer. "And Bonnie is mad because?"

"Because Chris said he was going with me."

Uncle sat back and waited.

"She's jealous—maybe embarrassed," Maggie said.

"She may not be used to having people say no to her."

"Uncle—she said I look like a frump in Virginia's hats and clothes."

Uncle patted her hand. "I would have to disagree with that. Virginia was anything but frumpy, and you aren't frumpy either. You look cute as can be when you leave this house in one of her outfits."

He took a sip of tea. "Maggie, you may not wear the same things all the girls are wearing, but that does not make you a frump. It makes you threatening—to Bonnie. You caught Chris's eye, and she's upset."

Caught his eye. Maggie couldn't help smiling. "A girl from Theater wore a beret to a basketball game."

"I'm not surprised."

"I wish I had stood up for Sharon, and Tina, and Alan. I'm such a chicken. They're my good, good friends. I've never had friends like them. Oh, I had a couple of sort-of-friends. But my friends here like me the way I am."

"I do too, Dear." Uncle took his cup to the sink.

"Maggie, there are going to be unpleasant times in school—in life for that matter. Just do the best you can. I'm proud you didn't get into an argument over this. Sometimes being quiet when someone is mad is the best approach."

Uncle leaned back against the counter. "Bonnie needed to blow off steam. It is human nature, sometimes, to strike out when we are hurt or embarrassed. You didn't strike back."

"I probably would have needed more stitches. Bonnie probably packs some weight behind one of her punches."

Maggie was suddenly exhausted by it all and put her head in her arms and cried.

Uncle brought a Kleenex box and sat down.

"I don't want to leave. I don't want to go back to Wisconsin or wherever they put me next. I'm so happy here. We get along, don't we?" She raised her head and asked, "I'm not a bother, am I? My grades are better than I've ever had. I have two A's and three B's. If it weren't for Typing, I'd have no C's. Sharon, and Chris, and Alan," She wiped her eyes. "And my friends like being here at the house."

"Of course, you and I get along, Maggie Girl—you're no trouble. You and your friends have made this house happy again."

Maggie hadn't cried that hard since the third grade. "I don't *want* to go back to Wisconsin. It makes my heart ache thinking about it, and it's *months* away."

The timer rattled, and Uncle drained the water off the potatoes. "Chris is going to be here in a little bit. Do you want me to tell him you don't feel well?"

"No." She sat up. "I'm feeling better. You always make me feel better. We read ahead last night so I wouldn't have homework. Sharon would say, enjoy what you have now, and don't fret about what might happen."

"Good advice."

Upstairs, Maggie washed her face, fixed her hair, and put on the outfit she had been saving. The magic of the conversation about staying in California had been broken by a tinny timer bell. Maggie longed to hear Uncle say, "You can stay here next year."

Uncle brought up a plate. When she gave up all sense of propriety and wolfed down meatloaf and mashed potatoes, he teased, "My mother would've said, 'You shouldn't bolt your food.'"

Maggie rolled her eyes but laughed.

After Uncle went down, Maggie whispered to the mirror, "Bonnie Schmonny. She's a little too much like Grandmother—nothing but an unhappy bully."

Special

"MAGGIE WILL BE DOWN in a minute," drifted up the stairs. When she came into the living room, Chris sat at the piano, playing "Only You," his eyes following her.

Maggie wanted to say, "Just the opposite, fella. The change is in *me*."

"You kids better go. Chris has to be with the team soon."

Chris got up. "Yeah, I have to keep moving. I'm looking forward to skating Saturday, Uncle T."

Maggie put her head on Uncle's shoulder and whispered, "Thanks for helping me today."

Uncle kissed her on the forehead. "You're a good girl."

In the car, Chris said, "How are you? I wanted to get to spend time with you. Sorry tonight is just the ride. Coach wants us in a pre-game meeting during the JV game."

"Chris, it's fine. Sharon and Wally'll be there." Maggie turned on the radio to mask her disappointment.

In the gym, Sharon and Maggie walked along the sidelines. Grace sat at the scoreboard controls, the clock counting down from three minutes.

She stopped near Grace. "How did it go at the school board?"

"Not that good." Grace stood. "After putting off the vote for three meetings, they voted 'No' to girls playing basketball. Mr. Tyler asked other schools if they were considering girls' sports, but none were. He really tried. It's a start." Grace eyed the clock. "I have to get back to the scoring table."

In the first minute, a Blackwater guard bounced the ball off the rim. Arcadia rebounded and made a quick score.

"So, I'm guessing that the basket is the same height for JV as for Varsity," Sharon said. "No wonder they don't do as well. They're younger and shorter, and yet they have to play with the same ball and same basket."

Maggie looked at Sharon. "Hmm?" She had avoided what she really needed to say to Grace.

"It seems curious. Same rules for the younger, shorter boys. I say they should lower the baskets. Look, there are ropes and pulley-things up there to raise the baskets out of the way. Why don't they fix them so they could be set for a reasonable JV height?"

"You have a funny brain."

"Think about it. They don't make little kids ride big bicycles when they're learning. They have little bikes with training wheels. So why does the JV have to play with baskets the same height as Varsity? Lower hoops and make the ball smaller too."

Wally took the stairs two at a time. "Hey, Sharon. Hey, Maggie."

"Sharon is explaining why the JV guys don't make as many baskets."

"Ah, the lower the baskets speech! It's one of her best." He took Sharon's hand.

"Smirk all you want. You know it's true. Speaking of the truth, there should be an award for watching this. Let's face it. None of our friends are on JV. The gym stinks. There are about fifty people in the whole place. I came to be with Maggie." She gestured toward Wally. "You came because you're a loyal boyfriend. Maggie got a ride with Chris, who's in a Varsity meeting and *not even having to watch* this! I declare we're loyal fans."

Sharon shook her head when Arcadia rebounded, moved the ball down court in two quick passes and scored. "So we should get a rating, like the tiers of high school. I mean, look at the center cheerleader, Susan Epperson. Now that's enthusiasm! She gets an E for effort. Me? I'm sitting here with no real basketball spirit. I suppose Susan is a level one, and I'm a level three. They give most valuable player awards. What happened to most valuable fan awards?"

Maggie stood up and clapped for a basket. She sat down and grinned at Sharon.

"So, Spirit-Girl is trying for level one?"

"Sure. I might as well be at the top in *one* of your groupings." She bumped Sharon with her shoulder.

At halftime, Maggie went down to where Grace stood with Coach Wiggins. "Can I talk to you for a minute?"

Grace moved to the side.

"I wanted to tell you I'm sorry I didn't speak up the day we tried out for the team. I was chicken."

Grace seemed surprised. "It's OK. I was just so mad and frustrated."

Maggie struggled to get the words right. "I should have told you sooner that I was—I don't know—I guess, half-hearted. You told me I was good, and I just went along. I wanted you to know I was sorry—and am sorry."

Grace checked the clock. "It really is OK. It's turned out better than I thought. Coach lets me help him at practice." She leaned forward. "Coach meets with the assistant coach each Monday morning. He lets me come, so I know what skills he's working on for the week." Grace lifted on her toes. "He's pretty good. I'm learning things about basketball I never knew before."

"I'm glad."

"Would you believe when two guys had the flu, I got to stand in during practice! I scored eight baskets! Coach is going to let me help assist again next year." Grace paused. "Would you be interested in helping?"

"I don't think I'll be here next year. I'm only here for one year." Maggie looked away, batting back tears. Even in her anguish, she could have said, "No, I am not interested in helping with basketball." "No" was an elusive word.

Maggie went back up in a daydream and didn't even remember who won the game.

The Varsity cheerleaders came in between games. Bonnie Douglas looked as pouty as ever, and Maggie avoided looking in her direction.

"Look at Bonnie." Sharon gave Maggie her one dimple smile. "Her lips are dripping with lipstick. She must go through three tubes a week!"

Maggie tried not to gawk, but Bonnie was pretty painted up.

Chris looked up and gave her that crooked smile. Maggie returned a low wave.

Blackwater moved into the lead early in the game. Chris played all but part of the third quarter, and Jimmy Smith played for several minutes. In the last seconds of the game, Chris took a bounce pass and drove under the basket to make a perfect layup. The final buzzer sounded, and Maggie was on her feet clapping and screaming.

Sharon looked amused. "Now that's some Level-One-Enthusiasm!" She nudged Maggie's arm. "Hey, we have to go. Wally has to help his dad before school."

"I'll be fine. Chris will be out in a few minutes. See you tomorrow."

Sharon bounced down the steps with Wally loping behind. She turned to say something to him, and they laughed.

When Chris came into the gym in his street clothes, Maggie started down to the floor. He walked tall and straight, and her heart fluttered. Bonnie intercepted Chris, and they stood under the basket. Maggie sat down on the bottom row.

Bonnie smiled and posed. She cocked her head sideways and touched Chris's arm. She said something, and Chris stepped back. Bonnie grabbed his other arm and stood on her tiptoes. She tried to kiss him on the cheek but had to settle for the neck. She looked up to where Maggie had been sitting, Chris pulled away, and Bonnie flounced out of the gym.

Maggie was tempted to ask what Bonnie had said but wasn't sure she wanted to hear the answer.

Chris rubbed his neck with his knuckles and looked at the back of his fingers. He took Maggie's hand and led her out of the gym, quiet until they got to the car.

He sat with his keys in his hands. "Maggie, did Bonnie say something to you?"

Her "Bonnie Schmonny" bluster evaporated.

Chris took her hand in his. "Seriously. Did Bonnie say something to you?"

Our hands look good together. "Yes."

"What?"

Maggie didn't want to have this conversation. "It was today, after school. I guess my locker is a good place for confrontations."

Chris gave a half-laugh. "What did she say? Did she say something about you and me?"

She wished Chris would drive. After a long time, he asked, "Did she say something about the Sadie Hawkins dance?"

"Yes."

Chris sighed. He put the keys in the ignition but didn't start the car. "And?"

"It doesn't matter."

"It does to me. What else?"

Maggie looked out the window and took a long, ragged breath. "She said my outfits make me look frumpy. She said terrible things about Sharon and Tina."

Chris slowly shook his head. "Oh, boy. She's really something."

He put his arm around her. "You always look so great—so unique. Tonight, you look like a sailor girl. It's great."

Maggie wiped a tear from her cheek. "What she said hurt. I can't compete with Bonnie. I don't feel unique."

Chris kissed her and brushed her cheek with the back of one finger. "You are to me." They kissed again.

Kissing Chris made all thoughts of Bonnie melt away.

He turned the key and touched the starter. The engine caught instantly, and he let it idle.

The low rumble helped Maggie forget Bonnie, the movie, and Wisconsin. She slid down and rested her head on the back of the seat as they started home.

And, Action!

MAGGIE PANICKED WHEN Coach Wiggins called a Friday practice in spite of there being no game. Mrs. Kavanagh stepped in and arranged for Chris to be late. Poor Coach Wiggins didn't stand a chance in the commanding presence of Mrs. Kavanagh.

"We will film Chris's scenes first," she said. "Movies are often filmed out of sequence."

Maggie found it unsettling.

Mrs. Kavanagh stood with Alan at the camera. They filmed the rescue scene first. Alan had placed a little "X" on the screen where the hat shadow was to be. Sharon marked where they were to stand with spike tape.

Mike clapped a piece of ruler down on a chalkboard in front of the lens. Scene 6.

Alan stopped the camera, and Maggie took her place. Her eyes followed the green spike tape marks, reviewing her moves in the scene.

"Ready, Aaand—action." Alan was in his element.

Mike called out the seconds. Jerk the door open. Enter. Rush to Chris in the chair by six. Struggle with the rope until fourteen. Help him up. Two exaggerated hugs, left and right, at twenty-two. *He smells so good!* Move to their marks. Backlight comes up. Lift her chin. Chris leans in at thirty. The hat shadow hits the mark. Chris comes close. Light fades. Hold until thirty-five. Their lips never touched, but it was so romantic!

"That's a take!" Alan declared.

"Well done, both of you," Mrs. Kavanagh said.

Maggie turned in a small circle, shaking the nerves out of her hands.

After filming the scene again, they shot the goodby scene as Chris left for Harmony Music. They exchanged exaggerated waves as Chris walked away, ending with Maggie holding her hands to her heart, lifting one leg behind her.

Mrs. Kavanagh laughed, "Well done, you two, well done!"

Chris moved through his remaining scenes with basketball court calm. In his overcoat and fedora, it was a film from another time, and Maggie resisted clapping at the end of his last scene.

He grabbed Maggie's hand. "Gotta go. This was great. You were perfect." He whispered, "I wanted to kiss you behind the screen."

She winked. "I'll get some spike tape and mark your spot."

In the street scene, Sharon turned to do a double-take as she passed Mike. Tina grabbed her arm and pulled her along. Sharon was what Mrs. Kavanagh called innovative on stage. The remainder of Maggie's scenes were in order, and she fell into a rhythm.

Mike placed the sign cards on an easel and called out ten seconds for each.

ALAN EASED THE LAST reel into its container and put on the lid. "Well, it's in the can."

Mrs. Kavanagh took off her glasses. "I believe you missed your calling, Alan. You should be on the camera side of film rather than the projector side." She handed Alan a brochure. "USC has the finest film school on the West Coast. There are scholarships available."

"Did you graduate from USC?"

Mrs. Kavanagh slipped her notepad into her purse. "Yes, I did. The School of Cinema had moved into the old Ag building." She chuckled. "We called it 'The Stables.' Think about it. I can talk to your counselor."

"I will—thank you." Alan took the brochure to his binder.

"Sharon, Margo, spring play practice starts in a couple of weeks."

Maggie couldn't imagine being in a play—yet.

They peeled up the spike tape, Alan pulled the flats up to the grid, and they carried the furniture to the props room. Mrs. Kavanagh let Maggie take a skimpy roll of tape.

When Alan told Mr. Mills it was the last day, Mr. Mills took off his hat and let Alan shake his hand.

Maggie stood in the middle of the empty stage as the lights clicked out.

Alan brought a handcart for the camera, lights, and suitcases, and they trundled them out to the Jeep. A deep tiredness pulled at Maggie, and she looked forward to the weekend.

Sharon pulled Maggie aside. "This was so much fun. We'll see you at the skating rink."

"Stay overnight, after?" Maggie asked.

"Yes! Popcorn!"

During supper, Maggie talked Uncle through each of the scenes. Chris called as she dried the last dish.

"Did the rest go as well as the first?"

"Yes. Sharon prissed around, pretending she was a starlet. It was pretty funny."

"What time did you get out of there?"

"I was home and we had everything put away by six."

Maggie was so tired she could hardly navigate the stairs.

Grandmother didn't visit Maggie's dreams, which was good because Maggie didn't have the energy to fight with her. Grandmother diminished in size, no longer wielding power. Like most bullies—there was no sand in her.

Spike Tape

MRS. BRICE LED MAGGIE through the art of waxing a kitchen floor. Maggie ran a little buffer with a rolling drum on the front.

Uncle admired the floor. "I'm leaving. I'll see you at the roller rink."

"Make beautiful music!"

Maggie played the piano and read *Anne of Green Gables*. Sharon suggested wonderful books.

Maggie tried on several outfits but knew which she would choose. She wore slacks Mrs. Kim called swing trousers. "I only took a small tuck," Mrs. Kim said.

The slacks were dark gray and buttoned down the left hip. The buttons were fuchsia with tiny white polka-dots that matched the collar and cuffs of the blouse. Virginia had taste, that was for sure. Maggie was sorry she would be wearing skates as the shoes matched the buttons.

She went out and put spike tape on the porch. When Chris stopped in front, she stood with her toes on her mark. He came up the steps, stood on his mark, leaned forward, and kissed her. They stepped over the tape, and she snuggled into his arms.

"Wow, best outfit yet!"

"Thank you. You don't look so bad yourself."

They ran down the drive, each on a ribbon of cement, stretching to touch fingers.

At a stoplight near the rink, Maggie said, "I love the chug of this car." The car created a safe place for them to simply be together.

Chris tapped the accelerator. The engine jumped in pitch and slowed to its normal lope. "My Uncle helped my brother put a racing cam in it. That's what makes it idle like that."

"Oh, I think I know this one." Maggie hesitated. "An itsycam!"

Chris laughed and nudged her shoulder. "Almost. Isky cam." He turned toward her. "You're fun."

"I hope so. I'm sure having fun."

They held hands, walking into the rink. Inside, Wally clung to the railing, and Sharon held his other hand. Tina, Laura, and Alan sailed around at terrific speed, all holding hands. Mike was on the inside, and Laura steadied him. Tina flew on the outside, her skirt ruffling in the breeze.

The music stopped and, "No crack the whip!" blared over the speakers.

Mike went down, and Laura helped him to the railing. Alan and Tina skated off together.

Maggie and Chris went to where Uncle was playing and thanked him for the invitation. *Uncle can play the organ and carry on a conversation at the same time!*

Maggie laced up her skates and stood. "OK. I have to tell you, I'm much better on ice skates."

"I'm not worried," Chris said. "We'll do fine."

Sharon looked cute, skating backward, holding Wally's hands. She towed him away from the railing.

As they came close, he said, "She's going to kill me, telling me her theories on life at the skating rink. I'm just trying to stay upright."

"Wally grew up on the farm. No sidewalks," Sharon sang. "Isn't Uncle T's playing the best? I told him he could get steady work here!"

Maggie and Chris made a few turns around the rink, falling into sync. It was like the movies, skating while holding hands. Maggie watched her pants ruffle around her ankles, saw the smile on Chris's face, and thought it was the perfect day.

Wally began to feel the rhythm of skating, and he and Sharon started gliding around. All eight were skating together when Wally fell backward, landing hard. Sharon and Alan helped him up. Wally insisted it was not as bad as football, but he agreed to take a break.

Sharon brought him water in a cone cup and took his skates off. She and Tina took turns skating backward, swinging each other into position.

Bonnie Douglas, Jenny, and the girl with the platinum hair arrived, skating in formation, like bombers in a war movie. Bonnie made a big deal of looking to where they sat and calling, "Hi Chris!" She led with her chest as she skated past, and Maggie had to admit it was effective. Boys loved girls who looked like Bonnie. Maggie brushed a hair off her knee and glanced up. Chris wasn't looking at Bonnie. Apparently, some guys liked slim girls in swing trousers.

Uncle took a break and got hotdogs and sodas. Chris started to object, but Uncle's eyes twinkled, "It is all part of the deal. I play, they let my young friends in, and we all get to eat!"

They sat and munched happily. Everyone laughed when Uncle got mustard in his mustache.

Sharon dabbed at him with a napkin. "Uncle T, you're always so dapper! We're having a bad effect on you."

"Quite the contrary. Quite the contrary."

"So, my theory of skating rinks is that they have organ music so we can glide around all swoopy." Sharon gestured up with her thumb. "But what's with the shiny ball making stars whirl around the room? Is that supposed to make us think we're going faster? I can skate pretty fast, but I can't keep up with the stars. The ball doesn't swoop."

"So, let's not slog around," Alan said. "Uncle T, what do you say we shake this place up a bit? When we get back out, could you do a little swing or boogie-woogie?"

Uncle's mustache crinkled. "I told them I'd play. I never said what I'd play."

Uncle began a bouncy rhythm, his feet dancing on the pedals. Alan, Laura, and Tina tap-danced on their skates.

Laura towed Wally while Sharon steadied him, patting the beat on his shoulders. Alan and Tina did the Charleston hands over the knees, and Maggie tried it half speed. Bonnie Douglas and her friends were at the side. Bonnie crossed her arms, her eyes shooting venom.

Bonnie kicked off toward Maggie when the song was over, her squadron trailing behind. "I hear that's your uncle playing. If he plays that kind of jive music again, I'm going to talk to Art, the manager."

Maggie stood her ground. "His name is Mr. Blackwater. He's the finest man I know."

Bonnie blinked.

Chris skated over. "What's the problem?"

"I'm going to complain about that music. I didn't pay to listen to that old-timey stuff."

"Bonnie, I want you to leave Maggie and my friends alone. It was one song. You can skate all evening to the regular music."

Bonnie put her hands on her hips. "Hey, I can have an opinion. I paid to get in here. Art said *Maaargo's* uncle got you guys in for free."

"No, Bonnie. Leave Maggie and my friends alone."

Bonnie looked up at Chris, her face slightly red. Tina and Alan skated to a stop next to Chris. Sharon and Wally clattered over, a smile dying on Wally's face.

"I think" Bonnie started, but Chris held up his hand.

"Enough, Bonnie! Enough. Let • it • go."

Bonnie glared at Maggie and skated away. Jenny hesitated. "I love your slacks." She touched a white bow above her ear. "Where do you get your hair done?"

"Polly's Final Touch."

"Thanks." She turned to follow Bonnie. Maggie wished she had the courage to say, "You don't have to follow her around like a puppy."

Maybe Jenny and I aren't so different, just hoping to get through the week without a disaster.

"Thanks, Chris," Mike said. "She's just not very nice. She called Laura 'Little Orphan Annie' a while ago."

Chris went to a bench, sat, and looked at his hands. "I don't usually do that kind of thing. Wow."

Maggie took Chris's hand and patted it. "Thank you," she whispered. "Nobody ever stuck up for me before."

Chris's lips pulled sideways. "She's never happy. She's always got a beef. It was no fun going anywhere with her. She was never happy with anything."

Maggie glanced at Sharon. "I've had good training in being happy with things the way they are."

Peru?

CHRIS AND MAGGIE LAUGHED and used their spike tape one more time. They wadded it into a ball, did two exaggerated hugs, and then a real hug. His arms went all the way around her, enveloping her in safety and happiness. She waved until his car taillights faded.

She brought in the mail and left it on the kitchen table. She carried a letter from Mother upstairs.

Dear Margo,

Your father has been offered another year from the fellowship, and he has accepted. It is a wonderful opportunity for further research for his thesis. It is a great honor.

I can't believe it! I am staying! I can graduate from Blackwater!

Because we are going to be here all next year, I have decided to have you spend the year in Lima. There is a very good boarding school for American students. It has an excellent academic standing.

I'm pleased by this opportunity as I know we haven't been there much for you the past few years. The school is only a five-hour bus ride from the dig, and I can come down every other weekend. We can have some weekends together!

I will write to T. Charles as well. I fear we've traded on his hospitality for too long.

We're scraping up the airfare and will fly you down the day school is out. School starts in the fall, which is March down here. You will only have missed three months. It should be exciting to do your Senior Year abroad.

Love,

Mother

Maggie felt sick. She went into the bathroom and sat on the edge of the tub, staring at the toilet for several minutes. She decided she wasn't going to throw up, so she sat on the bed and cried.

The doorbell disturbed the quiet, and she went down. Sharon waved as the old pickup chugged away.

"Maggie! What's wrong? Did you and Chris have a fight?"

Maggie shook her head miserably, handed Sharon the letter, and started upstairs.

Sharon read the letter twice, sat on the bed, and put her arm around Maggie. "Wow. Not good news."

Maggie wiped tears from her cheeks. "Sharon, I've never been as happy as I am now. I have friends. I have good grades. I have Uncle, who is wonderful. And Chri-" Her voice broke. "And I don't know what I would do without my bosom friend."

Anne Shirley had nothing on Maggie. Anne didn't want to leave Green Gables, and Maggie didn't want to be shipped to Peru.

Sharon laid the letter on the dresser. "We cannot control the things our parents do, but we can control the way we react." She shrugged. "We learn things like that at the meetings."

Maggie nodded. "I've been back and forth between two other high schools and several elementaries before that. I bounce around, never knowing—it's hard. I got by—hiding. But here, I don't hide. You and Uncle have helped me wake up and see things. Chris is my first boyfriend." She sighed. "I can't imagine letting all this go."

"It is not your fault that your parents gallivant all over." Sharon squeezed Maggie's shoulder. "You • are • not • to • blame. I've learned that much."

Maggie stood in front of the mirror. "I'm not even the same person. I—this is embarrassing, but I hardly recognize myself."

"Your figure's certainly nothing to sneeze at these days," Sharon laughed. "No wonder sturdy little Bonnie is jealous."

Maggie blushed. "What a nice thing to say. Polly, the hairdresser, said I'm willowy."

"I think the classification should be svelte."

Maggie choke-laughed and turned from the mirror. "Boarding school in *Peru!* Mother will come down the mountain every other *weekend*?" She raised her voice. "I don't want to go to Peru! I don't want another school! I don't want every other weekend!"

Maggie gained steam. "My father." She snatched the letter from the dresser, tearing off a corner, and it fluttered to the floor. "All my life there's been this thing about his father leaving Grandmother and him before he was born. He was exonerated from responsibilities in life." Maggie grabbed the letter and slapped it on the dresser. "It was his ticket to get to do what he wants. *Poor John.*"

Maggie took off her shoes. "And is *he* going to be coming down? He's left me with Aunt Louise ever since I can remember, to go on his precious digs. He likes his digs more than me." Maggie hung the swing trousers on a hanger and pulled on her capris.

"And my Mother just tags along." Maggie gestured toward the letter. "Off they go. 'You'll be fine, Margo.' And I pretended it was OK." Maggie fumbled with the buttons on her blouse.

"Then I landed here, and now I have a family! Well, a family of one." She had buttoned it wrong and started again. "Uncle pays attention to me. I have friends. I finally woke up and looked around—understood I'm supposed to live, and enjoy, and plan my life."

Maggie whispered, "All I ever did was keep my head down and hope it would get better. I waited for *them to come home.*" She finished the bottom button. "I just wanted them to notice me."

Maggie blew her nose. "You and Uncle and the gang showed me I have choices. This is home, now."

Maggie had stopped crying and gritted her teeth. "And now she wants me to go to a BOARDING SCHOOL?"

"Uncle T—I don't think he would mind you staying another year. Do you think?"

Old doubts circled. "The deal was for the school year." Maggie slipped her foot in her sneaker.

"Listen to me." Sharon turned Maggie's chin. "Uncle T loves you. He adores having you here. You told me Uncle T said you and us kids made this house happy again."

Maggie gave an angry jerk and broke the shoestring. She threw the lace on the floor, shoulders shaking.

Sharon knelt down and took off the shoe. "Here." She handed Maggie her slippers.

"Thanks. What a day! It was perfect until that letter came."

Maggie wiped her eyes. "We've talked about this long enough. This is our night for Ball of Wool and popcorn. I'm going to wait until Uncle gets his letter before I say anything." Maggie paused by the door. "I'm not going to Peru, Sharon! PERU?"

They made popcorn and played Ball of Wool. When the Packard purred past, they waited at the back door for Uncle.

"Ah-ha, girls, I smell popcorn. I'm guessing you're having a good time."

"It'll be better with you, Uncle T." Sharon hugged him around the neck. "Wally said to tell you thank you, again."

"I don't think Wally is cut out to be a skater, but he seemed to take the falls in stride."

"Wally is having the time of his life. A fall or two is worth it. Wally's so shy he just stood on the sidelines."

Maggie was familiar with the feeling.

"I think it may have been more than two falls, but you're right. He's a pleasant boy."

Maggie filled a bowl for Uncle. "Chris said to thank you again, too. Everyone had fun."

Uncle sat heavily. "I can tell you this. Playing theater organ for ten hours is more than I want in one day." He sighed. "Art, the manager asked me to play another boogie-woogie after you kids left. He said it livened up the place a bit."

Maggie winked at Sharon.

"Well, listen. I'm going to bed. Maggie and I have to be at the church at nine-thirty for choir rehearsal."

Uncle took a handful of popcorn. "For the road," he said.

"Let's get breakfast ready so we can serve Uncle T in bed," Sharon said,

"I'll soak the French toast. Pick some oranges. We can squeeze them in the morning."

"You have to stand by the door while I go out."

"My brother does that for me when I go out to feed the dog at night. I'll protect you." She made a muscle.

Maggie picked four. She wrapped them in the tail of her blouse and ran. She dropped one and squealed as she went back for it. A shiver went up her spine as she slipped past Sharon. "Made it!"

"Four may not be enough," Sharon teased, "but we will get more in the morning, when danger has passed."

They were up early and tapped on Uncle's door at seven-thirty.

"This is getting to be a habit. You're spoiling me."

———————◉———————

SHARON WENT TO CHURCH with them. She and Maggie settled in the back while the choir practiced.

"The director is good. He makes it fun," Sharon said.

"You should think about joining. You have a pretty voice."

"I'll think about it. We're supposed to work on our spiritual side. Maybe a little church would do me good."

During silent meditation, Maggie tried a prayer. She asked God to help her stay with Uncle. She added a quick prayer for Uncle and Sharon. Maggie slipped into a daydream, or maybe it was part of the prayer. She was thankful for all that had happened in California.

Uncle took them to In-N-Out for lunch before they dropped Sharon at home. Maggie didn't mention the letter, but she was not going to Peru!

The Premiere

MAGGIE HANDED MRS. Kavanagh a card. "We completed the movie editing. I'd like to invite you to my uncle's for the first showing. It will be a week from this Saturday."

"Ah, yes, the premiere! Exciting. How did it come out?"

"Alan says the exposure is good." She didn't mention they almost argued about which take of the rescue scene was best. "With the dialog cards, it will be about seven minutes long. Uncle took it to have a print made."

"This has been quite the adventure. I am proud of you. Of all of you."

"I know you might not be able to come, but I'd like it if you could. I want to thank you for helping us so much. You can bring your husband."

Mrs. Kavanagh looked at the card. "I appreciate your kind invitation. This has been a unique experience. Sometimes in teaching, we long for something special."

"Uncle will make popcorn, and he will play the music that will go with the movie. He's very good. It'll be like a real silent movie."

MRS. KAVANAGH DID COME. She was alone.

Alan, Tina, Mike, and Laura rolled up the drive and parked in the back. It had turned warm, and their hair was blown. Alan wore his tux, Tina, her green formal.

Maggie met Sharon and Wally at the French doors.

"This is my grand entrance. This is the first time Sharon Jackson has graced the silver screen! But, Maggie, when I disembarked, I expected a red carpet under the porte cochère."

"Oh my, and I forgot to get a searchlight."

Chris parked in front, and Maggie ran down to meet him. She took his arm and walked him to the house. "Glad you're here."

Chris nodded. "Me too. Never thought I'd be in a movie." He squeezed her hand. "Glad you're my girl."

My girl. Maggie paused. "Chris, what are you going to do after high school?" *If I spend a year in Peru, will Chris still be in town if I came back?*

He laughed nervously. "I want to be a dentist."

Maggie was surprised but was determined to not show it. "Would you go away to school?"

"I think I might stay in Southern California."

"I've been talking to Miss Gill about being a teacher." Maggie blushed at words so foreign, but that was looking back. Looking forward, they sounded right.

They jogged up the porch steps. *Even if my parents insist on Peru, I'm coming back!*

Uncle handed Maggie a reel of film with a ribbon tied in a bow. "I had another print made—just in case."

She hugged him. "Uncle, you're perfect. Just perfect." Thoughts of Peru evaporated.

Maggie had a short speech on little cards but decided not to use them. In her swing trousers, she felt like Katharine Hepburn.

"I want to thank you—each of you for coming. When I got off the plane last fall, I never dreamed I'd find such love." She looked at Uncle. "Friends. A good school with caring teachers." Maggie gestured toward Mrs. Kavanagh.

"I want to especially thank my Uncle and Sharon. Sharon, you believed in me from the beginning. Uncle, you gave me more than another place to live. You gave me a home."

Maggie wanted to memorize the room. Uncle at the piano. Chris, on a couch, with those gray eyes. Sharon's lovely smile, her hand in Wally's. Mike fiddling with the projector. Alan, leaning against the door jam as if he were a director from Hollywood. Laura sitting on the arm of Tina's chair.

"And Alan, Mike, and Chris. You have done such a great job. Tina, Laura, Wally, coming week after week. You are dear to me, and I thank you as well."

Maggie tipped her head slightly. "So on with the show. Maestro."

Uncle vamped as Mike started the projector.

Mrs. Kavanagh sat forward as the screen lit. The music and the movie on the screen gave Maggie chills. If only life could have turned out like the movie, Grandfather found, he and Grandmother kissing.

Everyone cheered, and Wally kicked over his popcorn.

"Ha, Ha!" Uncle exclaimed. "Maggie. Kids. That's pretty good if I do say so myself."

"Give us a fantastic idea, a fine camera, and a dedicated cast," Alan laughed, "and it was easy."

Sharon threw a piece of popcorn at him.

The second showing was as good as the first, and Mrs. Kavanagh drew Maggie aside. "Margo, I would like to show your movie to the theater class. I have taught for many years, and this is my first student film."

Uncle played quietly while Chris looked on. It was the beautiful song he had played before.

"What's that song, Uncle?"

"It is called 'An Affair to Remember.' It was in the movie a couple of years ago."

Aunt Louise had taken her to see the movie twice. They cried both times.

Uncle had an affair to remember. Perhaps Mrs. Kavanagh had an affair to remember. Are Chris and I beginning an affair to remember? She didn't think she would forget Chris, even if she moved and never saw him again.

Mrs. Kavanagh moved to the piano and spoke softly to Uncle. He played an introduction.

Mrs. Kavanagh began to sing, her voice rich and warm.

Alan and Tina sat on a couch with Wally and Sharon. Chris came and held Maggie's hand, Uncle watching for cues from Mrs. Kavanagh. When the song ended, there was a moment of quiet before everyone clapped.

"Wow, you two are great!" Tina said.

Sharon whispered in Uncle's ear. He laughed and played a quick bass run and sang "Great Balls of Fire," Alan and Sharon adding harmony.

I'm not trading this for Peru.

The kids danced, laughed, and showed the movie one more time.

"I need to be going," Mrs. Kavanagh said. "Thank you for the lovely evening."

Maggie walked her out, and Uncle joined them on the front porch.

"Thank you for inviting me." She turned to Uncle. "You have quite a menagerie here, Mr. Blackwater. It's good for kids to have a safe place to come."

Uncle put his arm around Maggie. "I'm afraid this old house was quite dull 'til my Maggie Girl arrived. I appreciate all you did for the play and for her."

Maggie didn't remember her father ever putting his arm around her.

Later, on the porch, Chris kissed her goodnight. "We have the best times," he said. "We don't just go to the movies; we make movies."

Maggie hung on his arm. "Part of that is Sharon—well, everyone here." They were members of the cast. The people who helped Margo become Maggie.

I've done more growing up—changing in seven months than I have in seventeen years. The minister had spoken about surrounding ourselves with people who make us better, who have a positive influence—people who are good soil for seeds trying to grow.

Maggie looked up at the glow of the house under the trees. This was good soil. Here was where she could grow, blossom.

Chris put his arm around her as they neared his car. "You're like a breath of fresh air because you are not afraid to be different, Sharon or no Sharon."

Maggie let the words, and his kiss, wash over her heart.

Virginia wasn't afraid to be different. I have always been afraid. Perhaps Virginia was nervous when she walked into that lobby on Grandfather's arm.

Chris's words, "not afraid to be different," resonated. She had given a short speech earlier. *Am I learning to be at ease?*

Chris waited until Maggie was back on the porch and blew a kiss. She stood with her arms around herself until the car was out of sight.

Sharon and Wally rumbled down the drive, followed by the Jeep.

Maggie and Uncle carried bowls and glasses to the kitchen. He ran the dishwater. "I got a letter from your mother."

The glow of the evening dimmed. Maggie sagged against the counter. "Did you get one too?"

"Yes." She shut her eyes against tears.

Uncle sat at the kitchen table. "What do you think?"

Maggie slid into the chair across from him. Tears rolled down her cheeks. "I don't want to leave." A glance told her Uncle was not letting her parents park her with him.

Uncle placed his fingers on the edge of the table. "You know, I cannot tell your mother what to do—it's not my place. You're her daughter, not mine."

Maggie shivered. In a perfect world, Uncle would convince her parents, save her from Peru. He would send a telegram or write, telling them she would be staying in California, but this was the real world.

"You've made this year alive for me. Oh, I suppose I was happy enough, but this has been—this is wonderful for me."

"I'm not going to Peru. I can't. It would kill me." Maggie wiped tears away and sat up a little straighter. "My grades are so much better. With summer school this summer, I could make up my credits. I could graduate on time. Miss Gill is helping me look at colleges I could go to." She paused. "Some are around here—if I could stay?"

Uncle reached across the table and took her hand. "I want what's best for you. And yes, you are always welcome here."

"This *is* what's best. I was lost. I spent my life hiding. Being invisible. I was..." Maggie dabbed at her eyes. "I was miserable." She shook herself. "I can't go to another school, start over—enrolling three months late. I've done that too many times."

No, that era had passed. She wanted to start school on time at Blackwater next year. *What is wrong with me? Shouldn't I want to be with my parents? Shouldn't I be homesick?*

The problem was, there weren't enough special times. Maggie could count Christmases with her parents on one hand.

"I'm going to write to Mother and tell her I'm not going to Peru."

"May I look at it before you mail it?"

"Yes. I want to share it with you."

Mr. Mills

THE THEATER CLASS SAT in the first two rows of the auditorium. Mike was in the projection booth, and Uncle was in the wings with the tape recorder. Mrs. Kavanagh arranged for the cast to be excused from their third-period classes.

Alan invited Mr. Mills, and he took off his hat in the back of the auditorium.

Maggie sat between Chris and Alan, tenth row, center. "Best seats in the house," Alan whispered.

Mrs. Kavanagh introduced the movie to the class and spoke about days of silent films.

When Alan signaled to Mike, Maggie reached for Chris's hand. Grandfather's theme rang through the auditorium. *Alan is a genius with wires and amplifiers. I had been a part of fixing that amplifier.* She laughed inside—a reluctant assistant, at best.

The piano played dark chords, and the next moment there were tinkling notes like a waterfall. Uncle used the organ for the suspenseful scene when Wally kidnapped Chris.

The movie faded as the last notes of Grandfather's song hung in the air.

The movie was Alan's idea, but I showed commitment—and the movie turned out fine, Grandmother! It turned out fine.

Maggie doubted Grandmother would visit her dreams regarding the movie. Finding fault was Grandmother's forte, and her air of superiority rang hollow that morning.

Mrs. Kavanagh held up her hand to quiet the applause. After making remarks, she asked that the movie be shown again. Maggie held her breath as Chris leaned into the hat's shadow, and the last scene faded.

"All right, class. Ten minutes until the bell. We will go back to the room. You are to write a short review of Margo's movie." She turned to Maggie. "Help your uncle and then get along to your next class."

"Great job, Old Girl," Alan said. "Mike had to leave, so I'm going up to get the film and close down the projection booth."

Uncle rewound the tape and slipped it in its box. Sharon hugged him around the neck. "Uncle T, your music really worked." She hurried up the aisle to where Wally waited.

When Uncle and Maggie were alone, he said, "Well done, Dear. Well done."

The stage piano began to play Grandfather's song, one warbling note at a time. Mr. Mills stood at the keyboard, undecided, and then repeated the line.

He sat, fumbling the notes. His left hand seemed to be lost, but his right hand began to play stronger. He stopped, rubbed the music rack with his fingertips, and stood. He reached out and played three notes.

"Daniel?" Uncle stood at the edge of the wings.

What? Maggie looked from Uncle to Mr. Mills. *Grandfather was from New York. Mr. Mills is the kind old janitor who repeats himself.* She watched a scene in a play unfold.

Mr. Mills took a half step toward Uncle. "No, I'm Tom Mills."

"Danny? It's Tom Blackwater. Tommy."

Mr. Mills turned and played a single note. "I work at Blackwater. It's a nice school." He paused. "Blackwater."

Uncle met Mr. Mills halfway across the stage. "Daniel? It's Tommy."

Margo's head swam. *Daniel?*

"I don't know—Tom is *my* name. I'm Tom. I..."

Maggie went closer, watching Mr. Mills' eyes.

"I liked your movie, young lady. It reminds me of the old days when we wore clothes like that." He turned to Uncle. "I'm glad to have met you, sir, but I have to eat. It will be noon by the time I get home. I have to get home and eat. It will be one-thirty soon. I take my pills at one-thirty. I need to be at school by ten to two—I'm always at school by ten to two." Mr. Mills went down the steps and up the aisle, never looking back.

"That's your grandfather." Uncle gazed up the empty aisle. "I knew as soon as I saw those hands on the keys."

"How can you be sure?"

"Mr. Mills is Daniel McKinney." Uncle unplugged the tape recorder. "It has been thirty-eight years—but that's Daniel. He tried to play his song."

"How could that be? He wasn't really playing." And yet, there had been a moment when his right hand played with the same ease as when Uncle played.

The sound system fan hummed quietly to itself.

"Something has happened to him." Uncle leaned heavily, hands on the counter. "He shows signs of a stroke, brain injury, or trauma." Uncle snapped the latches on the tape recorder and slid it to the edge of the counter.

Alan trotted up the steps from the dressing rooms. "I'll get that for you, Uncle T."

"Thank you." Uncle gave Maggie an almost imperceptible shake of his head. "You don't want to be late to class. We'll talk about everything when you get home."

Home! I can't wait another moment to find out more. But what was to be done? Follow Mr. Mills? Knock on his door? And say what?

Maggie kissed Uncle on the cheek. "I'll be home right after school."

After PE, she wandered toward the cafeteria, bumping a girl's arm. "Sorry," she mumbled.

Sharon rummaged in her lunch sack. "So how is director-actress-producer-girl? I'd say the morning was a success. Definitely a move toward tier two. Vivien Turner was pretty impressed—her curls were extra bouncy." She took out her sandwich. "Hey, Maggie? Are you there?" She waved her hand in front of Maggie's eyes.

Alan and Tina joined them. Maggie watched Chris talking to Wally near the band room. "Alan, please tell everyone I need to talk to Sharon for a minute. We'll be right back."

Alan drew a sideways triangle on one of his electronic schematics. Tina rolled her eyes and said, "OK."

Maggie towed a puzzled Sharon away.

On the quad side of the classrooms, Maggie said, "After everyone left, Mr. Mills went up on the stage and started playing the theme song from my movie. The song my grandfather wrote. He had trouble, but it was the song."

"Wow, he has a good ear," Sharon said.

"There's more. The next thing I knew, Uncle's calling 'Daniel,' my grandfather's name—my grandfather who disappeared!"

"OK. Hmmm." Sharon cocked her head. "OKaaay."

"Uncle thinks Mr. Mills is my grandfather!" Maggie wrapped her arms around herself. "Mr. Mills was confused. Uncle said Mr. Mills has had a stroke or brain trauma."

"Well, we all know Mr. Mills is—different." Sharon shook her head. "Your grandfather working here at school. What are the chances?" Sharon turned in a little circle. "Mr. Mills? Oh, Maggie!"

Maggie grabbed Sharon's arm to stop her from turning. "What are you thinking? Is this possible?"

"It is possible." Sharon's eyes were bright. "Grandpa McKinney gets conked on the head and forgets who he is. He wanders the country looking for clues to his past."

"Sharon, it's a big country." Maggie pulled her toward the center of the quad. Two girls hurried by.

"I'm serious. He tries out for a job here at Blackwater High because…" Sharon grabbed Maggie by the shoulders. "Because the name—Blackwater—is in his head, rattling around in there somewhere."

"I don't know." It seemed as though days had passed since they showed the movie to the theater class. Maggie felt tired and jumpy at the same time. California was too far. Mr. Mills didn't even drive.

Maggie wanted to believe it was possible. She wanted Mr. Mills to suddenly wake up from his fog, recognize Uncle, have his memory click back into gear, put his arms around her, and say, "Hello, Granddaughter."

Sharon's eyes sparked. "But here's the proof. One day, when I got to the auditorium, Mr. Mills was leaving. He looked right at me as natural as can be and said, 'Ginny is already inside.' I thought he was just his usual confused self."

Sharon stood on her toes. "Virginia—Ginny! Ooooh, I got a shiver."

Maggie rubbed goosebumps off her arm.

"It makes perfect sense," Sharon said. "He looks at you so oddly and tells you your clothes remind him of the old days."

It's like Cary Grant finding Debrah Kerr hiding in her apartment, seeing his painting, realizing she was injured, and her saying, "Anything can happen, don't you think?"

"In the movie, you are wearing his sister's clothes! Uncle T says you look like Virginia."

Grandfather may have seen Virginia wear that very dress in New York. The years compressed, the distance from New York to California diminished. If the dress made the journey, Grandfather could too.

"I never noticed Mr. Mills' eyes before today. He has green eyes, my eyes." The two girls scurried back across the quad. "What should I do?"

"Nothing!" Sharon gave Maggie her no-nonsense face. "Absolutely nothing—wait until you have talked to Uncle T. We don't need Mary Suttle getting ahold of this."

Sharon started for the lunch tables. "Alan knows where Mr. Mills lives. I'll get the address. Uncle T will know what to do."

At the table, Sharon didn't wait for questions. "So, I've been thinking about Orson Bean. They say someone came up to him and said, 'Say something funny,' and Orson said, 'Belly button.'"

Alan choked on his cookie. It was hard to tell if Tina was laughing at Sharon or Alan.

"Don't look at me like that. I mean the word belly button is pretty odd, don't you think? Who makes up these words?"

Chris turned to Maggie. "So, what's the big secret?"

"Maybe we were talking about how handsome I think you are," she teased.

The Truth

SHARON HAD ASKED FOR Mr. Mills address, telling Alan that Maggie and Uncle T wanted to write a thank you note. Sharon's misdirection jogged Maggie into action, and she wrote a card to Mr. Mills. *Did I just write a thank you card to my grandfather?*

Uncle planned to visit Mr. Mills in the morning. Maggie begged to go with him, but he said, "After all your progress, we cannot let your grades suffer because of this. We are not sure where this is going."

It was another three-week-long day. The clocks only relented during lunch, speeding to make up for lost time.

After History, Maggie hurried to Room 54. Mr. Mills pushed a broom with little skips, rolling papers, and clutter ahead. She leaned against the door jam and watched his back. *Those are Father's shoulders, or maybe it's wishful thinking.*

"Mr. Mills?"

He turned and leaned the broom against the wall.

"I brought you a card to thank you for letting us in the auditorium and locking up." She handed him the envelope, wondering if she should shake hands, anything to touch him. She settled for a smile.

"It was my pleasure. I liked watching you practice." He read the card slowly. "This is a nice card, but I have to finish this room. I need to be in Room 56 by three forty-five."

Maggie came away flustered. *He's my flesh and blood and yet still a stranger.*

She and Sharon stood under the oak tree when Uncle pulled to the curb.

"Hi, Uncle T!" Sharon called.

Uncle waved.

Maggie touched Sharon's shoulder. "I have to go. I'll see you at the game—I think?"

Sharon whispered, "Good luck," and wiggled her fingers.

218

Maggie hurried to the Packard. "So, did you see Mr. Mills? Did you talk?"

"Yes. He is your grandfather. But it's very complicated. We need tea and cookies. Lots of cookies. It's a long story."

Maggie watched the scenery go by. She felt unsettled, as she had the day she arrived in California. However, this time she became calmer the closer they got to home.

Home. For how long? Will finding Grandfather bring Father running? Will this change my chances of staying here? Will he go back to Wisconsin with us?

Uncle turned into the drive. "He doesn't remember—anything. He was in an accident."

"So, he didn't run away?" It was the question she longed to ask but hadn't because Grandmother was convinced that Grandfather was a deserter.

"No, he didn't run away."

Maggie felt great relief. The man in the picture had kind eyes and looked directly at the camera in an easy way. Shifty people rarely looked you in the eye. Maggie suspected it might be the same as the eye of the camera. The man sitting at the piano with Uncle wouldn't run away.

"Why don't you go in and get the tea started? I'll park the car."

The house seemed extra quiet. Maggie started the fire under the kettle and got the teapot ready. The kitchen was a peaceful place—safe when life became a jumble.

Uncle came in and leaned back against the counter. "The conversation was not very satisfying, I'm afraid. Daniel doesn't know me. I'm not sure he believes me—or can grasp it all may be a better way to describe it."

They sat at the kitchen table, Maggie feeling numb.

Uncle pulled his cuffs down. "Even my visit upset his routine. This is not something he can process quickly or understand."

He got up and poured the water, the kettle spitting. "I went to his house about ten o'clock and Daniel—Mr. Mills, let me in. I believe he remembered me from yesterday, but it's hard to be sure. He looks at me in such an odd way."

"He always seems puzzled." Maggie got the good cups.

"Yes. His world is—foggy."

Maggie polished a spot on the red kitchen table with a tea towel.

"I asked him if he had ever lived in New York. He said he hadn't lived there, but he remembered New Jersey."

"The conversation got a bit confusing. Daniel was unable to tell me how he got to New Jersey—in fact he doesn't remember where he was raised. I could tell he was reaching into a distant part of his mind. When words failed, he brought out a box with important papers. 'Always keep them,' were his words."

Maggie poured the tea.

"A police report tells of how your grandfather was in a terrific accident." Uncle turned his saucer, the cup handle pointing this way and that. "Witnesses say he was being robbed, tried to run, and was hit by a car. It was in the dead of winter—early January. The hospital report describes traumatic head injury. He was in a partial coma for months." Uncle sighed. "What a waste."

Maggie got the cookies and put three on Uncle's dessert plate.

"Thieves took his wallet, his identification, so he was declared a John Doe. He was there for sixteen months."

Grandmother, you were so sure he ran away. But that story was always about Grandmother and her misfortune. Grandmother loved a good story in which she was the long-suffering star. Poor Mr. Mills—Grandfather, in the hospital. Maggie sat on the edge of her chair.

"Your grandfather was vague about what happened next, but he was eventually released. His doctor, Dr. Koehler, noted that Daniel stayed in a studio apartment near the hospital. He must have been a very kind man as I'm not sure who would have paid for an apartment. There was a phone number, but Dr. Koehler passed away before the war. So, I guess that's all we know."

"Can we visit?"

"Not for a bit. I didn't try to tell him he had a child or a grandchild. He has no memory of your grandmother or Virginia."

Maggie had wanted Uncle to say they could visit, but she was relieved. She sipped her tea, hoping it would calm the shifting feelings. *Mr. Mills is my grandfather, but he might not ever know that I am his granddaughter.* Sadness settled heavily.

"I took a picture of Virginia, one taken in New York. He said, 'Oh, the pretty girl in the movie.' I didn't think it could be explained."

Uncle took a sip of tea. "He told me he opened the auditorium for you at three-thirty-five to let you work on your play. He said the play was like the movie you showed." Uncle smiled sadly. "So, you see, I'm not sure he's made the connection between the practice and the movie. Poor Daniel."

Peace came over Maggie. "I came to California, and I answered questions that have always bothered me. I suppose I've found my grandfather." She searched for the right words. "But what I really found was you." She leaned around the table and kissed Uncle on the cheek. "Coming here was the best thing in my life."

Uncle adjusted his cuffs. "Yes. It was the brightest day since—well, for years."

"I've scribbled several versions of the letter I'm going to send to Mother. Tomorrow, after we 'get after the dust,' I'd like you to help me with it. I want the letter to be just right."

Uncle brightened. "That will be fine." He looked toward the clock. "You better get moving if you're going to impress Chris with that jumper you've been dying to wear!"

"Do you want me to stay with you? I can skip the game."

"I am fine—I really am. I too have found an answer to something that I have wrestled with for years. Perhaps not the one we wanted, but Virginia would be so relieved. You go. Have fun. I will see you when you get home."

Maggie told Chris about Mr. Mills on the way to the game. "I don't think we should say anything. I mean, he doesn't remember or can't make sense of it. I hardly can. Anyway, I think it should be kept quiet. Mary Suttle would go nuts with this." She listened to the car's rumble. "But I wanted you to know."

"So, your movie about finding your grandfather, found your grandfather."

"Yes," Maggie whispered. *Grandfather's song found him.*

No Misdirection

Dear Father and Mother,

A most wonderful thing has happened, but it's hard to explain. My movie was a great success. Mrs. Kavanagh showed it to the class in the auditorium. She arranged for everyone who helped with the filming to be there. Uncle came to operate the tape recorder for the music. Alan, who I have mentioned helped with the filming and editing, invited the janitor who was kind enough to open the auditorium on practice days.

After the movie, the strangest thing happened. The janitor, Mr. Mills, went up on the stage and started fiddling with the piano, playing Grandfather's melody.

When Uncle heard him, he recognized Grandfather! Uncle tried to talk to him, but he kept saying he was Tom Mills.

Since then, Uncle has gone to Mr. Mills' house, and Mr. Mills is Grandfather McKinney! He cannot remember anything of his past. He showed Uncle papers he keeps about his condition.

Father, you might not believe this, but the papers tell of Grandfather being in a hospital for sixteen months while you were born. A witness saw a robbery, Grandfather tried to run, and was hit by a car. He suffered what Uncle calls Traumatic Brain Injury. He was declared a John Doe.

Uncle showed him a picture of your Aunt Virginia, but he thought it was a picture of me.

Grandfather didn't desert his family! He was in the hospital and then wandered around for years. We guess he came to California because Uncle had told him about orange groves and Pasadena. Mr. Tyler, the Vice-Principal, helped him get the job. He never changes the order of his day and doesn't miss anything he's supposed to do.

Grandfather didn't desert Grandmother or you, Father. He's just not well from the accident.

I have one other thing to tell you, and I'm sorry this letter may contain information that you're shocked by or don't want to hear. But I am not coming to Peru. It's too much. It would be my fourth high school. I cannot do that. I'd get there after school started, be behind, and I can't do that again.

You see that my grades are very good- amazing for me. My counselor, Miss Gill, has arranged for me to go to summer school to make up the credits I missed because I flunked biology last year.

I have talked all this over with Uncle. You have to believe me that it's fine if I live here. Uncle did not try to talk me into this idea, and it has nothing to do with Grandfather McKinney, although sometimes I go to see him after school. He won't know I am his granddaughter, but I want to know him better.

Please try to understand. I hope the project goes well there.

Love, Margo

UNCLE LAID THE LETTER back on the table. "I wouldn't change a word. It is perfect."

"I wrote it over and over. I think all our studying is having a good effect on me. Miss Johnson says I'm writing better all the time." Maggie tapped the letter. "We won't get this in an airmail envelope. I couldn't make it any shorter."

"I think we can scrape up the extra postage."

———————=◉=———————

MAGGIE BAKED COOKIES for Mr. Mills. She made them small, bite-sized, so he could put some in his supper bag. He seemed surprised but gingerly took a cookie from the tin, sampled a bite, and smiled.

He offered one to Maggie, and they stood and ate their cookies together. *I'm eating with my grandfather!*

Maggie found Sharon under the oak. "I wrote a letter to my folks, telling them I am not going to Peru. I didn't want to say anything in front of the others."

Sharon leaned her back against the trunk.

"The trouble is, I'm going crazy. I only sent it Saturday, and already I can't wait to find out what they say."

Sharon laid her binder down. "I have never been very good at being patient. I'm sure I could be more patient if it didn't involve so much waiting."

"I should be better at it. I have spent my life waiting for my parents." Flowers pushed up around the base of the school sign. One pink blossom stretched to the afternoon sun. "I guess I thought telling them would make me feel better."

"What does Uncle T say?"

Maggie gave a crooked grin. "He said I need to be patient."

"There we are, back to waiting."

"I haven't told Chris about Peru, and I don't know why. I think I am afraid if I told him I might be leaving the day after school is out, he will exit, stage right."

"Doesn't seem like Chris. If he's anything, he's loyal."

"I guess I wish I knew he was—well, more than loyal."

"One day at a time. We can't ruin today by worrying about what might happen."

"You sound like Uncle."

Sharon looked up into the tree. "Dad had a little relapse. Not big, but he stopped by the bar and had a few drinks with his old buddies. He was home in time for supper."

Surprised, Maggie said, "When?" She had fallen into her old habits of only worrying about herself.

"Friday." Sharon sighed. "He thinks he can handle it."

"Can he? Do you think he can?"

"He needs to go to meetings."

Maggie was confused. "I don't—like your meetings?"

"AA—Alcoholics Anonymous. He has to admit he cannot do this by himself."

"So, I guess you are waiting, too?"

"Yes, in a way, I suppose. But only he can decide it's time to go to a meeting. I need to get on with my life—with the things I can control." She picked up her binder.

"You're so smart, Sharon."

"Pay no attention to the girl behind the curtain. I have no idea what I am doing." Sharon pretended to reach up and pull a lever. "I am Oz!" she breathed.

Maggie shook her arms like Scarecrow. "You're not a humbug, but I'll have straw for a brain if I don't finish my English paper."

"Trig, for me." Sharon rippled her fingers. "Smile. Talk to Chris."

⸻ ◉ ⸻

MAGGIE SAT IN FRONT of her diary before bed and thought about basketball. With the season over, she would miss the Tuesday and Friday games. Chris had started an afternoon job at the hardware store, and Maggie longed to see him. Maybe she would join the Welcome and Hospitality Club. Uncle said the best way to quit worrying about yourself was to help someone else.

Aunt Louise

MAGGIE'S LATEST LETTER to Aunt Louise was returned, "Moved. No forwarding address." Another card explained.

Dear Margo,

Your aunt passed away Tuesday afternoon. I want you to know she went easily. She didn't suffer. I sent a note to your mother as well.

She read your letters over and over. You were very special to her. Even though she couldn't speak, Mrs. Carter always had a smile and said "Yagan" when we helped her. We knew she meant thank you. We at Shady Cove will miss her.

Sincerely,

Jean Frasier

Maggie felt numb. She hadn't seen Aunt Louise for nearly a year. She wasn't overwhelmed with missing her, but it felt odd to think of the world without Aunt Louise. Maggie had stayed with her since she was five, mostly during the school year. She didn't know a summer Aunt Louise.

Maggie didn't put the letter in the desk with Mother's. She carried it to the top drawer of her dresser. She didn't open the envelope; she knew what she had written. "No forwarding address." The post office had an odd way of doing things.

Sadie Hawkins Dance

ALAN BROUGHT TINA TO talk to Uncle. Maggie and Alan fiddled with the player piano while Tina and Uncle were in the kitchen. When Tina came through, she had not been crying.

"Tina is going to look at some of the costumes upstairs for the Sadie Hawkins Dance," Uncle said. "Come on up. This should be fun."

Maggie was fascinated as Tina held up different dresses. She selected a high necked Victorian corset dress. Uncle insisted Tina look at shoes.

When they were leaving, Tina whispered in Uncle's ear and hugged him. Alan nodded a smile at Maggie.

At the dance, Sharon had fixed ponytails on both sides of her head and drew huge freckles. Maggie wore Virginia's overalls with one strap hanging down over a three-button Henley shirt that Sharon said accented her shape. Maggie was pretty impressed to have a shape after being a toothpick all her life. Wally and Chris dressed in plaid shirts and jeans with one pant leg rolled up.

Alan and Tina were late. Alan wore his tux and a top hat. A monocle on a ribbon and a walking stick completed the picture. Tina came in on his arm, and the dress was perfect. She had hemmed it, so it swept the floor. The crowd seemed to sense that Alan and Tina were moving up a tier.

"Looking pretty sharp, you two," Sharon said.

"I would like to present Miss Tina May Cort-TEE," drawled Alan.

Tina gave a curtsy and batted her eyes. She smoothed the dress. "We went by Uncle T's, but you were already gone. I wanted him to see us. He is so wonderful to let me use these things."

"Those costumes have been stored up there for years. He's tickled someone is wearing them," Maggie said.

Bonnie filled out a scoop neck peasant blouse cinched with a wide black belt that turned boys heads. Maggie felt sorry for her; her makeup was overdone. According to Uncle, Virginia said some women try too hard.

While Bonnie flirted with Craig Waller, Jenny gave Maggie a shy smile and whispered, "We're twins." She hooked her thumbs in the bib of her overalls. She wore her hair shoulder length with bangs.

Maggie surprised herself by giving Jenny a quick hug. She wasn't trying to take her away from Bonnie but sensed Jenny to be lonely and a bit lost. "Your hair is cute."

"Thank you! I went to Polly's to get it cut like yours." Jenny blushed. "I think your hair is so cute. Polly said with my hair, this length worked better."

"She's the best." Jenny was one of those redheads with alabaster skin. Glorious hair like hers shouldn't be bobbed. Maggie reached down and unclipped the right strap of Jenny's overalls to match hers. "There, twins for sure."

She beamed. "Thanks!"

When Bonnie was done with Craig and on the prowl, Jenny moved toward the punch bowl.

Mike came in with Linda Laurence.

"Alan, Laura didn't ask Mike?" Maggie asked.

"She did, but Linda asked first." Alan rolled his eyes. "He was flattered that Linda asked and said yes before he—well, he goofed it up."

"How's Laura?"

"Miffed. She and Mike talked. Tina says she'll be OK." Alan put his cane out in front of him and leaned on it with both hands. "If you can believe Mary Suttle, Linda asked Mike to make Peter Fredrickson jealous."

Frankie's brother's band played "Get a Job," with Frankie playing the saxophone.

Maggie led Chris to the floor. "Harder work than standing under the clock?" she teased.

"Never wanted to stand under the clock after I saw you in the red beret."

"You say the nicest things."

The band played, "Put Your Head on My Shoulder." Maggie put her head on Chris's shoulder as she had wanted to before and hummed along with the words. She refused to think about Peru.

Later, Maggie went into the bathroom and heard crying in the third stall. "You OK in there?"

"Margo?"

She didn't recognize the voice. "Yes." Maggie waited.

"It's Jenny—from before." She sniffled.

Maggie stood by the door. "Can I help?" A muffled "Mr. Blue" drifted in from the cafeteria, filling the moment.

"I planned to ask Tim Watkins to the dance. Bonnie was in one of her moods because Chris was going with you. She said we would go stag." Jenny blew her nose. "I have liked Tim all year." She sighed. "She's flirting with every boy out there as if she is determined to break up as many dates as possible."

Two giggling sophomores came in to check their faces. Maggie fiddled with a curl in front of her ear until the girls scurried out, shoulder to shoulder.

"Did Tim come tonight?"

"No."

"Does he know you like him?"

Jenny's voice became a whisper. "No, probably not."

Sometimes the world comes full circle. The one who needs lessons in how to live through the perils of high school ends up being the teacher—and Maggie knew the lessons well. She leaned close. "Jenny, when you're ready, come out."

The door clicked open, and Jenny fell into her arms. She felt like a small bird, hardly coming to Maggie's shoulder. "Bonnie saw you make my overalls match yours, and she had a fit."

The strap was fastened to the steel button again.

"I rode with her, and now she says I am walking home." Jenny shook her head miserably.

"You are not walking home. Come here and splash cold water on your eyes." Maggie held her hair.

"I have been Bonnie's neighbor since second grade. She gets meaner and meaner, but she's never left me somewhere!" She sniffed. "I don't even have a dime to call my mom."

"You can ride with us. There's room."

"You are so nice. Bonnie said you stole Chris and spread rumors about her."

Maggie handed Jenny a paper towel. "Jenny, look at me. Talk to Tim. Tell him you wanted, well almost asked him to the dance. That's not a lie. You were going to, and then—well, you didn't." She watched Jenny in the mirror.

"What if he's—he doesn't like me back. What if I make a fool out of myself?"

Maggie lifted Jenny's chin. "Then he's a fool. You're cute, and if you don't say anything, you'll never know."

Maggie caught a glimpse of herself delivering this advice. *I should take my own medicine and tell Chris about the letter, Peru, the whole mess.*

Maggie turned Jenny to the mirror, moving her head side to side as Polly had done. "Look. You're pretty. The day you talk to Tim will be his lucky day." She turned Jenny toward the door. "Now, when we get outside, walk beside me. Don't tag along behind."

Maggie stood tall as they walked back to the dance floor. Bonnie looked up, but she didn't come their way. "Alan, we are going to teach Jenny how to do the swing."

Maggie's friends gathered around Jenny while Alan went to request songs.

Virginia's Ford

A CUTE LITTLE CAR SAT under the porte cochère. Maggie was at the French doors when Uncle met her.

"It was Virginia's."

The bougainvilleas reflected in the paint. "Where has it been?"

"It has been in the other garage. I never had the heart to sell it."

Maggie put her books by the door.

"I thought it was time you learned to drive. Miss Gill said you're scheduled for Driver's Education soon. We'll get your learner's permit." He handed her a DMV study book. "It should be easier to handle than the Packard for a beginner. Virginia drove the Packard, but she preferred her little Ford."

Has mother written? Am I staying? No. Uncle would tell me if a letter arrived.

Uncle opened the driver's door. "Some folks call these suicide doors. They open from the front. You want to make sure they are shut tight because the wind will catch them and pull them open." He brushed his mustache.

Inside, the cab was tiny compared to the Packard. The single seat was hardly wide enough for three.

"Get in—see if it fits."

Uncle got this car out for me. He wants me to stay. She slipped into the seat.

"It has been sitting for eight years. I had the garage pick it up and get it ready for the road. It has new tires, and the brakes have been adjusted. I had them wax it." He rolled down the window and closed the door.

"Virginia loved this car. I suggested we get her a new one, but she said the post-war cars were too big. She ran around town in this little rig. It doesn't have many miles on it."

Maggie put her hands on the steering wheel. "I'd be afraid to dent it."

Uncle got in on the other side. He sighed and rubbed his hand along the dash.

He opened the glove box, took out a pair of brown gloves and sniffed them. When he handed them to Maggie, there were tears in his eyes. "I had forgotten the gloves. She kept them in here for when it was cold, or sometimes the sun made the steering wheel hot." He took a deep breath. "She was so sweet."

"I know, Uncle. I know." When Maggie heard a quiet sob, she didn't know what to say.

Uncle shook his head. "I'm sorry. I don't do this in front of others. I haven't cried like this—for a long time." He dabbed his eyes with his handkerchief. "It overwhelms me sometimes."

"Would you like to go have some tea?"

He sat up straighter. "No. We're going to have your first driving lesson."

They traded places, and Uncle flipped a switch and reached out with his foot. "You step on the starter in this car." He pressed down on a plunger, the engine turned and caught. Maggie could hardly hear it idling. *Little car, you have been waiting for me.* She ran her fingers along the windowsill.

"I'll back into the backyard, and then you can try pulling it forward."

When Uncle put the car in gear, Maggie said, "Uncle, it has two floor shifts!"

He chuckled. "All the old cars had floor shifts, but this one is the parking brake."

She had a lot to learn.

Uncle showed Maggie where the gears were, and they switched places.

She practiced shifting between gears. At least she didn't have trouble reaching the pedals. She remembered Sharon saying, "You'll see this clutch and gas pedal and shifting takes some doing."

Uncle was very patient, and Maggie learned to move the car forward and back, without stalling.

Maggie caught a glimpse of her hair in the tiny rearview mirror. Virginia had looked at herself in that mirror. She pulled the curl in front of her right ear further forward. "What kind of car is this?"

"Thirty-four Ford, three-window coupe. We bought it new the year we moved to California."

Maggie repeated the model several times. Her friends would want to know.

Uncle showed Maggie a seat in the back trunk.

"Uncle, that's so cute!"

"It's called a rumble seat."

At school, Maggie recited, "It is a thirty-four Ford, three-window coupe with a floor shift!" She gave Sharon a satisfied smile. "It has a rumble seat."

"Well, I must say, I'm impressed. Uncle T seems determined to spoil you."

"Do you think I'm spoiled?"

"Not at all. I actually think it's high time you were spoiled a little."

"I'm not telling everyone at lunch. I told Chris, and he came by last night to see it. He said the wire wheels are what makes it perfect."

"I cannot speak for wire wheels. Apparently, that is not a topic for the Driver's Ed boys. But, it will be quite the thing, you driving around in a three-window-coupe-with-a-floor-shift. This may move you to tier two. Even Bonnie has to drive a Nash!"

Maggie raised her eyebrows in curiosity.

"Oh, Maggie! You're catching up pretty fast, but a Nash is not the cool car. Ford or Chevy, Ford or Chevy."

"But, a couple of years ago, there was that silly song about the little Nash Rambler passing the Cadillac."

"I know. Cute song, but the Driver's Ed boys assured me it's still not cool, and I'm sure the Driver's Ed boys would know." She winked. "Besides, Bonnie's car is not a Rambler. It is just a Nash."

"I don't know if I'll ever get to drive it. I am only starting Driver's Ed next week. I feel like time is running out. What if my folks decided to come home early, and I end up back in Wisconsin? I wish a letter would come." That wasn't quite true. Each day without a letter was a relief. No news was good news.

Marching Orders

THE LETTER WAS IN THE mailbox. A note on the kitchen table reminded Maggie that Uncle had a dentist appointment, so she laid the letter on the kitchen table and walked through the quiet house. She didn't know how long she would be able to stay there. She wanted to see it all, keep it perfectly in her mind.

In the study, the pictures, the player piano, the rolls Grandfather had made, the rolls Uncle had made, all waited. Maggie leaned close to the photo taken in Santa Monica. She wandered into the living room and touched the Bechstein. Such beautiful music.

In the library, she pulled down Virginia's copy of *Pride and Prejudice* and held the marker close to her heart.

"I'm scared, Virginia." She thought of how it must have been with her in the house. They couldn't have children, and she kept Maggie's little card in her book.

"I can't leave here. I belong here. I feel..."

Maggie ran upstairs, put on the cream-colored dress and hat, and went back to Uncle and Virginia's picture. She studied her face in the large entry hall mirror and then the photo. She adjusted the hat.

Maggie held the picture over her shoulder and looked at the three of them in the mirror, Virginia's face reflected next to hers, and she saw it. Mirrors reversed images. She brought the picture closer to the glass and stepped back as far as she could. Uncle's words, "You're going to look like her," mirrored back to her.

In her room, Maggie put on the swing trousers and blouse and got the picture of Virginia wearing the outfit. At the dressing table mirror, she thought of Miss Johnson reading Shakespeare's third sonnet so beautifully:

Thou art thy mother's glass and she in thee
Calls back the lovely April of her prime;

It seemed disloyal to feel closer to Virginia than to her own Mother.

She got out the cable-knit sweater and slipped it on over her blouse. In the mirror, she said, "Twins for sure."

Maggie gathered strength. Virginia's doctor told her she was sick—told her she was dying. Maggie only had a letter to read.

Dear Margo,

Your letter was upsetting, to say the least. It is unacceptable that you would not come to Peru. It is an opportunity to see and learn about a new country. You will learn Spanish and about a fascinating people and their culture.

We want you to call us on Sunday, the 10th, at two PM, your time. We will be down to get supplies. The number—

She skimmed the rest of the letter. There it was, her marching orders. There was no hiding from that.

San Dimas Canyon

CHRIS WALKED MAGGIE to her locker.

"You said you don't work Saturday afternoon. Could we go for a drive?"

"How about a picnic? We could double with Sharon and Wally. We could go to San Dimas Canyon Park. It is a nice drive out Foothill Boulevard."

Maggie hated the idea of not inviting Sharon and Wally. "How about just us. I want to tell you about my family."

"Oooh. Sounds serious," Chris teased.

Maggie laughed at herself. "No, not all *that* serious, but I want—I want it to be the two of us." But it was serious. This was what Miss Johnson called a defining moment. She either was going to begin taking charge of her life, or she was going to revert to the girl she had been a few months ago—a girl who didn't make waves, who went along, taking the path of least resistance.

"Sounds good. My mom can pack a lunch. I have to help unload a truck at the store early. I can pick you up at eleven.

"Mrs. Brice will be wearing out by then. I will check with Uncle, but it should be fine." Jenny and Tim Watkins were talking near a crepe myrtle.

Chris put his hand behind Maggie's neck and rubbed her cheek with his thumb.

Taking charge of her life scared her. She didn't want to be in charge! She wanted guidance from people who cared. She found herself, at seventeen, longing to be raised. She wanted Uncle, Mrs. Kavanagh, Miss Johnson, Miss Gill—she wanted to be in California, where these marvelous adults would take time to help her plan her life.

I want Chris to choose me. If I am gone for a year, will he wait? Dread rippled through her, taking her breath away. Telling him was the only way to know.

Uncle insisted on sending food in a picnic basket. Two plates, cups, and flowered napkins lay in perfect order.

They put the basket in the trunk next to the one Chris's mother had sent. *We won't starve; that's for sure.*

Chris touched the starter and squeezed Maggie's hand. "This is nice—fun."

The drive was peaceful. The foothills were green, and white-rimmed clouds billowed in bunches. Maggie leaned forward to look at the sky. "Is it going to rain?"

"Not for a while. The news said mid-afternoon." Chris glanced over. "I pay attention to these things."

Maggie leaned back as they turned off the highway and drove past sycamore trees. "This is pretty."

The park was huge, with grass and oak stretching into the hills. They brought both baskets and a blanket. They used Virginia's place settings.

"Fried chicken. Your mother went all out."

"It's her thing. She likes nothing better than to make lots of food."

They ate in peaceful silence, watching three small boys kick a ball.

"We should go to a movie tonight. I could pick you up after supper."

"My parents want me to go to Peru. Next year. I have known for a while—since the skating party. I didn't know how to tell you. I was pretty shocked." Her delivery was not as delicate as she had planned, but there it was.

Chris's head came up quickly.

"I don't want to go. I love my life here. Uncle watches over me, loves me. He is interested in what is happening in my life." She paused.

"It's not that my parents don't care, but in a distracted way. Well—they're gone a lot. I don't know why I haven't told you much about this." *He hasn't looked away.* "I wanted to pretend I had always been here and would always be here. The day I met you, the day you showed me around? That was the fifth time I changed high schools."

"No wonder you could work a new combination so fast! You were so relaxed and natural your first day."

"I was not relaxed. Inside, I was scared to death."

"You were—statuesque." Chris shook off the word. "In control."

Maggie hissed air between her teeth. "Control? No. But the minute you came into the office, I had a crush on you."

"Really?" Chris cocked one eye.

"You were great that day."

"Thanks. I try, when I'm not ganging up on people getting them knocked down." Chris chuckled and then paused. "I remember you. I thought you were—I don't know—the way you held your head. Comfortable with yourself. You didn't ask a million questions. You seemed to know where you were already."

Maggie traced the pattern on the quilt. "Oh, Chris—I can't believe that. I was not at all at ease. I was miserable—too scared to say anything."

"You had me fooled." Chris pulled at one of the ties near her hand. "When would you have to leave?"

"If my mother has her way, the day school is out." Maggie nibbled on a carrot stick. "I would go to a school in Lima, to a boarding school."

"Boarding school? Wait! You wouldn't be with your folks?"

"No, they would be five hours away. My mother says she would come down the mountain every other weekend."

"What's the point of going at all?" Chris huffed.

"Exactly. But they do that. They park me while they're gone. Up to now, mostly at my aunt's. When she had the stroke, I suggested coming here." Maggie sighed. "Best thing I ever did." *That was the one time—the moment I actually took a chance on upsetting Father.*

"So, you would be gone all year, and then what? Back to Wisconsin?"

"I don't know. I never know for sure."

"I would hate to see you go," Chris said quietly.

"Well, I have written and told them I'm not going."

Chris searched Maggie's face. "I can't imagine—I don't buck my parents."

"I have never openly defied my parents, especially Father, but I can't go to Peru. I would get there three months after school started. It's fall down there, and school is starting now. So, I wrote and said I am not coming."

"What did they say?"

"They're pretty unhappy and want me to call them. Tomorrow." she leaned toward Chris. "What are you thinking? Am I a bad person for not obeying my parents?"

"No, not at all. No." He sat back with his arms around his knees. "I've been lucky. Same house. Same town. Same schools."

Maggie rambled about things she never dared tell him. "Father gets to do what he wants. Grandmother thought Grandfather ran away. She played that record over and over. It became a free pass for Father; he was entitled, special. Don't disturb Father—his research is important. Don't upset Father. Mother learned the lessons well."

Maggie watched Chris to see how he was taking the information.

"The trouble is, I was not in the equation. Father wanted to go here or there, so they left me with Aunt Louise." Maggie gave a half-laugh. "One time, they left me with Grandmother. I guess having me around was 'bad for her nerves.' Oh, she approved of leaving me behind but didn't want the inconvenience." A long tiredness filled her. "Sorry."

"Hey, it's OK." Chris traced a quilt square. "You call your dad Father?"

"I guess we aren't very close." *Dad? Mom? It sounds like "Leave it to Beaver."*

"I'm glad you told me."

"It's so frustrating." Maggie started to add maddening, but that was Sharon's word. "I'm scared."

Chris reached for her hand and held it. The boys had stopped their game.

A drop of water plopped on the back of Maggie's hand, and Chris squinted at the sky. "We better pack up."

Rain started coming down hard. They laughed as they scrambled to get everything into the car. Maggie leaned over the seat to spread the damp blanket to dry. She nestled beside Chris, shivering, rain rattling on the roof.

Chris rubbed his hands together and started the engine. "Neither my mom or Uncle T thought to send towels."

They laughed together.

Maggie turned on the heater as they drove on past the park. It was quite beautiful, with orange groves to the left and a rocky river bottom on the other side.

"What if you invited them to visit? Maybe if they saw you and your life with Uncle T, they would understand."

She tried to imagine her parents visiting, being in the house, strangers in her home. She idly watched two boys walking on stilts in a mud puddle along a country drive.

"It might be a halfway point," Chris said. "Middle ground. Maybe it would help."

At the mouth of the canyon, drops from trees arching over the road made tinny plops on the roof. "That's a good idea—a visit gives me hope." Maggie patted his arm. "Thank you."

The rain let up when they came to a place where the road made a loop and met itself.

"Is this the end of the road?"

"No, it goes on. This is the lower ranger station. Do you want to go on up? The dam is up ahead."

"It's beautiful here—peaceful. This is what I needed. Yes, let's go on."

The road got narrower, turning back on itself, brown rocks glistening. Further up, they came to a flat and passed a cottage with pea gravel in the yard.

"This is like a storybook," Maggie said. Sometimes, Uncle sang, "Let the Rest of the World Go By."

Those words suited her fine. Let her parents do whatever they did. They were part of "the rest" of the world. Her place in the west was a safe nest. Chris stopped near banks of mailboxes under huge oaks.

She listened to the heater whirring. "I had no idea so many people would live up here."

Chris turned off the engine and put his arm around her. The rain pattered on the roof. Maggie turned toward him. "I don't want to leave. I don't want to go to Peru. I want to stay here." She hugged Chris tight, not wanting to let go. They kissed.

Chris chuckled. "Oops."

The mail carrier was starting to put mail in the boxes. He gave them a sideways glance and grinned.

Maggie blushed and sat back in the seat. "Caught necking," she giggled.

"Yup." Chris started the car, and they drove back down the canyon. The watch on the knob said four o'clock. Twenty-two hours.

The Call

A FAINT GLOW BREWED in the east. Maggie dreaded the call. Panic hovered, and she turned on her side.

Why am I so scared? It was more than the fear of having to go to another new school in Lima. Maggie squirmed in the bed. Being ordered to go to Peru brought another burning wave of panic.

Uncle said he would arrange the call. The same old uncertainty loomed; Father went whenever he wanted, Mother trotting along. Maggie was no longer willing to sit, waiting—hoping it would be OK.

The first morning here, I buried my head in the covers, but not today.

She got up, put on a sweater over her pajamas, and sat at the writing desk. "Things I need to say to Father." Fear evaporated, and she began to write.

———◦———

AFTER CHURCH, MAGGIE and Uncle went to In-N-Out. At home, they puttered, neither of them able to settle on any task.

Maggie put the picture of Virginia with the "I don't think so look" on the end table next to the phone.

Uncle placed the call with the operator and handed her the receiver. She returned his smile. "Hello?"

"Margo, is that you?"

"Yes." The connection was good.

"You are to come to Peru. Your father is not happy—with your refusal to obey."

Mother was not usually that direct, and her forcefulness gave Maggie pause. She opened her diary.

"Margo, are you there?"

"Yes."

"What do you have to say for yourself?"

Mother doesn't get to be Father's spokesperson. "I want to talk to Father, please."

It was Mother's turn to be quiet. Maggie waited.

"Margo, this is not like you—being difficult."

Maggie tapped "Things to say to Father" with her pencil. She kept her voice even. "Please let me speak with Father."

There was a muffled sound; Mother had her hand over the mouthpiece. Maggie began to relax.

"Hello?" Father sounded smaller than she remembered.

"Hello."

"Your mother says you want to talk to me. You have upset her."

"I only asked to talk to you." Maggie traced a small square in the margin of the diary.

There was a long pause. "Margo, you know about my research, the foundation's extension of the grant. The discovery of these sherds will have significant impact on the conclusions for my thesis. We cannot come home right now."

"I am not asking you to come home. I simply want you to understand I am not coming to Peru."

"Margo, this call is too expensive for silly arguments. I have worked too hard to put up with you being stubborn. Your mother wants you to come to Peru. That is the end of this foolishness."

He has real nerve! Uncle was paying for the call. Father breathed into the phone. Maggie kept her voice level but decisive.

"I can't come. I explained in the letter. It would be the fourth high school I have gone to and my sixth transfer. I would be three months behind."

"This is *not* a discussion. I am telling you, you are to get on that plane the day school is out and fly to Lima."

"No. I have made up my mind. I know you don't like it, but please try to understand. You continue your project there. I know it is important." She didn't say "to you." *I'm not going to let this be about Father and the dig.* "I am finishing high school here next year. I am planning to go to college in California after that. This is my project."

She put a checkmark beside "Project." It was the first time she could remember saying "No" out loud to Father.

"Young lady, that is about enough of this!"

Young lady. Grandmother's words. Maggie closed the diary, her finger marking the page. "Do you remember when I found out you were going on the third trip to Chilé and I was crying? Grandmother was there and told me that it was time I grew up?" She waited. "I was eight years old."

Maggie heard nothing but a faint hum. "This year, I did what Grandmother said. I grew up." *And you still haven't finished your thesis.*

"Don't make me fly up there to get you."

Now he's flying up and taking me back! Three tickets! Mother wrote you were scraping the money together to get me down there.

They're gonna put the bite on Uncle. Good old Uncle. Ostracize him from the family, but let him pay for Grandmother's funeral. Let him pay for my ticket to California. What's two more tickets?

"I am not coming to Peru." Maggie opened the diary and began to trace a square around those words.

Father was quiet. "What's gotten into you? You have never given us trouble before."

"That's because my life has always been controlled by a dig. Now I have a future here in California. I have hopes. Dreams." She circled the words: "Don't mention Chris."

"Did T. Charles put you up to this?"

Maggie gasped. "No! No, not at all!" *He didn't even read my letter.* "Why would you even think such a thing?! I love it here, but..." She began to put checkmarks next to the points in the diary.

"I am doing well in school." She paused, letting each point sink in. "My school counselor is helping me plan for college. This is what is best for my future." She improvised. "Now I need to go to summer school. I have credits to make up. I need to visit colleges." *Did you think I was going to Blakemore College, where you are still an adjunct professor?*

The other end of the line was quiet. She heard Father say, "You talk to her." Maggie waited. Mother either didn't take the phone, or she was very quiet.

"Hello?"

"Yes," Father said.

"I will write to you next week. But I will not spend a year in Peru."

Maggie started to wonder if the connection had been broken when Father said, "Your mother and I will talk it over."

"Thank you. Put Mother on, please."

"Now, Margo, let's not be rash and say something—we'll regret." It was Mother's "keeping the peace" voice, but she lacked conviction.

"Father has to understand I can't wait for another dig to be over. I live in California now. I am happy and doing well." At the bottom of the page, Maggie circled the words, "You should be proud of me," and sighed.

After the call, they went to the kitchen for tea and cookies.

"What do you think?"

"You stood your ground."

"They were upset."

"Maggie, *you* have been upset. You have been worrying for weeks."

Months. Uncle understands. Why can't Father understand?

"I have never heard Father sound like that. In a way, the call settled nothing. He talked about flying up here to get me."

"You'll be eighteen in July. You are starting to be independent."

"I don't want to be independent. I want..." She started again. "You let me choose my way, but you guide me." She wished for the right words. "I can depend on you."

Uncle smiled. "It is wonderful watching you mature." He poured the tea. "Did your father mention Daniel? Mr. Mills?"

"No."

Uncle had talked with some of his former colleagues about Mr. Mills. Advancement in treatments could make Grandfather's life easier. Maggie had taken him a tin of brownies, and his smile was Virginia's smile as they each ate one in silence. *Father didn't even bother to ask. Mother didn't mention Aunt Louise.* Maggie let out a long breath. The dig took precedence over everything.

Maggie got the cookie jar, letting her parent's world fade. Their world was not her world. "I feel like Virginia is helping raise me. I know that sounds odd, but the stories you tell, the clothes, the records, this house—having her picture beside me helped me stay calm on the phone."

"I know she would have loved every moment of you being here." Uncle turned to look at her. "Just as I do."

They sat, each with an uneaten cookie on dessert plates. Maggie felt very loved.

Home

MAGGIE COULDN'T DECIDE if it was the ending of a great story or the beginning. The piano at M'Goo's hammered out, "The Sidewalks of New York."

"We have a guest pianist who will play a number not on the song sheet, in honor of this group right down here." The piano player gestured to their table. "Tommy Blackwater, playing, 'Uptown Ivories,' by Daniel McKinney."

Uncle played the whole song with a jazzed up second chorus. Sharon hugged him around the neck when he came back to the table.

Alan said Uncle had let Mike drive the Packard to the freeway entrance. Uncle sat in front because Mike only had a learner's permit. Mike was grinning as if Uncle had allowed him to drive a rocket ship to the moon.

Tina said, "If we'd gone any slower, we would of had to weave back and forth to keep from falling over."

Laura patted Mike's shoulder.

The pizza came, and Uncle stood. "Everyone, we are here to celebrate the movie, the good times we have at our little gatherings, and..." He looked at Maggie with great love. "And, Maggie is going to be living here for the summer and next year."

Chris reached for her hand.

Uncle raised his soda. "Maggie's parents are flying here in August for a *special* visit, and we are going to Disneyland. But, our Maggie Girl will be completing her senior year at Blackwater High."

"And college after that," Maggie said firmly. She squeezed Chris's hand.

Sharon gave her a slow wink.

Acknowledgments

Thanks to our son Matthew who said, "Dad, why don't you write something?"

I want to thank my family, Ruth, Rachel, and Matthew, who have spent hours on this book.

A special thanks to Gail Carriger, author of the *Soulless* (The Parasol Protectorate, 1) and many other books. Gail, with degrees in archaeological studies, set me straight on the difference between shards and sherds.

I'm grateful for my critique partners, Harlow, Abby, and Beth who have supported me and taught me a great deal.

Thanks to Donna, PamX2, and Kerri.

Two editors helped along the way, Ann Creel and Jess Lawrence

And to all my #LineByLineTime friends on Twitter—thanks for helping polish the rough places.

Don't miss out!

Visit the website below and you can sign up to receive emails whenever George Beckman publishes a new book. There's no charge and no obligation.

https://books2read.com/r/B-A-XNBN-SOFLB

Connecting independent readers to independent writers.

About the Author

As an educator, George spent his life stamping out illiteracy in sixth-grade classrooms. He and the kids had a great time, and George learned a great deal.

George and Ruth live in an old stone house that was named Graestone long before they came.

George doesn't always wear a tux.

Read more at https://graestonewriter.com.

About the Publisher

Books from Graestone is pleased to bring you this book.
Graestone is a beautiful old stone house nestled on four acres. My writing has blossomed since arriving at Graestone.

Made in United States
North Haven, CT
05 March 2022

16827089R00141